高等学校"专业综合改革试点"项目（ZG0295）
山东省高等教育本科教改项目（Z2018S002，Z2016Z029）阶段性成果

大学英语实用写作教程
（科技类）

主　编　张锦辉
副主编　马应心　孙如军
编　委　宋　辉　黄　倩　蔡　静
　　　　庄三生　王　翠　吴颖芳

北京理工大学出版社
BEIJING INSTITUTE OF TECHNOLOGY PRESS

版权专有　侵权必究

图书在版编目（CIP）数据

大学英语实用写作教程．科技类/张锦辉主编．—北京：北京理工大学出版社，2018.12

ISBN 978 – 7 – 5682 – 6566 – 9

Ⅰ．①大…　Ⅱ．①张…　Ⅲ．①英语 – 写作 – 高等学校 – 教材　Ⅳ．①H315

中国版本图书馆 CIP 数据核字（2018）第 296475 号

出版发行 / 北京理工大学出版社有限责任公司
社　　址 / 北京市海淀区中关村南大街 5 号
邮　　编 / 100081
电　　话 / (010) 68914775（总编室）
　　　　　 (010) 82562903（教材售后服务热线）
　　　　　 (010) 68948351（其他图书服务热线）
网　　址 / http：//www.bitpress.com.cn
经　　销 / 全国各地新华书店
印　　刷 / 三河市华骏印务包装有限公司
开　　本 / 710 毫米 × 1000 毫米　1/16
印　　张 / 15.25　　　　　　　　　　　　　　　责任编辑 / 张慧峰
字　　数 / 287 千字　　　　　　　　　　　　　　文案编辑 / 张慧峰
版　　次 / 2018 年 12 月第 1 版　2018 年 12 月第 1 次印刷　责任校对 / 周瑞红
定　　价 / 49.00 元　　　　　　　　　　　　　　责任印制 / 李志强

图书出现印装质量问题，请拨打售后服务热线，本社负责调换

前　　言

教育部在2017年颁布了《大学英语教学指南》，对大学英语教学提出了新的教学指导意见。大学英语课程是基础教育阶段英语教学的提升和拓展，主要目的是在高中英语教学的基础上进一步提高学生英语听、说、读、写、译的能力。其中，对书面表达能力从基础目标、提高目标和发展目标三个层次提出了相应的要求，如书面表达能力的基础目标应达到"能用英语描述个人经历、观感、情感和发生的事件等；能写常见的应用文；能就一般性话题或提纲以短文的形式展开简短的讨论、解释、说明等，语言结构基本完整，中心思想明确，用词较为恰当，语意连贯；能运用基本的写作技巧"。为了适应《大学英语教学指南》新的要求，切实提高学生的书面表达能力，夯实学生的语言基本功，作者结合一线写作教学实践编写了本书。

本书针对学生英语写作学习的语用能力与语言水平测试需求，从词汇、段落、篇章等写作的基础知识到信件、海报等应用文的写作，从大学英语四六级考试、研究生入学考试、国际人才英语考试的写作命题到常用的规范句型及各类文章的写作要点，都进行了详细的阐述。

本书选取的例句、范文和素材广泛、新颖、实用。首先，为配合大学英语课程的学习，本写作教程依托《全新版大学进阶英语综合教程》的学习，大量例句出自教程课文，并将综合教程中的写作部分作为案例进行分析，充分发挥"输入－输出"相互促进的作用，推进学生将读写有效结合，切实提升写作能力。另外，教材为拓宽学生的知识面，增加学生对日常话题的分析与表述能力，注重讲练结合，运用了大量例句、图片与例文，很多素材选自英文报刊网站China Daily、大学英语四六级考试历年真题、研究生入学考试英语真题、《朗文当代高级英语辞典》、《肖立齐考研英语写作》、《新东方考研英语写作》、原版经典名著、各大英语学习权威网站等，语言地道，涉及面广。本书还编选了英语美文、部分常用词汇和短语供学习者阅读、参考。

由于作者水平有限，书中难免有错误和疏漏之处，恳请专家和读者不吝赐教。

张锦辉

2018 年 9 月

目 录

第一章 英语词汇的使用 …………………………………………… (1)

  美文赏析 ………………………………………………………… (1)
  第一节 名词的用法 …………………………………………… (3)
  第二节 动词的用法 …………………………………………… (8)
  第三节 形容词的用法 ………………………………………… (16)
  第四节 副词的用法 …………………………………………… (19)
  第五节 写作词汇的使用 ……………………………………… (20)
  第六节 写作常用词汇 ………………………………………… (24)
  Exercises ………………………………………………………… (46)

第二章 英语句子的写作 …………………………………………… (51)

  美文赏析 ………………………………………………………… (51)
  第一节 英语句子的结构 ……………………………………… (54)
  第二节 英语句子的成分 ……………………………………… (60)
  第三节 标点的用法 …………………………………………… (65)
  第四节 英语句子的规范化 …………………………………… (70)
  第五节 写作常用规范句型 …………………………………… (80)
  Exercises ………………………………………………………… (92)

第三章 英语段落的写作 …………………………………………… (100)

  美文赏析 ………………………………………………………… (100)
  第一节 段落的构成 …………………………………………… (103)
  第二节 段落的组织 …………………………………………… (116)
  第三节 段落的模式 …………………………………………… (125)
  Exercises ………………………………………………………… (138)

第四章　英语篇章的写作 (142)

美文赏析 (142)
第一节　英语写作的谋篇布局 (145)
第二节　大学英语四、六级写作 (156)
第三节　研究生入学考试英语写作 (163)
第四节　国际人才英语考试写作 (169)
Exercises (173)

第五章　英语应用文写作 (175)

美文赏析 (175)
第一节　应用文的写作要求 (178)
第二节　书信体应用文写作 (180)
第三节　其他类型应用文写作 (189)
Exercises (192)

第六章　数字化时代的英语写作学习 (194)

美文赏析 (194)
第一节　数字化学习的理论基础 (196)
第二节　英语写作数字化平台建设 (197)
第三节　基于网络的写作训练 (198)

附录 (204)

附录一　练习参考答案 (204)
附录二　科技类专业词汇 (214)
附录三　常用前缀、后缀与词根 (219)
附录四　常用英语谚语与名人名言 (228)

参考文献 (234)

第一章

英语词汇的使用

美文赏析

When You Are Old
——W. B. Yeats

When you are old and gray and full of sleep,
And nodding by the fire, take down this book,
And slowly read, and dream of the soft look
Your eyes had once, and of their shadows deep;

How many loved your moments of glad grace,
And loved your beauty with love false or true,
But one man loved the pilgrim soul in you,
And loved the sorrows of your changing face;

And bending down beside the glowing bars,
Murmur, a little sadly, how Love fled,
And paced upon the mountains overhead,
And hid his face amid a crowd of stars.

▶ 赏析：

《When You Are Old》（译为《当你老了》），是叶芝广为传诵的一首爱情诗，此诗写于1893年，当时叶芝一直追求年轻貌美的茅德·冈（Mand Gonne，后成为爱尔兰独立运动领导人），对方对诗人的若即若离使其对爱情感到无望与痛苦，他这段时间写下了很多诗歌，《当你老了》是其中一首。

　　文中词汇的使用朴实无华，但极具张力（词汇使用统计见下表）。诗人想象若干年后年迈的恋人在炉火旁阅读诗集并陷入回忆的情景。诗中各种词性综合运用，其中名词最多，主要表现在诗人丰富的想象场景，对方的 look、shadows、grace、sorrows 犹在眼前，所处环境中的 book、fire 则烘托了回忆的深沉；诗人年老后的恋人依旧饱含深情，主要体现在形容词与副词的使用上，如 soft、glad、sadly 等词。文中运用 full of sleep 与 nod 的现在分词形式，使"充满倦意、正在昏昏欲睡"的状态跃然纸上；slowly 的使用，展现了读书的动作缓慢，也渐渐陷入回忆。Murmur 与 sadly 体现了在诗人想象中恋人回忆时对爱情消逝的遗憾。

名词	动词	形容词	副词
sleep	nodding	old	slowly
fire	take	gray	once
book	read	full	sadly
look	dream	soft	overhead
eyes	loved	deep	
shadows	bending	many	
moments	murmur	glad	
grace	fled	changing	
beauty	paced	glowing	
pilgrim			
sorrows			
face			
bars			
mountains			
stars			

　　诗人未用华丽的辞藻，平常的词汇便凸显了诗的意境，引领读者一起想象，为作者的爱情唏嘘感叹。由此可见，写作词汇的使用，重要的不是堆积华丽辞藻，而是恰当选词。最浓艳的妆不是最美的，恰到好处精心雕

饰的才是最赏心悦目的。写作中，词汇的使用要反复推敲。"推敲"一词便来自贾岛精心选用词汇的典故。唐朝的贾岛是著名的苦吟派诗人。为何被称为苦吟派？即为了诗中的一个词或句，煞费苦心，花费工夫。贾岛在作"鸟宿池边树，僧敲月下门"这句诗时，因为拿不定主意是用"推"还是用"敲"而苦心思考，一时忘我闯进了大官韩愈的仪仗队里。推敲也就成了脍炙人口的常用词，用来比喻做文章或做事时，反复琢磨，反复斟酌。英文写作的词汇选用亦是如此。

第一节　名词的用法

一、名词的基本用法

（一）名词的用法

名词是表示人、事物、概念等名称的词，如 fellow 同伴，peer 同龄人，idea 主意，creation 创造，news 消息，progress 进步，strategy 策略，John 约翰，Netherlands 荷兰，France 法国，dishware 餐具等。名词根据其词汇意义，通常分为专有名词和普通名词。专有名词主要指人、地方、组织、机构等专有的名称，专有名词的首字母通常要大写，如 Mark 马克，Miss Jane 简女士，New York 纽约等；普通名词通常指人、物、概念等的一般名称。普通名词又可以细分为个体名词、物质名词、集合名词和抽象名词四类。

个体名词表示人或事物的个体，如 company 公司，psychologist 心理学家等；

物质名词表示无法分为个体的实物，如 steel 钢铁，oxygen 氧等；

集合名词表示由若干个体组成的集合体，如：audience 听众，people 人民等；

抽象名词表示性质、行为、状态、感情等抽象概念，如 loyalty 忠诚，harmony 和谐等。

（二）名词的数

1. 名词的可数性

名词根据其可数性，可分为可数名词与不可数名词。通常情况下，个体名词和大部分集合名词是可数的，专有名词、物质名词、抽象名词以及少部分集合名词则通常是不可数的。

（1）专有名词的可数性。在通常情况下，专有名词具有"独一无二"的含义，因此它通常没有复数形式，即不可数。但是，专有名词的独一无二性通常是相对的，会随着使用范围的扩大而有所改变。如星期几，指一个星期内特定的一天，但是范围扩大到一个月或一年中，便有多个了。所以专有名词有时可数。如 We have spent many happy Sundays in this park. 我们在这个公园度过了许多个愉快的周末。另如人名，在小范围内指特定的一个人，但在范围较大时则可能有多个同名的人，便会出现复数形式，如：There are two Marks in my friends. 我有两个叫马克的朋友。

（2）个体名词的可数性。个体名词表示的是人或事物的个体，通常是可数的，如 one apple。

（3）物质名词的可数性。物质名词在通常情况下不能分成独立的个体，所以它通常是不可数的。但是，在某些特殊情况下（如表示种类等），有些物质名词也可以连用不定冠词或用复数形式：sheep 绵羊（不可数），a sheep 一种绵羊（可数）；meet 肉（不可数），a meet 一种肉（可数）；fish 鱼，鱼肉（不可数），fishes 鱼的种类（可数）。如：

The stonefish is the most deadly of all fishes. 石鱼是所有鱼类中最致命的。

One usually drinks white wine with fish. 人们一般配鱼喝白葡萄酒。

（4）抽象名词的可数性。抽象名词表示事物性质、行为、状态、感情等抽象概念，因此通常不可数，如 creation, happiness, peace, pride。但有时抽象名词也可转化为可数的具体名词，用于表示具有某种性质的人或事物，如failure失败（不可数），a failure 失败的人或事（可数）；sadness 悲伤（不可数），a sadness 令人悲伤的人或事（可数）。

（5）集合名词的可数性。集合名词表示若干个体组成的集合体，通常是可数的，其复数形式表示多个集合体，如 a club 一个社团, three clubs 三个社团；an organization 一个组织, many organizations 多个组织。另外，在使用集合名词时若视其为整体，表示单数意义，若考虑其个体成员，表示复数意义。比如：

Her family is large. 她的家是个大家庭。

Her family are all going to visit her aunt. 她全家人一起去拜访她姑妈。

This class consists of 30 students. 这个班有30名学生。

This class are reading Chinese now. 这个班的学生在读语文。

上述名词的可数性区分规则并非绝对。英语中很多名词的可数性取决于语境，在不同语境中既是可数也可以是不可数的，如下列两句话中，experience作"经历，阅历：event or activity that affects one in some way; event or activity that has given one experience"时是可数名词，作为"经验，体验：knowledge or skill acquired from seeing and doing things"时则不可数。

Veiseh began to remember the details of his everyday experiences after he met his first young love. Veiseh 开始记得他的日常经历的细节，在他遇到第一次年轻的爱情之后。（CET-4，2017-06）

Their parents' bad experience still haunts them. 他们父母糟糕的体验仍然困扰着他们。（CET-4，2017-06）

2. 名词复数的构成方法

（1）在一般情况下，加词尾-s：

achievement/achievements 成就；assignment/assignments 分配

（2）以 s，x，z，sh，ch 等结尾的名词，通常加词尾-es：

bunch/bunches 束；speech/speeches 演讲；dish/dishes 盘子

注：有些以 ch 结尾的名词，由于其发音是 [k] 而不是 [tʃ]，那么其复数形式应加词尾-s，如 stomach/stomachs 胃。

（3）以 y 结尾的名词，其复数构成要分两种情况：以"辅音字母+y"结尾的名词，将 y 改为 i 加-es；以"元音字母+y"结尾的名词，直接加词尾 s：

ability/abilities 能力；　　　　activity/activities 活动；
toy/toys 玩具；　　　　　　　key/keys 钥匙

（4）以 o 结尾的名词，有些加词尾-s，有些加-es，有些加-s 或-es 均可：

radio/radios 收音机；　　　　tomato/tomatoes 西红柿；
buffalo/buffaloes 水牛；　　　echo/echoes 回声

（5）以 f 或 fe 结尾的名词，也有两种可能，即有些直接加词尾-s，有些则把 f/fe 改为 ves：

chief/chiefs 首领；　　gulf/gulfs 海湾；　　loaf/loaves 一条面包；
dwarf/dwarves 矮人；　wolf/wolves 狼

（6）单数与复数同形式的名词，例如：

species 物种；cattle 牛；aircraft 飞行器；means 方法；series 系列

（7）不规则的复数名词。有的名词单数变复数时，没有一定的规则，例如：

medium/mediums 或 media 媒介；　　basis/bases 基础；
analysis/analyses 分析；　　　　　　phenomenon/phenomena 现象；
criterion/criteria 标准；　　　　　　alumnus/alumni 男校友

注：一些以 man，woman 结尾的合成词，在构成复数时与 man，woman 的变化形式相同，如：policewoman/policewomen 警察，gentleman/gentlemen

绅士。

(8) 复合名词的复数形式。通常是将其主要名词变为复数：

pencil-box/pencil-boxes 铅笔盒

gate-keeper/gate-keepers 守门人

moon-cake/moon-cakes 月饼

waiting-room/waiting-rooms 等候室

mother-in-law/mothers-in-law 岳母

passer-by/passers-by 过路人

若没有主要名词，则通常在最后一个词加 s：

get-together/get-togethers 聚会

know-all/know-alls 万事通，无所不知的人

注：由 man/woman 用于另一名词前构成的合成名词，变复数时两者均变为复数：

man writer/men writers 男作家；woman doctor/women doctors 女医生

(9) 字母、文字、数字、符号等的复数形式。原则上加词尾-'s：

There are two o's in the word "foot." 单词 foot 里有两个字母 o。

All the -'s should be changed to +'s. 所有的负号应改为正号。

(10) 度量衡单位的缩写词的复数形式，一般不加词尾-s：

m (meter, meters) 米；   g (gram, grams) 克；

kg (kilogram, kilograms) 千克；   mm (millimeter, millimeters) 毫米

有的缩写词也加 s，如 hrs (hours) 小时。

(三) 名词的格

名词有三种格，即主格、宾格和所有格。名词的主格和宾格形式相同，统称作通格。当名词用作主语、宾语、表语及同位语时，用通格。名词的所有格表示所属关系，它分-'s 所有格和 of 所有格两种形式。

Mary likes flowers. (Mary 为主格，flowers 为宾格，均为通格形式)

Mary's best friend is Lucy. (Mary's 是所有格，Lucy 为通格)

The photos of this park are very beautiful. (of this park 为所有格)

-'s 所有格的构成方法：

(1) 一般情况下，单数名词和不带词尾 s 的复数名词直接加 's：

Children's toys 儿童玩具；Tom's house 汤姆的房子

(2) 带词尾 s 的复数名词加 '：

the Smiths' house 史密斯家的房子；adults' school 成人学校

the students' reading room 学生阅览室

注：带词尾 s 的单数名词，通常仍加 's：
the boss's idea 老板的想法

（3）用 and 连接的并列名词的所有格分两种情况：若表示各自拥有时，要在并列的名词后分别加 's；表示共同所有关系时，只在最后一个名词后加 's：

Mary's and Lucy's rooms. 玛丽和露西（各自）的房间
Mary and Lucy's room. 玛丽和露西（共同）的房间

二、名词的句法功能

（一）在句中作主语

This picture is very beautiful.
The students are going to have English lesson tomorrow.

（二）作表语

My brother is a driver.
She is a writer.

（三）作宾语或宾补

She finished her homework on time.
Just one week after Obama was elected president, participants were less ready to support policies designed to address racial inequality than they had been two weeks before the election. (CET-6, 2010.06)

（四）作定语

Well, I know in my case, I did an English literature degree and I didn't really expect to end up doing what I am doing now. (CET-6, 2011.12)

注：名词作定语修饰名词，通常表示事物的属性、本质特征、内容、材料、目的等。这些形容词化的名词与形容词作定语在语义上有一定的区别。如：

a golden medal 金色的奖牌（颜色，非材料）
a gold medal 金牌（质地材料为金子）

（五）作状语

The sports meeting lasted two days.
It has been the subject of your close scrutiny every morning since you were tall enough to see into the bathroom mirror. (CET-6, 2013.12)

（六）作同位语

For example, Arne Sorenson, the president of Marriott hotels, likens the crisis to the downturn that hit his business after September 11th, 2001. （CET-4, 2013.06）

We students should study hard.

（七）作称呼语

Good morning, ladies and gentlemen.

第二节 动词的用法

一、动词的分类

动词可以依据其含义及在句中的作用分成四类，包括即实义动词、系动词、助动词和情态动词。

（一）实义动词

实义动词是用来表示行为、动作或状态的词，其词义完整，可单独作谓语。例如：

But chariots maintained their place in parades and triumphs right up until the end of the Roman Empire 1,500 years later. （CET-4, 2014.06）

Without social pressures to keep pair-bonds, romantic love plays a key role in maintaining long-term relationships. （CET-4, 2013.06）

（二）系动词

系动词也称连系动词（Link Verb），后边必须跟表语构成系表结构说明主语的状况、性质、特征等情况。

The problem is that such an impulse is hard to sustain Across the country, many similar families were unable to maintain the initial boost in morale （士气）. （CET-4, 2012.06）

But it gets complicated.

The latest congressional report acknowledges the critical importance of technical training, but also asserts that the study of the humanities and social sciences must remain central components of America's educational system at all levels. （CET-4, 2014.06）

Almost all said that their cell phone was the way they stayed in touch with peers, one-third had used the cell phone to help a peer in need, and about 80% said the phone made them feel safer. (CET-6, 2013.12)

Though the Swedish model appears workable for most American parents, it may not be accepted by them in its entirety. (CET-6, 2014.06)

Goldman Sachs, an investment bank, canceled a conference in Las Vegas at the last minute and rebooked it in San Francisco, which cost more but sounded less fun. (CET-4, 2013.06)

The flower smells good.

Surveys show that the number of worried Americans has been steadily growing over the years as the computer becomes increasingly efficient, easier to operate, and less costly to purchase and maintain. (CET-4, 2013.06)

The college admission essay contains the grandest American themes — status anxiety, parental piety, intellectual standards—and so it is only a matter of time before it becomes infected by the country's culture of excessive concern with self-esteem. (CET-6, 2013.12)

It proves profitable to both sides. (CET-4, 2014.06)

The change cut their expenditures in half, but the new living arrangement proved too challenging. (CET-6, 2012.12)

(三) 助动词

助动词（Auxiliary Verb）是指协助主要动词构成谓语动词词组的词。被协助的动词称作主要动词（Main Verb）。助动词自身没有词义，不可单独使用，例如：

He doesn't like physics. (doesn't 是助动词，无词义，协助主要动词 like 构成谓语)

助动词协助主要动词可以用来表示时态、语态、语气等，如：

She is going to visit Tianjin.

He has left here.

He was sent to Shanghai.

—What do you want? —Noodles, please.

Do not wait for fortunate things to happen to you. You need to walk towards happiness.

The woman feels lucky to have got a ticket.

Many people do not have clear memories of past events.

The officers are facing large challenges.

The students were encouraged by teacher.
By the end of last month, they had finished more than half of their task.
Don't do this!
I did attend the meeting.
Mark suggests that we should stop and think carefully about our plan.

（四）情态动词

情态动词本身虽有意义，但不能单独作谓语，与实义动词的原形一起作谓语，表示说话人的能力、说话人的语气或情态，例如：

They can only afford a second-hand car.
I must arrive there before the meeting.

二、谓语动词用法

（一）动词的时态

动词时态是表示动作和状态在各种时间条件下的动词形式。"时"是指动作发生的时段或状态存在的时间，包括"现在、过去、将来、过去将来"四种；"态"是指动作发生时所处的状态，包括"一般、进行、完成、完成进行"四种。动作的时与态结合，形成16种时态（见下表）：

时态	现在	过去	将来	过去将来
一般时态	一般现在时	一般过去时	一般将来时	一般过去将来时
进行时态	现在进行时	过去进行时	将来进行时	过去将来进行时
完成时态	现在完成时	过去完成时	将来完成时	过去将来完成时
完成进行时态	现在完成进行时	过去完成进行时	将来完成进行时	过去将来完成进行时

1. 一般现在时

表示当前的状态或习惯性的动作、主语的属性等。

时间状语：always, usually, often, sometimes, every day, once a week, on Sundays 等。

基本结构：主语 + be/do。如：

This technological problem remains to be solved.

2. 一般过去时

表示过去的时间发生的动作或存在的状态，过去经常或反复发生的动作。

时间状语：two years ago, yesterday, last week, in 1981, just now, at the age of 5, long long ago, once upon a time 等。

基本结构：主语+动词的过去式/主语+系动词过去式+表语。如：

She often went to Beijing to attend meetings last year.

3. 一般将来时

表示将要发生的动作、打算、计划。

时间状语：tomorrow, soon, in a few minutes, the day after tomorrow 等。

基本结构：主语 + is/am/are going to + do sth；主语 + will/shall + do sth。如：

They are going to have a speech contest.

4. 一般过去将来时

基于过去某一时刻，从过去看将来，常用于从句中。

时间状语：the next day (morning/year…), the following month (week…) 等。

基本结构：主语 + was/were + going to + do；主语 + would/should + do。如：

He said he would go to NewYork the next day.

5. 现在进行时

表示说话时或当前阶段正在进行或发生的动作。

时间状语：now, at this time 等。

基本结构：主语 + be + doing。如：

He is playing basketball now.

6. 过去进行时

表示过去某时间正在发生或进行的动作。

时间状语：at this time yesterday, at that time 或表示过去的时间状语。

基本结构：主语 + was/were + doing。如：

When Mary came in, I was listening to music.

7. 将来进行时

表示将来某个时刻正在进行的动作。

时间状语：soon, tomorrow, this evening, on Sunday, in two days, tomorrow evening 等。

基本结构：主语 + shall/will + be + 现在分词。如：

He will be coming to the party this evening.

8. 过去将来进行时

基于过去某一时间，在将来某一时刻正在进行的动作。

基本结构：should/would + be + 现在分词。如：

She said he could not come because she would be having a meeting.

9. 现在完成时

动作在过去时间发生一直持续到现在，或已完成但对现在产生影响。

时间状语：already，just，never，ever，so far，by now，since + 时间点，for + 时间段，recently，lately 等。

基本结构：主语 + have/has + 过去分词。如：

Large changes have taken place in the countryside in the past few years.

10. 过去完成时

以过去某个时间为基准，在此以前发生的动作对基准时间行为产生影响，或在过去某动作之前完成的行为。

时间状语：before，by the end of last year 等。

基本结构：主语 + had + 过去分词。如：

By the end of last year, he had stayed in London for four years.

11. 将来完成时

在将来某一时刻之前开始的动作并一直持续或对将来产生影响。

时间状语：by the time of，by the end of + 时间短语（将来），by the time + 从句（将来）等。

基本结构：主语 + be going to/will/shall + have + 过去分词。如：

By the time you get back, great changes will have taken place in this area.

12. 过去将来完成时

表示在过去某一时间发生并对将来某一时刻产生影响的动作，常用在虚拟语气中。

基本结构：should/would have done sth。如：

If I had known that you were coming, I would have met you at the airport.

13. 现在完成进行时

表示从过去某一时间开始一直延续到现在的动作，可能仍在继续，并可能延续到将来。

基本结构：主语 + have/has + been + doing。

时间状语：since + 时间点，for + 时间段 等。如：

I have been here for an hour.

14. 过去完成进行时

表示某个过去正在进行的动作，持续到过去某个时刻或将继续持续。

基本结构：主语 + had been + doing。如：

They had been expecting the news for three months.

15. 将来完成进行时

表示动作从某一时间开始一直延续到将来某一时间。

基本结构：shall/will have been doing。如：

Dahlia will have been in China for 9 years by the end of this year.

16. 过去将来完成进行时

表示从过去某时刻看至将来某时刻以前会一直在进行的动作。

基本结构：should/would + have + been + 现在分词。如：

Dahlia told me that by the end of the year she would have been living in China for eight years.

（二）动词的语态

主动语态中，主语是谓语动作的实施方，即谓语的动作源自主语并施加于宾语。相反，被动语态中，主语是谓语动作的承受方，如果有宾语的，宾语往往是谓语动作的发出者。在语法结构上，主动语态直接使用动词原形作为谓语，然后再在该动词原形的基础上依据时态要求对动词形式进行相应变化；而被动语态则使用系动词 + 动词的过去分词作为谓语，各种时态的表现形式主要由系动词的形式体现。

例句：

主动语态：Mike writes a letter every week.

被动语态：A letter is written by Mike every week.

主动语态：He has read two novels so far.

被动语态：Two novels have been read by him so far.

（三）动词的语气

语气是动词的一种形式，它表示说话人对某一行为或事情的看法和态度。

1. 陈述语气

陈述语气表示动作或状态是真实的、符合现实的或确定的，用于陈述句、疑问句和某些感叹句。如：

（1）He didn't go to school yesterday.（陈述句）

（2）What a beautiful girl she is!（感叹句）

2. 祈使语气

祈使语气表示说话人的建议、请求、邀请、命令等,一般主语为第二人称并省略。如:

(1) Open the window, please. (请求)

(2) Turn off the light. (命令)

3. 虚拟语气

虚拟语气表示动作或状态不是客观存在的事实或与现实情况相反,是说话人的主观愿望、假设或推测等,主要表达"非真实意义"与"假设意义"。主要用在 if 非真实条件句、wish、suggest 等情况中。如:

(1) I wish I were a bird.

(2) If there were no gravity, we should not be able to walk.

(3) If you had been here yesterday, you would have seen him.

三、非谓语动词的用法

非谓语动词主要包括动词不定式与分词。非谓语动词不能够作谓语,但仍保留动词的特征,可带有宾语和状语,并可有时态与语态的变化。

(一)动词不定式

不定式短语可做主语、宾语、宾语补足语、表语、同位语、定语及状语等句子成分。

1. 不定式做主语

不定式短语可放在句首充当句子的主语。或将 it 做形式主语放在句首,而将真正的主语——不定式放到句末。

To learn English well is very important.

It is very important to learn English well.

Is it necessary to bring an umbrella today?

注意:当不定式做主语时,逻辑主语应用 for sb. 或 of sb. 如:

It is very important for you to memorize the new words if you want to learn English well.

It is very kind of you to help us.

2. 不定式做宾语

He agrees to go with us.

I want to buy a English-Chinese dictionary.

注意:

(1) 不定式并非可做任何及物动词的宾语。能接不定式做宾语的动词有：ask, decide, desire, demand, like, long, love, intend, want, wish, determine, afford, agree, arrange, attempt, begin, care, choose, continue, dare, expect, fail, hate, hesitate, hope, know, learn, manage, need, plan, prepare, refuse, wait, wonder 等。

例如：

Can you afford to buy such an expensive house?

He planned to go travelling with you.

（2）做宾语的不定式如果跟有自己的补足语，则需用 it 做形式宾语，而将真正的宾语置于补足语之后。

例如：

I find it interesting to play games with you.

3. 不定式做宾语补足语

The guide advised us to buy some local specialties after walking around West Lake.

4. 不定式做表语

不定式短语可用来做系动词的表语，且一般不定式前面的 to 不能省略。

例如：

My dream is to become a successful businessman like Jack Ma.

My job is to teach English.

What I want to do is pass the CET－4.

What he wants to do is playing basketball after class.

5. 不定式做定语

不定式做定语时，一般需后置，即放在被修饰的名词、代词之后，表示即将发生的动作。

例如：

We have a lot of house work to do.

I have some clothes to wash.

I have a dream to travel around the world.

6. 不定式做状语

不定式做状语，主要用于表达动作的目的、结果和原因。

To catch the train, we get up at four in the morning.

He goes the shop to buy some fruits.

Lily bought some vegetables and meat to cook dinner for her family.

I hurried to the railway station yesterday only to find that the train had left.
We set out too late to catch the early bus.
I'm very glad to hear that Lucy has been elected monitor of the class.

（二）分词

分词主要包括现在分词和过去分词。一般来讲，现在分词表示主动、正在进行的动作，而过去分词表示被动，或表示动作已经完成。

1. 分词作定语

We can see the rising sun.
His mother is a retired teacher.
There were ten kids sitting around the teacher.

2. 分词作状语

Not receiving any information from him, I gave him a call.
Listening to music, Mary danced to the rhythm.
Seen from the mountain, the village looks very small.

3. 分词作补语

通常在感官动词和使役动词之后，例如：

I found the story very touching.
I'll have my bike repaired.

4. 分词作表语

She looked tired with cooking.
He remained standing beside the table.
He is interested in the story.
The book is so interesting that he was reading for the whole morning.

第三节　形容词的用法

形容词有其结构特点和句法特点。从构词上讲，以-able，-al，-ful，-ic，-ish，-less，-ous，-y 等后缀结尾的词，一般是形容词，如：sympathetic（同情的），specific（明确的），cheerful（快乐），typical（典型的），intellectual（智力的），imaginary（想象的），gradual（逐渐的），sensible（明智的），available（可利用的）等。从句法功能上讲，大多数形容词都可以作定语和表语，可用副词来修饰，有比较级和最高级形式。如：

The park is very beautiful.（作表语）
There is a beautiful park.（作定语）

第一章 英语词汇的使用

一、形容词的一般用法

（一）用作定语

形容词可以用来修饰、限定、说明名词的品质或特征。

We can infer from the passage that strong family and community ties can contribute to stable marriages. （CET-4，2013.06）

The result of constant muscle tension and stiffness of joints, many of them are avoidable, and simple flexibility training can prevent these by making muscles stronger and keeping joints lubricated. （CET-4，2013.06）

By 1973, domestic US sources of oil were peaking, and the nation was importing more of its oil, depending on a constant flow from abroad to keep cars on the road and machines running. （CET-6，2013.06）

However, many complain that their school libraries do not have enough up-to-date interesting books and magazines （CET-4，2013.06）

Twitter's huge success is rooted in the simple but profound insight that in a medium with infinite space for self-expression, the most interesting thing we can do is restrict ourselves to 140 characters. （CET-6，2013.12）

如果出现不同层次的形容词做前置修饰语，词序是：限定词→大小、形状、新旧→颜色→国别，来源，材料→用途，目的→名词类别→名词中心词。如：

a large black German military jeep.

（二）用作表语

形容词作表语用来说明主语的性质、特征和状态，常位于系动词（be, become, appear, seem, look, sound, feel, get, smell 等词）之后。

Almost every child, on the first day he sets foot in a school building, is smarter, more curious, less afraid of what he doesn't know, better at finding and figuring things out, more confident, resourceful, persistent and independent than he will ever be again in his schooling—or, unless he is very unusual and very lucky, for the rest of his life. （CET-4，2010.06）

The supervisor of the laboratory is beginning to get headaches and dizzy spells because she says it's dangerous to breathe some of the chemical smoke there. （CET-4，2011.06）

They are interesting for the fact that they are very plain and undecorated for the time, with only one plain central panel at the back and no armrests. （CET-

6,2013.12)

（三）用作宾语补足语

They need to keep teams small and focused：giving in to pressure to be more inclusive is a guarantee of dysfunction.

She speculated that professors might try even harder to make classes interesting if they were to compete with the devices. （CET－6，2013.06）

注：有些形容词只能作表语，不能作定语，这些形容词包括 ill, asleep, awake, alone, alive, well, worth, glad, unable, afraid 等。例如：

Don't be afraid. （正）　　　　　Mr Li is an afraid man. （误）
The old man was ill yesterday. （正）　This is an ill person. （误）
This place is worth visiting. （正）　That is a worth book. （误）

有些形容词只能作定语，不能作表语，这些形容词包括 little, live 等。例如：

This is a little house. （正）　　　The house is little. （误）
Do you want live fish or dead one? （正）
The old monkey is still live. （误）

二、形容词比较级与最高级

大多数形容词有三种形式：原级、比较级和最高级，以表示形容词说明的性质在程度上的不同。形容词的比较级和最高级形式是在形容词的原级形式的基础上变化的，分为规则变化和不规则变化。

（一）变化规则

1. 规则变化

（1）单音节形容词的比较级和最高级形式是在词尾加-er 和-est 构成。例如：

great（原级）　　greater（比较级）　　greatest（最高级）
small（原级）　　smaller（比较级）　　smallest（最高级）

（2）以-e 结尾的单音节形容词的比较级和最高级在词尾加-r 和-st 构成。例如：

wide（原级）　　wider（比较级）　　widest（最高级）

（3）以-y 结尾，但-y 前是辅音字母的形容词的比较级和最高级是把-y 去掉，加上-ier 和-iest 构成．

happy（原形）　　happier（比较级）　　happiest（最高级）

（4）以一个辅音字母结尾、其前面的元音字母发短元音的形容词的比较级和最高级要双写该辅音字母再加-er 和-est。

  big（原级）   bigger（比较级）   biggest（最高级）

  （5）双音节和多音节形容词的比较级和最高级用 more 和 most 加在形容词前面来构成。

beautiful（原级） more beautiful（比较级） most beautiful（最高级）

important（原级） more important（比较级） most important（最高级）

2. 常用的不规则变化

原级	比较级	最高级
good	better	best
many	more	most
much	more	most
bad	worse	worst
far	farther; further	farthest; furthest

（二）形容词各等级的用法

1. 原级（同级）

比较：as...as...；not as（so）...as...

We'll give you as much help as we can.

She isn't as（so）active in sports as before.

2. 比较级

表示"A 比 B 更……"，形容词比较级可用状语 much, a little, even 等修饰。

He made fewer mistakes than I did.

He is even richer than I.

3. 最高级

形容词最高级前必须加 the，后面加用"of.../in..."短语表示比较范围。

It was the most/least interesting story I have ever listened.

He is the tallest in the class.

第四节 副词的用法

  副词修饰动词、形容词和其他副词等，用来说明时间、地点、程度、方式、频率等，如：often, here, very, quickly, always 等。除本身就是副词的，如 now 现在、there 那里、rather 非常，部分副词是由形容词加词尾

-ly转换来的，如firmly坚决地，happily幸福地，也有部分副词与形容词同形，如straight adj. 直率的，straight adv. 坦率地；enough adj. 充足的，enough adv. 充足地；long adj. 长的，长久的；long adv. 长久地。副词可分为普通副词（如together, well, seriously, slowly, carefully）、疑问副词（如when, where, how, why）、关系副词（where, when）与连接副词（如then, so, therefore, however, hence, thus, nevertheless, otherwise, still）。

副词在句中可用作状语、表语等，最主要的功能是作状语，如：

What makes monarch butterflies particularly interesting is they migrate, all the way to California or Mexico in back. （CET-6, 2014.06）

It's quite interesting because the man is obviously used to teaching man. （CET-4, 2012.12）

Its informal conversational style would make interaction comfortable, and yet the machine would remain slightly unpredictable and therefore interesting. （CET-6, 2013.06）

Finally, he had a speech that was interesting and perfectly understandable to his audience. （CET-6, 2010.06）

Researchers having contributed greatly to psychology. （CET-4, 2012.12）

Since much of this energy comes from the utilization of fossil fuels, wastage of food potentially contributes to unnecessary global warming as well as inefficient resource utilization. （CET-6, 2013.12）

第五节 写作词汇的使用

一、词的语体色彩

词是构成篇章的最小单位。从写作的角度讲，词可以根据其语体特色分为普通词（例如begin, buy, drink）、书面词语（如commence, purchase）、口语体词汇（如kid, vim）。对于写作初学者，在写作中根据语体来选择词汇是比较困难的，但尽量要避免使用俚语，也不要追求书面语词汇。力求准确地使用普通词汇即常用词汇，应是我们写作的原则。例如：

People often collect things. Stamps, books and records are fairly common. But the strangest collection I have ever seen belongs to a man who possesses

150 clocks. There are clocks in every room of his house. Each clock keeps its own time, so chimes can be heard almost any time during the day and night. In her opinion, however, there is something even worse than dust and noise. Even with so many clocks around, she never knows what time it is!

本段通篇均使用普通词汇，但表达语意到位，浅显易懂，幽默风趣，语言可读性非常强。对于写作初学者，建议使用常用词，通俗易懂，直接明了，非常用词则抽象难懂应尽量避免，例如：

常用词	非常用词
make	manufacture
buy	purchase
ask	interrogate
finish	accomplish
begin	commence
end	terminate
use	utilize
love	affection
agree	accord
discussion	controversy
tell	inform
enough	sufficient
speed	velocity
car	vehicle
live	dwell
open	unclose
put	dispose
choice	alternative

二、辨析词义与正确选词

（一）词汇的本意和引申意

词汇的本意指其基本含义，引申意义往往指从本义发展出来的意义、暗示的意义或感情色彩。例如 country，nation，state 和 land 的本义均含有"国家"的意义，但其引申意义却各有不同。Country 着眼于国家的版图领土，nation 着重于一个国家的民族，state 强调国家的政体，land 较模糊地从地理学角度着眼于一个国家，但常含较浓的感情色彩，因此常构成 mother-land，father-land，home-land 等复合词和词组。

试比较：

Japan is an island country.

Please name your neighboring countries.

We are a peace-loving nation.

The modernization program has won the support of the whole nation.

China belongs to the Third World states.

Ours is a state-owned enterprise.

He died for his mother-land.

（二）词汇的广义与狭义

词汇均有广义和狭义两种意义，因而在表达某一具体思想时，需要予以选择。如：

（1）农业是国民经济的基础。

Agriculture is the foundation of the national economy.

（2）在这一地区，农业和林业同等重要。

In this area, farming is as important as forestry.

（三）词汇的多义性

英语词汇十分丰富，与汉语词汇一样，常常一词多义、一词多性，一个词语有多种具有相互联系的词义、不同的词性，在不同的语境中可以表达多种不同的意义，也可呈现不同的词性。如多义词 develop，《朗文当代英语辞典》中列出的 develop 动词义项有：

（1）to grow or gradually change into a larger, stronger, or more advanced state. 如：

Knowledge in the field of genetics has been developing very rapidly.

（2）to make a new idea, plan, or product become successful over a period of time. 如：

Scientists are developing new drugs to treat arthritis.

（3）to start to have a feeling or a quality that then becomes stronger. 如：

It was in college that he developed a taste for rugby football.

（4）to make an argument or idea dearer, by studying it more or by speaking or writing about it in more detail. 如:

We will develop a few of these points in the seminar.

(5) to use land for the things that people need. 如:

The land was developed for low-cost housing.

(6) to make a photograph out of a photograph film. 如:

Did you ever get the pictures developed?

再如 major 一词有三种词性:

(1) 形容词, adj. very large or important, when compared to other things or people of a similar kind.

There are two major political parties in the US.

(2) 名词, n. the main subject that a student studies at college or university.

Her major is history.

(3) 动词, v. to study something as your main subject at college or university.

He is majoring in political science.

(四) 词义的强弱

在写作中要结合语境与语气的强弱选择恰当的词汇。如:

(1) 他极其生气。

His anger knew no boundness.

(2) 反动派的暴行激起了人民极大的愤怒。

The atrocities of the reactionaries roused the people to great indignation.

indignation 比 anger 显得更有力量,因为这个词的外延含有"义愤"的意思,其语体色彩较为正式和庄重。

再如 surprised 和 shocked 都表示"惊讶",但词义强弱有很大区别,surprised 表示吃惊,而 shocked 表示震惊。

(五) 词义的褒贬色彩

文以表意。人们通过文字表达感情与对事物的态度,态度不同就会使用含有不同感情色彩的词,或肯定、赞扬、否定、鄙视。在写作中,应依据词义的褒贬色彩选择恰当词汇来表达作者的感情色彩。

如 I like to work with that (resolute/stubborn) person. 此句中由 like 来看,应选用褒义词,resolute 表示"坚决的,刚毅的",stubborn 表示"倔强的",因此选用 resolute。

再如 They preach idealism whereas we advocate materialism. 其中用 preach (宣扬) 和 advocate (提倡) 来表达对 idealism 与 materialism 的不同态度。

第六节　写作常用词汇

语言表达是作文成功的关键。选择恰当的词汇来表达自己所确定的内容，才能表达清楚，文字连贯，突出中心。大学生在学习英语写作时应积极拓展词汇，力求准确表达。本节内容主要聚焦热点话题，帮助学习者掌握相关领域的词汇，主要包括科技类、教育类、经济类、社会生活类等各领域的词汇，并结合作文命题进行写作，每部分附有相关主题图画或图表，作为写作命题启发学习者思考主题词汇的运用与组织相关话题内容。另外，介绍图画图标常用词汇以及起连接作用的关联词。

一、科技类词汇

1. advanced science　尖端科学
2. scientific invention　科学发明
3. exert a far-reaching impact on…　对…产生一种深远的影响
4. double-edged sword　双刃剑
5. earth-shaking changes　翻天覆地的改变
6. pave the way for the future development　为未来的发展铺平道路
7. lay a solid foundation for…　为…打下良好的基础
8. energy crisis　能源危机
9. depletion of resources　能源消耗
10. milestone　里程碑
11. sophisticated equipment　尖端设备
12. technical innovation　科技创新
13. over-commercialized　过度商业化的
14. a heated discussion　热烈的讨论
15. exhaust gas　废气
16. disastrous　灾难性的
17. compared to/with…　与…相比
18. speedy and comfortable　既快捷又舒适
19. opposite forces　负面影响
20. potential hazards　潜在危险
21. pose a threat to…　对…有一种威胁
22. promote relative industries　促进相关产业发展

23. accelerate　加速…

24. means of transportation　交通方式

25. transportation tools　交通工具

26. social status　社会地位

27. environmentally-friendly resources　环保的能源

28. make people's life easier　使人们生活更方便

29. alternative fuel　可替代燃料

30. sustainable development　可持续性发展

31. scientific exploration　科学探索

32. air travel　航空旅行

33. ridiculous　可笑的

34. absurd　荒唐的

35. substitute　取代

36. overcome difficulties　克服困难

37. make progress　取得进步

38. a sense of national pride　民族自豪感

39. unprecedented　前所未有的

40. soaring　不断上升的

41. give a great push to the economic growth　极大地推动了经济发展

42. see dramatic breakthroughs　取得突破性进展

43. aggravate　使恶化

44. cure-all solution　万能良药

45. portable　便携的

46. innovative　创新的

47. cutting-edge　尖端的

48. cost-effective　性价比高的

49. augment/enhance/boost/efficiency/productivity　提高生产效率

50. be addicted to/be obsessed with　对…着迷/上瘾

51. technological progress/advances　科技进步

52. be accessible to　容易获得的

53. with the advent of　随着…的到来

54. pay a heavy price for sth.　为…付出惨痛的代价

55. theory of circuit　电路理论

56. analog electronics technology　模拟电子技术

57. digital electronics technology　数字电子技术
58. power electronics technology　电力电子技术
59. electromagnetic field　电磁场
60. automatic control theory　自动控制理论
61. modern control theory　现代控制理论
62. intelligent control　智能控制
63. principle of microcomputer　微机原理
64. computer control technology　计算机控制技术
65. process control system　过程控制系统
66. principle and application of single-chip computer　单片机原理与应用
67. programmable logical controller system　可编程序控制器系统
68. power supplying technology　供电技术
69. computer simulation　计算机仿真
70. signal analyzing and processing　信号分析与处理

◆ **Practices**

Directions：For each picture, write an essay of 160 – 200 words with the words about Education. In your essay you should describe the drawing briefly, explain its intended meaning, and give your comments.

Picture 1：Smart phones, the new lifeline

图片来源：http：//www.chinadaily.com.cn/a/201811/07/WS5be227afa310eff303286f9d.html

Picture 2: Duplicity By Li Min

图片来源：http://www.chinadaily.com.cn/a/201811/22/WS5bf5edd2a310eff30328a457.html

二、教育类词汇

1. diplomas and certificates 文凭

2. the craze for graduate school study 考研热

3. the examination-oriented education 应试教育

4. compulsory education 义务教育

5. interdisciplinary talents 复合型人才

6. the rich cultural deposits 文化底蕴

7. the university students' innovative undertakings 大学生创业

8. expand enrollment 扩招

9. be granted an official certificate 被授予学位

10. good scores but low qualities 高分低能

11. drop out of the school 退学

12. frame an elimination system 形成淘汰制度

13. impart knowledge and educate people 教书育人

14. teach students according to their aptitude 因材施教

15. place undue emphasis on the proportion of students entering schools of a higher level 片面追求升学率

16. be a students of fine qualities and fine scholar 品学兼优

17. improve the health and psychological quality 提高学生身心素质

18. adjust to the social changes quickly 适应社会的改变

19. meet the urgent need of the society 满足社会的急需

20. protect the intellectual property　保护知识产权

21. be wanting in ability and shallow in knowledge　才疏学浅

22. reduce the heavy burdens　减轻负担

23. a more vigorous, colorful and dynamic life　更加有意义和丰富的生活

24. education in patriotism　爱国主义教育

25. be innovation-minded; to have a creative mind　创新精神

26. school dropout/leaver　辍学/失学青少年

27. to combine ability with character; equal stress on integrity and ability　德才兼备

28. to give scope to students' initiative and creativeness　发挥学生的主动性、创造性

29. interdisciplinary talents　复合型人才

30. open class　公开课

31. intercultural communication　国际文化交流

32. extracurricular activities　课外活动

33. to cultivate the ability of analyzing and solving concrete problems independently　培养独立分析问题和解决问题的能力

34. to foster students' ability to study on their own　培养学生自学能力

35. to help develop the ability of students to think things out for themselves　启发学生独立思考的能力

36. exhaustion of human resources　人才枯竭

37. social practice　社会实践

38. cramming/forced-feeding method of teaching　填鸭式教学法

39. coordinated and balanced development　协调发展

40. graduate student; postgraduate (student)　研究生

41. graduating student; this year's graduates　应届毕业生

42. optimize the teaching staff　优化教师队伍

43. new regulation on preschool education　学前教育新规

◆ **Practices**

Directions: For each picture, write an essay of 160 – 200 words with the words about Education. In your essay you should describe the drawing briefly, explain its intended meaning, and give your comments.

第一章　英语词汇的使用

Picture 1：Life of a student

By Hao Yanpeng
图片来源：http：//www.chinadaily.com.cn/a/201810/12/WS5bbfe7cba310eff303281ed4.html

Picture 2：Spending childhood online

By Hao Yanpeng
图片来源：http：//www.chinadaily.com.cn/a/201809/13/WS5b99ac28a31033b4f4655bb8.html

Picture 3：Burden of children's eyes

By Hao Yanpeng

图片来源：http：//www.chinadaily.com.cn/a/201806/08/WS5b19bb03a31001b82571ec9b.html

Picture 4：Happy children or not?

By Hao Yanpeng

图片来源：http：//www.chinadaily.com.cn/a/201806/01/WS5b1089c0a31001b82571d8f4.html

三、经济类词汇

经济类话题是大学生常常面对的话题，如下列图片反映的网购话题"Upgraded online shopping can meet demands"：

第一章　英语词汇的使用

Upgraded online shopping can meet demands

By Zhang Zhiye

图片来源：http：//www.chinadaily.com.cn/a/201811/03/WS5bdd0023a310eff303286543.html

In a recent China Youth Daily survey covering 1,969 respondents aged between 18 and 35, 68.1 percent said they value the price-performance ratio when shopping, while 58.3 percent said they would take into consideration the practicality and necessity of the goods they purchase, and 61.1 percent said they believe young people should purchase goods online to fulfill their real interests and for self-improvement.

Experts believe today's youths have a more rational approach to consumption, and the incorporation of knowledge and the fitness element into their daily lives has increasingly become a habit among them.

That young people attach more importance to the quality and price-performance ratio of the goods and services they purchase, and have a more mature consumption approach suggest they are nurturing "higher-quality consumption" as a result of China's qualitative economic development in recent years.

During the four decades of reform and opening-up, China's consumption has grown rapidly—for instance, total retail sales of social consumer goods increased from 155.86 billion yuan ($24.39 billion) in 1978 to 36.6 trillion yuan in 2017.

Once people's "quantity" demand for consumer goods is met, they tend to demand "quality" goods. This is true for consumption habits in any country.

No wonder an increasing number of young people in China are bidding adieu to indiscriminate "one-click purchase" on the internet. The rapid growth of non-living necessities in China's consumption market in recent years indicates people's consumption demands have become increasingly diversified. In general, people today attach more importance to quality products and seek more value experience from shopping. If the unrestrained online shopping in the past was a "lower stage" of consumption, then the current trend means the upgrading of consumption from quantity to quality.

Good quality and fast delivery of goods constitute the core of good online shopping experience. Many Chinese people like online shopping because the prices of goods online are lower compared with those in brick-and-mortar stores. But online shopping may not necessarily ensure the supply of quality goods. So, the guarantee of quality goods in online stores can give consumers a true and assured sense of gain.

If the price advantage in online shopping is offset by shoddy products, then the advantage could become a disadvantage. As consumers focus more on rational shopping and quality goods, it means that the consumption supply chain is being upgraded.

Given these facts, it is important to build a scientific and efficient quality control mechanism, introduce at-source quality management, and establish a set of mature basic service and after-sales service system, to address the rising diversified needs of consumers.

Some e-commerce platforms have been working hard to meet consumers' diversified demands for high-quality shopping. For example, JD.com, one of China's leading e-commerce giants, set up a special customer experience department this year to improve a series of services for consumers, from assured purchase and quick refund, to compensation for delayed delivery, replacement of old products with new ones through home calls, and other tailored after-sales services.

Fast delivery can bring consumers a sense of instant gratification, which is particularly important during big shopping events such as "Double Eleven" when there is a high probability of express delivery congestion. So it is of vital importance to have an independent and high-quality logistics platform. The business of providing comprehensive and integrated logistics solutions for the diversified demands of consumers and consumption scenarios, and of offering better quality services to consumers and merchants, is becoming a competitive area for major e-commerce platforms.

That young Chinese have become more mature means that during shopping galas such as "Double Eleven", every link in the demand and supply chain—from production and sales to delivery, after-sales services, technology upgrading and operation mode optimization—must be continuously strengthened to provide high-quality services for consumers. In other words, only when the online shopping supply chain is upgraded can it meet the needs of rational and high-quality consumption.

(The article was first published in China Youth Daily.)

1. give play to the regulatory role of the market 发挥市场的调节作用
2. excessive growth 发展过快
3. take precautions against and reduce financial risks 防范和化解金融风险
4. public ownership 公有制
5. joint venture 合资企业
6. exercise macro control 实行宏观控制
7. active fiscal policy 积极的财政政策
8. a mechanism that combines planned economy and market regulation 计划经济和市场调节相结合的机制
9. liberate/unshackle/release the productive forces 解放生产力
10. reform in economic structure 经济结构改革
11. fuel economic growth 拉动经济增长
12. per capital income 人均收入
13. commodity economy 商品经济
14. foreign-funded enterprise 外资企业
15. effectively control inflation 有效控制通货膨胀
16. sustainable development strategy 可持续发展战略
17. to fuel economic growth 拉动经济增长
18. to open up and enliven the economy 开放搞活经济
19. to expand domestic demand 扩大内需
20. integration with the global economy 全球经济一体化
21. to turn losses into gains 转亏为盈
22. decline/recession/depression 萎缩/衰退/萧条
23. to increase consumption 增加消费
24. net profit 净利润
25. to extend cooperation 扩大合作
26. economic prosperity 经济繁荣
27. real estate 房地产
28. stock market 股市

29. macro-regulatory measures/policies 宏观调控手段/政策
30. consumption goods 消费品
31. a financial crisis 金融危机
32. to demand exceeds supply 供不应求
33. with low price and high quality 物美价廉
34. after-sale service 售后服务
35. during peak selling seasons 旺季
36. the peak of the tourist season 旅游旺季
37. the golden week for tourism 旅游黄金周
38. trade mark infringement 商标冒用
39. stabilize the commodity prices 稳定物价
40. raise the purchasing power 提高购买力
41. keep the market in good order 保持市场的良好的秩序
42. be good for sale 适销对路
43. out of stock 脱销
44. stimulate the desire to buy 刺激购买欲
45. clearance sale 清仓甩卖
46. premature consumption 超前消费
47. term of validity 有效期
48. retail price 零售价
49. whole price 批发价
50. forged and fake commodities 假冒伪劣
51. international tourist deficit 国际游客赤字
52. lazy economy 懒人经济
53. countryside tourism 乡村旅游

◆ **Practices**

Directions：For each picture, write an essay of 160 – 200 words with the words about Economy. In your essay you should describe the drawing briefly, explain its intended meaning, and give your comments.

Picture 1：The price of love

By Hao Yanpeng

图片来源：http://www.chinadaily.com.cn/a/201707/28/WS59bbf3dfa310ded8ac18f4b7.html

Picture 2：Avoid the travel trap

By Hao Yanpeng

图片来源：http://www.chinadaily.com.cn/a/201709/26/WS5a0bde44a31061a7384049ca.html

Picture 3：Alibaba sets new record

By Cai Meng

图片来源：http://www.chinadaily.com.cn/a/201811/13/WS5bea1442a310eff303288397.html

四、社会生活类词汇

1. farmer laborer   农民工
2. noble career   崇高职业
3. white-collar workers   白领
4. job-hopping   跳槽
5. probationary period   试用期
6. talent flow and a dual-way selection   人才流动和双向选择
7. freelance work   自由职业
8. money worship   拜金主义
9. achieve fame and wealth   获得名利
10. develop fully one's potential and creativity   充分发挥个人的潜力
11. steadfast and earnest in one's work   实干精神
12. excel in one's work   工作出色
13. be care-free   无忧无虑
14. social and personal esteem   社会和个人的尊重
15. a bread and butter issue   生计问题
16. living subsidies   生活补助
17. talents exchange   人才交流
18. cultivate talents   培养人才
19. recommend the virtuous and able   推荐人才
20. brain drain   人才外流
21. cut off the overstaffed offices   精减人员
22. improve the comprehensive quality   提高综合素质
23. tackle the problem of labor force utilization   解决劳动就业问题
24. be persistent in the reform progress   坚持改革
25. bring about the unemployment problem   造成失业问题
26. the laid-off workers   下岗人员
27. give preferential treatment   给出优惠政策
28. enjoy unemployment pension   享受失业救济金
29. need a sense of security and guarantee of life   需要安全感和生活保障
30. shortage of labour   劳动力短缺
31. enhance their cultural and moral quality   提高文化、智慧、品质修养
32. white-collar   白领

33. strive for a relatively comfortable life 奔小康

34. the social security system in urban areas 城镇社会保障体系

35. get advanced in the society 出人头地

36. （passenger）transport during the Spring Festival 春运

37. a well-paid job 待遇优厚的工作

38. pay close attention to cultural and ethical progress 高度重视精神文明建设

39. matters vital to national well-being and the people's livelihood 关系国计民生的大事

40. to rationally readjust the employment structure 合理调整就业结构

41. ensure that the correct orientation is maintained in public opinion 加强舆论监督

42. family virtues 家庭美德

43. to establish a market-oriented employment mechanism 建立市场导向的就业机制

44. build a clean, diligent, pragmatic and efficient government 建设廉洁、勤政、务实、高效政府

45. to expand employment and reemployment 扩大就业和再就业

46. help people develop practical abilities and a spirit of innovation 培养创新精神和实践能力

47. aging of population 人口老龄化

48. implement the policy of vigorously increasing employment 实施积极促进就业的政策

49. foster the morally sound values and outlooks on the world and life 树立正确的价值观、世界观、人生观

50. push ahead with education for all-around development 推进素质教育

51. modern city; culturally advanced city 文明城市

52. supervision by public opinion 舆论监督

53. ethics of profession 职业道德

54. starting from scratch 白手起家

55. over consuming; excessive consumption 超前消费

56. foster integration with the global economy 促进全球经济一体化

57. regional protectionism 地方保护主义

58. combat corruption and build a clean government 反腐倡廉

59. internationalization strategy　国际化战略

60. economic globalization; economic integration　经济全球化

61. streamline government organs　精简机构

62. refuse to take passengers　拒载

63. rely on science and education to rejuvenate the nation　科教兴国

64. courtesy calls for reciprocity　礼尚往来

65. bubble economy　泡沫经济

66. show special preference (favor) to…　情有独钟

67. take-out　外卖

68. (of two countries or companies) have complementary advantages　优势互补

69. strategic partnership　战略伙伴关系

70. transform/shift the government function　政府职能转变

71. make government affairs public　政务公开

72. virtual nursing home　虚拟养老院

73. new occupation population　新职业人群

◆ **Practices**

Directions: For each picture, write an essay of 160 – 200 words with the words about Social Life. In your essay you should describe the drawing briefly, explain its intended meaning, and give your comments.

Picture 1: Jumping through hoops

By Cai Meng

图片来源: http://www.chinadaily.com.cn/a/201811/29/WS5bff2e2fa310eff30328bac3.html

Picture 2：Traffic congestion

By Chen Jianhui

图片来源：http：//www.chinadaily.com.cn/a/201810/08/WS5bbaadd6a310eff303280f30.html

Picture 3：Focused

By Lu Nan

图片来源：http：//www.chinadaily.com.cn/a/201706/15/WS59bbeb7aa310ded8ac18ce7a.html

五、环保类词汇

1. environmental（air/water/noise）pollution 环境（空气/水/噪声）污染
2. resources exhaustion 资源枯竭
3. wildlife extinction 野生动物灭绝
4. endangered species 濒危物种
5. natural habitat 自然栖息地
6. reserved areas 野生动物保护区
7. sand/dust storms 沙尘暴

8. clear-cutting/deforestation 滥砍滥伐
9. over-fishing 过度捕捞
10. overgrazing 过度放牧
11. soil erosion 土壤侵蚀
12. water and soil conservation 水土保持
13. desertification 沙漠化
14. natural disaster 自然灾害
15. drought 旱灾
16. famine 饥荒
17. disruption of ecological balance 生态失衡
18. devastate/ruin/destroy 毁坏
19. shortage of water resources 水资源短缺
20. harmful chemicals 有害化合物
21. poisonous/toxic gases 有毒气体
22. urban smog 城市烟雾
23. industrial waste 工业废料
24. hazardous nuclear waste 有害核废料
25. waste gas sent off from automobiles 汽车排放废气
26. throw-away lunchbox 一次性饭盒
27. recyclable product 可循环产品
28. renewable resources 可更新资源
29. solar energy 太阳能
30. conserve natural resources 保护自然资源
31. greenhouse effect 温室效应
32. global warming 全球变暖
33. energy crisis 能源危机
34. shortage of fresh water 淡水资源短缺
35. environmental awareness 环保意识
36. survival of the fittest 适者生存
37. food chain 食物链
38. ecosystem 生态系统
39. garbage disposal 垃圾处理
40. greenhouse effect 温室效应
41. pursue the strategy of sustainable development 推行可持续发展战略

42. promote fundamental shifts in the economic system and mode of economic growth　促进经济体制和经济增长方式的转变

43. policy of prevention in the first place and integrating prevention with control　预防为主、防治结合的政策

44. raise environmental awareness among the general public　提高全民环保意识

45. industrial solid wastes　工业固体废物

46. protect forests from over exploitation　防止过度利用森林

47. water and soil erosion　水土流失

48. environment-friendly agriculture; eco-agriculture　生态农业

49. sea water desalination　海水淡化

50. protect fishing resource　保护渔业资源

51. develop renewable resources　开发可再生资源

52. environmental degradation　环境恶化

53. uncontrolled urbanization　城市化失控

54. air pollution concentration　空气污染浓度

55. acid rain　酸雨

56. suspended particles　悬浮颗粒物

57. industrial dust discharged　工业粉尘排放

58. motor vehicle exhaust　汽车尾气排放

59. cell-driven vehicles; battery cars　电动汽车

60. zero-waste cities　无废城市

61. green industrial project　绿色产业项目

62. unbounded forest　无界森林

63. ban on catching wild birds　禁猎野生鸟类

◆ **Practices**

Directions: For each picture, write an essay of 160 – 200 words with the words about Environmental Protection. In your essay you should describe the drawing briefly, explain its intended meaning, and give your comments.

Picture 1: Melting polar regions

By Hao Yanpeng

图片来源：http://www.chinadaily.com.cn/a/201812/03/WS5c047dd6a310eff30328e8f3.html

Picture 2: Protect animals

图片来源：http://www.chinadaily.com.cn/a/201811/01/WS5bda3539a310eff303285c88.html

Picture 3: Climate change

By Zhu Shaowei

图片来源：http://www.chinadaily.com.cn/a/201808/20/WS5b79ffc6a310add14f386918.html

六、图画图表作文常用词

（一）图的种类及相关表达

漫画　cartoon
图片　picture
照片　photograph
饼状图　pie chart
柱状图　bar chart/column chart
表格　table
流程图　flow chart

（二）图表数据的种类及表达

数字　figure /number
数据　data
统计数据　statistic
比例　proportion
百分比　percentage

（三）数据变化及表达

不变　remain stable
在一系列时间段中转变　change over time
增加　increase, rise, go up, surge, climb, mount
减少　decrease, grow down, drop, fall, descend, decline, reduce, lessen
波动　fluctuate, undulate, wave, rise and fall, up and down
迅速的　rapid/rapidly
戏剧性　dramatic/dramatically
有意义的　significant/-ly
急剧的　sharp/-ly
稳固的　steady/steadily
逐渐的　gradual/-ly
缓慢的　slow/-ly
略微的　slight/-ly
一些较大变化　significant changes

（四）表比较的常用词汇

占20%比例　account for 20 percent, make up 20 percent

位居第一　rank the first
仅次于　be second to
居第二位　in second spot
与…相比　compared with

◆ **Practices**

Directions: For each picture, write an essay of 160 – 200 words with the words about Environmental Protection. In your essay you should describe the drawing briefly, explain its intended meaning, and give your comments.

Picture 1: Global warming alert

By Luo Jie
图片来源：http://www.chinadaily.com.cn/a/201808/10/WS5b6cc9a8a310add14f384f6a.html

Picture 2: The last supper

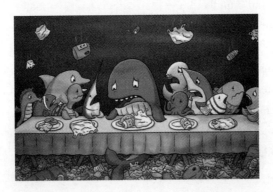

By Hao Yanpeng
图片来源：http://www.chinadaily.com.cn/a/201807/26/WS5b5913c7a31031a351e9032c.html

七、常用关联词

（一）表层次的关联词

first, firstly, to begin/start with, in the first place, second, secondly, still, furthermore, third, thirdly, what is more, last but not least, also, and, then, next, besides, and equally important, too, moreover, in addition, finally

（二）表转折的关联词

by contrast, although, though, yet, at the same time, but, despite the fact that, in contrast with, nevertheless, even though, notwithstanding, on the contrary, however, in spite of, on the other hand, otherwise

（三）表因果的关联词

therefore, consequently, because of, for the reason, thus, hence, due to, owing to, so, accordingly, thanks to, on this account, since, as, for, as a result, as a consequence

（四）表递进的关联词

furthermore, moreover, likewise, what is more, besides, also, not only… but also…, too, in addition

（五）表举例的关联词

for example, for instance, for one thing, to illustrate, as an illustration, a case in point

（六）表解释的关联词

as a matter of fact, frankly speaking, in this case, namely, in other words

（七）表总结的关联词

in summary, in a word, thus, as has been said, in brief, in conclusion, altogether in other words, in simpler terms, in short, in other words, on the whole, to put it differently, in consequence, hence namely, all in all, therefore, to summarize

◆ **Practices**

Directions: For each picture, write an essay of 160 – 200 words with the words about Environmental Protection. In your essay you should describe the drawing briefly, explain its intended meaning, and give your comments.

Picture 1: Water crisis

By Cai Meng

图片来源：http://www.chinadaily.com.cn/a/201704/06/WS59bb42fba310d4d9ab7e1b6f.html

Picture 2: Bike-sharing

By Cai Meng

图片来源：http://www.chinadaily.com.cn/a/201704/20/WS59bb7bb1a310d4d9ab7e8a98.html

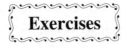

I. Multiple choice

Direction: Identify the choice that best completes the statement.

1. The computer revolution may well change society as ____ as did the Industrial Revolution.

    A. comparatively   B. certainly
    C. fundamentally   D. insignificantly

2. Petrol is refined from the ____ oil we take out of the ground.

    A. fresh   B. original

    C. rude   D. crude

3. If America insists on using fuel-efficiency standards to cut ____ emissions, then tough ones are better than weak ones.

    A. ship   B. boat

    C. vehicle   D. vessel

4. As the country with the largest military expenses in the world, even a single soldier's ____ is rather expensive.

    A. dress   B. uniform

    C. costume   D. gown

5. Scientists have found new uses for some ____ such as mercury and lead.

    A. stuff   B. matters

    C. substances   D. materials

6. The engineer ____ a rare disease when he was working in Africa.

    A. took   B. suffered

    C. caught   D. infected

7. Without the friction between their feet and the ground, people would ____ be able to walk.

    A. in no time   B. by all means

    C. in no way   D. on any account

8. Tall-growing crops should be planted where they will not shade or ____ with the growth of smaller crops.

    A. interrupt   B. interfere

    C. disturb   D. distract

9. The mechanic examined the car engine ____ but could find nothing wrong with it.

    A. exactly   B. completely

    C. thoroughly   D. throughout

10. The melting of the snow has caused flooding by ____ rivers.

    A. increased   B. expanded

    C. overgrown   D. swollen

11. As a result of the radio ____ for help for those who lost their homes in the earthquake, over a million pounds has been raised.

A. appeal				B. call
C. program				D. demand

12. An ambulance must have priority as it usually has to deal with something of ____ .

A. urgency				B. danger
C. crisis				D. emergency

13. Our compass and maps proved ____ to us in the walking tours.

A. valuable				B. worth
C. profitable			D. valueless

14. The fundamental ____ , which govern all physical processes, are related to many everyday occurrences.

A. rules				B. regulations
C. principals			D. principles

15. He told me his digestive trouble is cured ____ and all.

A. for long				B. for life
C. for ever				D. for good

16. The liquid was heated until the temperature ____ 1000℃.

A. arrived				B. reached
C. achieved				D. attained

17. Half the planet always faces the sun, while the other half is ____ dark.

A. clearly				B. consequently
C. continually			D. continuously

18. The noise was so faint that only those with excellent ____ were aware of it.

A. ear					B. listening
C. hearing				D. ears

19. It is said that a heavy ____ is imposed on foreign radios.

A. tax					B. fine
C. duty					D. rate

20. The doctor took X-rays to ____ the chance of broken bones.

A. make sure			B. rule out
C. break down			D. knock out

II. Reading Comprehension

Directions: In this section, there is a passage with ten blanks. You are required to select one word for each blank from a list of choices given in a word bank following the passage. Read the passage through carefully before making your choices. Each choice in the bank is identified by a letter. Please mark the corresponding letter for each item. You may not use any of the words in the bank more than once.

Passage One

When we think of green buildings, we tend to think of new ones—the kind of high-tech, solar-paneled masterpieces that make the covers of architecture magazines. But the U. S. has more than 100 million existing homes, and it would be __ 1 __ wasteful to tear them all down and __ 2 __ them with greener versions. An enormous amount of energy and resources went into the construction of those houses. And it would take an average of 65 years for the __ 3 __ carbon emissions from a new energy-efficient home to make up for the resources lost by destroying an old one. So in the broadest __ 4 __, the greenest home is the one that has already been built. But at the same time, nearly half of U. S. carbon emissions come from heating, cooling and __ 5 __ our homes, offices and other buildings. "You can't deal with climate change without dealing with existing buildings," says Richard Moe, the president of the National Trust.

With some __ 6 __, the oldest homes tend to be the least energy-efficient. Houses built before 1939 use about 50% more energy per square foot than those built after 2000, mainly due to the tiny cracks and gaps that __ 7 __ over time and let in more outside air.

Fortunately, there are a __ 8 __ number of relatively simple changes that can green older homes, from __ 9 __ ones like Lincoln's Cottage to your own postwar home. And efficiency upgrades (升级) can save more than just the earth; they can help __ 10 __ property owners from rising power costs.

A) accommodations	B) clumsy	C) doubtful	D) exceptions
E) expand	F) historic	G) incredibly	H) powering	I) protect
J) reduced	K) replace	L) sense	M) shifted	N) supplying
O) vast			

Passage Two

For a while, biologist Arjan Boonman lived in Indonesia and spent much of his time traveling the country to make __ 11 __ recordings of bats. "There's a lot of deforestation there, and lots of bats are __ 12 __ going to go extinct," says

Boonman, now a post doctoral researcher at Tel Aviv University in Israel. __13__ by the bats, he decided to gather as much information as __14__ about the various species in Indonesia, before they're gone. One day Boonman sat down on a bus next to a friendly man, who told him he'd heard a species __15__ cave nectar bats making a clicking sound with their wings, perhaps using it to echolocate. Echolocation is the process whereby bats and other animals bounce sound off their surroundings to help them navigate, especially in the dark. Boonman was __16__. Bat biologists, including Boonman, pretty much all assumed that bats only echolocate __17__, by making sounds in their larynx. It was also generally thought that the vast majority of species in this family, known as Old World fruits bats, didn't echolocate at all, says bat expert Nancy Simmons, the curator – in – charge at the department of mammalogy at New York's American Museum of Natural History.

Boonman was convinced that it was a story worth looking into, and together they and a third scientist went to Thailand to record several different unrelated species of fruit bats (one of the better travel excuses out there). They found that several species of bats did __18__ make clicking sounds with their wings, increasing the frequency of these clicks more than fivefold when they turned out the lights. This and other experiments led them to __19__ that the bats use these wing clicks to find their way around, and the clicking appears to function as a primitive form of echolocation, says Simmons, who wasn't involved in the study, which was __20__ in the journal Current Biology.

| A) called   B) published   C) vocally   D) feasible   E) possible |
| F) probably   G) primarily   H) stop   I) indeed   J) conclude |
| K) Interested   L) Fascinated   M) identical   N) skeptical   O) audio |

第二章

英语句子的写作

  美文赏析

Speech by President Barack Hussein Obama

Vice President Biden, Mr. Chief Justice, Members of the United States Congress, distinguished guests, and fellow citizens:

Each time we gather to inaugurate a president, we bear witness to the enduring strength of our Constitution. We affirm the promise of our democracy. We recall that what binds this nation together is not the colors of our skin or the tenets of our faith or the origins of our names. What makes us exceptional—what makes us American—is our allegiance to an idea, articulated in a declaration made more than two centuries ago:

"We hold these truths to be self-evident, that all men are created equal, that they are endowed by their Creator with certain unalienable rights, that among these are Life, Liberty, and the pursuit of Happiness."

Today we continue a never-ending journey, to bridge the meaning of those words with the realities of our time. For history tells us that while these truths may be self-evident, they have never been self-executing; that while freedom is a gift from God, it must be secured by His people here on Earth. The patriots of 1776 did not fight to replace the tyranny of a king with the privileges of a few or the rule of a mob. They gave to us a Republic, a government of, and by, and for the people, entrusting each generation to keep safe our founding creed.

For more than two hundred years, we have:

Through blood drawn by lash and blood drawn by sword, we learned that no union founded on the principles of liberty and equality could survive half-slave and half-free. We made ourselves anew, and vowed to move forward together.

Together, we determined that a modern economy requires railroads and highways to speed travel and commerce; schools and colleges to train our workers.

Together, we discovered that a free market only thrives when there are rules to ensure competition and fair play.

Together, we resolved that a great nation must care for the vulnerable, and protect its people from life's worst hazards and misfortune.

Through it all, we have never relinquished our skepticism of central authority, nor have we succumbed to the fiction that all society's ills can be cured through government alone. Our celebration of initiative and enterprise; our insistence on hard work and personal responsibility, these are constants in our character.

But we have always understood that when times change, so must we; that fidelity to our founding principles requires new responses to new challenges; that preserving our individual freedoms ultimately requires collective action. For the American people can nomore meet the demands of today's world by acting alone than American soldiers could have met the forces of fascism or communism with muskets and militias. No single person can train all the math and science teachers we'll need to equip our children for the future, or build the roads and networks and research labs that will bring new jobs and businesses to our shores. Now, more than ever, we must do these things together, as one nation, and one people.

This generation of Americans has been tested by crisis that steeled our resolve and proved our resilience. A decade of war is now ending. An economic recovery has begun. America's possibilities are limitless, for we possess all the qualities that this world without boundaries demands: youth and drive; diversity and openness; an endless capacity for risk and a gift for reinvention. My fellow Americans, we are made for this moment, and we will seize it—so long as we seize it together.

For we, the people, understand that our country cannot succeed when a shrinking few do very well and a growing many barely make it. We believe that America's prosperity must rest upon the broad shoulders of a rising middle class. We know that America thrives when every person can find independence and pride in their work; when the wages of honest labor liberate families from the brink of hardship. We are true to our creed when a little girl born into the bleakest poverty knows that she has the same chance to succeed as anybody else, because she is an American, she is free, and she is equal, not just in the eyes of God but also in our own.

We understand that outworn programs are inadequate to the needs of our time. We must harness new ideas and technology to remake our government, revamp our tax code, reform our schools, and empower our citizens with the skills they need to work harder, learn more, and reach higher. But while the means will change, our purpose endures: a nation that rewards the effort and determination of every single American. That is what this moment requires. That is what will give real meaning to our creed.

We, the people, still believe that every citizen deserves a basic measure of security and dignity. We must make the hard choices to reduce the cost of health care and the size of our deficit. But we reject the belief that America must choose between caring for the generation that built this country and investing in the generation that will build its future. For we remember the lessons of our past, when twilight years were spent in poverty, and parents of a child with a disability had nowhere to turn. We do not believe that in this country, freedom is reserved for the lucky, or happiness for the few. We recognize that no matter how responsibly we live our lives, any one of us, at any time, may face a job loss, or a sudden illness, or a home swept away in a terrible storm. The commitments we make to each other—through Medicare, and Medicaid, and Social Security—these things do not sap our initiative; they strengthen us. They do not make us a nation of takers; they free us to take the risks that make this country great.

▶ 赏析：

奥巴马在宣誓就职第四十四任美利坚合众国总统时发表的就职演说堪称句式运用的典范。该篇演讲内容丰富、深刻，追溯了美国民主传统和宪法精神，强调了民众的力量，演讲中涉及了包括就业、医保、移民等多项议题，演讲中句子多为陈述句，分句、从句使用频率高，能够引发听众情感上共鸣。多处运用了反复、排比等修辞，使演讲词更具美感与号召力，如 Together, we determined that...; Together, we discovered that...; Together, we resolved that...。We must harness new ideas and technology to remake our government, revamp our tax code, reform our schools, and empower our citizens with the skills they need to work harder, learn more, and reach higher. 平行结构的使用使语调上富有韵律，能够充分表现演讲者的情感、渲染气氛，更能打动人心。

第一节　英语句子的结构

英语的基本句型是构成所有句子结构的根本。学习者在掌握基本句型的基础上，在写作中要使用多样化的句型，如错综使用长句与短句、简单句与复合句，从而丰富写作表达力，但初学者对主从复合句的使用往往存在困难。本节结合实例分别讲解英语句子的基本结构与主从复合句的构成及用法。

一、英语的基本句型

英语句子有长有短，有简有繁，但分析其基本结构可以归纳成五种基本句型，这五种基本句型是构成各种英语句子结构的基础。英语五种基本句型包括主+谓、主+系+表、主+谓+宾、主+谓+双宾与主+谓+复合宾语。

（一）"主+谓"结构

此句型的句子可分为两个部分，即主语部分和谓语部分，主语部分主要由名词、代词、名词短语或名词性从句来构成，谓语部分主要由不及物动词构成并能表达完整的意思。如：

It begins in the west, passes through three ninety-degree turns, and exits to the south. (Peter Hessler, New Progressive College English Integrated Course 4, abbreviated as NPCEIC in the following part)

These structures stand behind walls of gray brick. (NPCEIC)

Street vendors pass through regularly, because the hutong are too small for supermarkets. (NPCEIC)

For the past five years, I've lived about a mile north of the Forbidden City in an apartment building off a tiny alleyway in downtown Beijing. (NPCEIC)

On warm evenings, men sit idly on the machines and smoke cigarettes. (NPCEIC)

（二）"主+系+表"结构

此句型由主语、系动词和表语构成。系动词起连接作用，其中 be、look、keep、seem 等用来表示状态，get、grow、become、turn 等表示变化。如：

Indeed, the change was dramatic. (NPCEIC)

At dawn and dusk, they are especially busy—older people meet in groups to chat and take a few rounds on the pendulum. (NPCEIC)

The workout stations are perfect for the ultimate hutong sport: hanging around in the street with the neighbors. (NPCEIC)

Like many Beijing people I knew, Wang Zhaoxin was practical, good-humored, and unsentimental. (NPCEIC)

He kept silent in the dinner.

（三）"主+谓+宾"结构

此句型中谓语由及物动词构成，动词是主语实施的动作，且该动作要有承受者，即宾语。如：

Dozens of households might share a single entrance, and although the old residences have running water, few people have private bathrooms, so public toilets play a major role in local life. (NPCEIC)

At the end of 2000, as part of the citywide pre-Olympic campaign to improve sanitation facilities, the government rebuilt the public toilet at the head of Ju'er Hutong. (NPCEIC)

Wang Zhaoxin modestly refused the title of Chairman although he was the obvious choice, because nobody else had seen so many changes in the neighborhood. (NPCEIC)

(四)"主+谓+双宾"结构

此句型中的谓语动词是及物动词且必须跟有两个宾语才能表达完整的意思。两个宾语中,一个是动作的直接承受者,称为直接宾语,另一个是动作的间接承受者,称为直接宾语。

She brought me a new book.
He showed me a picture.
My mother told me a story.

(五)"主+谓+复合宾语"结构

此句型的句子的共同特点是:动词虽然是及物动词,但是只跟一个宾语还不能表达完整的意思,必须加上一个补充成分来补足宾语,才能使意思完整。宾语和宾语补足语统称为复合宾语,常接复合宾语的动词有believe、choose、consider、find、elect、keep、make等。如:

Just one week after Obama was elected president, participants were less ready to support policies designed to address racial inequality than they had been two weeks before the election. (CET-6, 2010.06)

He has been successfully elected Prime Minister. (CET-6, 2011.12)

We consider it a compliment to be called "conservative."

二、主从复合句

主从复合句由主句与一个或一个以上的从句构成,主句为句子的主体,从句不能独立,只用作句子的一个成分。一般来说,英语中一个句子只能有一个谓语,如果要出现两个或两个以上谓语动词,那么谓语动词要用并列连词连接以并列形式出现,或者其中一个谓语动词在主句中出现而其他谓语动词在从句中出现。从句是指从属于主句的句子,借助从属连词与主句连接,表达不同的逻辑关系,起不同作用。根据从句的性质和作用,从句可以分为名词性从句、形容词性从句(即定语从句)与副词性从句（即状语从句）三大类。

（一）名词性从句

在句子中起名词作用的句子叫名词性从句。名词性从句和名词在句子中的功能一致，在复合句中可以充当主语、宾语、表语、同位语等。

1. 主语从句

作句子主语的从句叫主语从句。引导主语从句的关联词有从属连词 that/whether、关系代词 who/ what/ which/ whom/ whose/ whatever/ whoever/ whomever/ whichever、关系副词 when/ where/ how/ why/ however/ whenever/ wherever 等。也可用 it 做形式主语，主语从句放在句末。另外，用 that 引导主语从句时，连接词 that 不能省略。如：

Whatever he bought was not attractive to her. （以 whatever 为引导词）

It is imperative that we keep pushing the limits of our ocean. （以 that 为引导词）（NPCEIC）

That she suddenly came to visit me made me surprised. （以 that 为引导词）

Whether he is coming or not doesn't matter. （以 whether 为引导词）

What we care about is, when faced with a problem and you're a member of a team, do you, at the appropriate time, step in and lead. （以 what 为引导词）（NPCEIC）

What's critical to be an effective leader in this environment is you have to be willing to relinquish power. （以 what 为引导词）（NPCEIC）

2. 宾语从句

作宾语的从句叫作宾语从句，在句中可以作动词、介词、形容词的宾语，由从属连词 that whether、if，关系代词 what, who, whose, which 和关系副词 when、where、how、why 等引导。如：

I am not certain whether he will come here this afternoon. （以 whether 为引导词，作形容词 certain 的宾语）

This discovery means that we may find other fishlike creatures, supposedly extinct but still living in the sea. （以 that 为引导词，作动词 means 的宾语）（NPCEIC）

As long as it keeps ticking, you will know what time it is. （以 what 为引导词，作动词 know 的宾语）（NPCEIC）

You can't understand what the problem is by just looking. （以 what 为引导词，作动词 understand 的宾语）（NPCEIC）

Yet despite the similarity in how we employ technology to explore both the ocean and space, there is a great disparity between the amount of funding put toward space exploration and ocean exploration. （以 how 为引导词，作介词 in 的宾语）（NPCEIC）

That is, until 2012, when Drs. Edith Widder, Steve O'Shea and Tsunemi Kobodera filmed the elusive and mysterious giant in its natural deep-sea habitat for the first time—a landmark moment in ocean exploration and an example of how technology and ingenuity can overcome the monumental challenges we face in exploring the deep. （以 how 为引导词，作介词 of 的宾语）（NPCEIC）

All of these types of findings fit together in a jigsaw puzzle that, as it reaches completion, reveals to us how people fit into the picture and how we can best manage, conserve and protect the oceans for our own benefit. （以 how 为引导词，作介词 to 的宾语）（NPCEIC）

3. 表语从句

用作表语的从句叫作表语从句，它位于主句中 be、look、remain、seem 等连系动词之后，引导表语从句的词有从属连词 that/whether/as though 等、关系代词 who/what/which/whom/whose/whatever/whoever/whomever/whichever 等、关系副词 when/where/why/how/however/whenever/wherever 等。

What's critical to be an effective leader in this environment is you have to be willing to relinquish power. （省略引导词 that）（NPCEIC）

What we've seen is that the people who are the most successful here, who we want to hire, will have a fierce position. （以 that 为引导词）（NPCEIC）

Culture has a way of evolving and that's exactly what we're experiencing with language. （以 what 为引导词）（NPCEIC）

4. 同位语从句

用作同位语的从句叫同位语从句，一般跟在抽象名词 fact/idea/news/plan/advice/belief/thought/truth/suggestion 等之后，对这些名词的具体内容展开说明或解释。引导同位语从句的词包括连词 that/whether、关系代词 what/which/who 及关系副词 how/when/where/why 等。

The teachers have got the information that 65% of the graduates in this class have been admitted into universities. （以 that 为引导词）

I've come from Mrs Li with a message that she will go to Beijing with you next week. （以 that 为引导词）

He didn't receive the news that the show had been put off. （以 that 为引导词）

（二）形容词性从句

同形容词的作用一样，在整个句子中作定语起修饰作用的从句叫做定语从句。定语从句往往跟在名词、代词或句子后面。被修饰的词叫先行词。定语从句分为限制性定语从句和非限制性定语从句。限制性定语从句对被修饰词起到限制修饰的作用，一般不可缺少，若缺少会影响句意表达。非限制性定语从句起补充、附带说明的作用，缺少也不会影响句子主要内容的表达。定语从句常用关系代词 who/whom/whose/that/which/as 等与关系副词 where/on which/when/why 来连接。定语从句引导词的选择取决于先行词在定语从句中的成分。

Healthy oceans can help ease the increasing burden our population is placing on this planet. （先行词是 burden，在从句中作 placing 的宾语，引导词 that 被省略）（NPCEIC）

As a scientist, I want to explore the great wonders our ocean has to offer. （先行词是 wonders，在从句中作 offer 的宾语，引导词 that 被省略）（NPCEIC）

And in an age when innovation is increasingly a group endeavor, it also cares about a lot of soft skills—leadership, humility, collaboration, adaptability and loving to learn and re-learn. （NPCEIC）（先行词是 age，在从句中作状语，引导词为 when）（NPCEIC）

He arranged a tiny space for her at the Municipal School of Industrial Physics and Chemistry where he worked. （先行词是 Municipal School of Industrial Physics and Chemistry，在从句中作 he worked 的状语，引导词为 where）（NPCEIC）

（三）状语从句

状语从句指在句子中起副词的作用、用作状语的从句。状语从句可以用来修饰谓语、非谓语动词、定语、状语或整个句子。状语从句一般由连词引导。常用引导词包括 when/as/while/as soon as/before/where/because/since/so that/if/unless/whether 等，根据其作用可分为时间、地点、原因、条件、目的、结果、让步、方式和比较等从句。

When Maria registered at the Sorbonne, in Paris, she signed her name as "Marie" to seem more French. （以 when 为引导词）（NPCEIC）

Although we did not get to film the giant squid or observe any species new to science, we did manage to film an important and often overlooked part of the ocean life cycle. （以 although 为引导词）（NPCEIC）

When animals in the ocean, particularly large ones like whales, die and sink to the bottom, they create their own micro-ecosystem, sort of like an oasis in the desert. （以 when 为引导词）（NPCEIC）

Many jobs at Google require math, computing and coding skills, so if your good grades truly reflect skills in those areas that you can apply, it would be an advantage. （以 if 为引导词）（NPCEIC）

When it was time for the final examinations, she was first in her class. （以 when 为引导词）（NPCEIC）

第二节 英语句子的成分

句子成分是句子的组成部分。清楚句子成分对规范写作与正确表达至关重要。一般来说，写作中常涉及的英语句子基本成分包括主语（subject）、谓语（predicate）、宾语（object）、表语（predicative）、定语（attribute）和状语（adverbial）。本节将对这六种句子成分依次作简要介绍。

一、主语

主语是一个句子的主题，是句子表达的主体。主语一般位于句首，放在谓语或系动词的前面，可用作主语的有名词、代词、名词短语、非谓语动词以及从句等。多数情况下，在主动句中，主语是动作的发出者，而在被动句中，主语是动作的承受者。在倒装句中，主语要放在谓语或助动词的后面。

Marie was buried next to Pierre, but in 1995, their remains were moved and interred in the Pantheon in Paris alongside France's greatest citizens. （NPCEIC，下同）

After the war, she worked hard to raise money for her Radium Institute, including a trip to the United States.

The nominating committee objected to including a woman as a Nobel Laureate, but Pierre insisted that the original research was Marie's.

Reaching it requires the same kind of methods, technology and expertise required for exploring space.

Making these kinds of observations are incredibly important to understanding how the ocean works.

There are no doubt countless discoveries to be made under the surface of the sea, whether they are species we know to exist but have yet to observe in their own habitat, species new to science or those species thought long extinct.

What we care about is, when faced with a problem and you're a member of a team, do you, at the appropriate time, step in and lead.

There's little room to worry about grammar in 140 characters, goes the argument, and besides, conforming to the rules of engagement in the Twitter-sphere is far more important than old grammatical rules.

It is imperative that we keep pushing the limits of our ocean.

二、谓语

谓语是对主语动作的陈述或说明，一般在主语之后，经常用动词或动词与名词搭配来充当。在主动句中，谓语表示主语发出的动作，而在被动句中则表示主语所承受的动作。谓语有其时态和语态的变化，因此在写作中要注重谓语动词形式的变化。

She decided to use Pierre's instruments to measure the faint electrical currents she detected in air that had been bombarded with uranium rays.

Together, they found that two ores, chalcolite and pitchblende, were much more radioactive than pure uranium.

Marie suspected that these ores might contain as yet undiscovered radioactive elements.

We are now hearing people actually saying "sad face" at the end of a sentence as in The weekend was a disaster.

Several tons of pitchblende were donated by the Austrian government, but the space Marie was using for a lab was too small.

At the exercise stations, people can spin giant wheels with their hands, push big levers that offer no resistance, and swing on pendulums like children at a park.

谓语动词的形式，除时态与语态变化外，还要注意与主语的搭配，遵循主谓一致原则，即谓语动词在人称和数上要和主语保持一致，主谓一致包括语法一致、意义一致和就近一致，语法一致即谓语动词在单复数形式上要和主语保持一致，意义一致即谓语动词要和主语意义上的单复数保持一致，就近一致即谓语动词要和靠近它的主语部分保持一致。在写作中，需要注意下列情况：

　　a. 当主语后面有 as well as、with、along with、together with、but、like、rather than、except 加名词或代词短语时，谓语动词要与最前面的主语保持一致，如 A as well as B 作主语时，句子的谓语与 A 一致，A rather than B 作主语时，句子的谓语与 A 一致。

　　b. not only A but also B 作主语时，句子的谓语与 B 一致。either A or B 或 neither A nor B 作主语时，句子的谓语与 B 一致。

　　c. "more than one + 单数名词" 作主语时，句子的谓语用单数形式。"many a + 名词" 作主语时，从意义上看是复数，但谓语动词常用单数。

　　d. "one and half + 复数名词" 作主语时，句子的谓语用单数形式；"one or two + 复数名词" 作主语时，句子的谓语用复数形式。

　　e. "a set/kind/piece/type/sort/form/pair of + 复数名词" 作主语时，句子的谓语一般要用单数形式。

　　f. 表示时间、距离、温度等的复数名词作主语时，句子的谓语常用单数形式。

　　g. 如果在由 and 连接作主语的两个单数名词前面有 every，each，no 等修饰的话，谓语用单数形式。

　　h. there be 的单复数形式一般与靠近的第一个名词一致。

　　i. 有些集合名词作主语时，如果作为一个整体看待，则谓语用单数形式；若强调其成员时，则谓语用复数形式。

三、宾语

　　宾语在主动句中作谓语及物动词所发出动作的承受对象，或者在句中作介词的对象。宾语由名词、代词、非谓语动词或从句来担任。英语中及物动词后必须有宾语，否则语法结构残缺、表达不完整。有时当句子带有宾补时，要采用形式宾语 it 的句型。

　　At the exercise stations, people can spin giant wheels with their hands, push big levers that offer no resistance, and swing on pendulums like children at a park.

　　Her studies showed that the effects of the rays were constant even when the uranium ore was treated in different ways.

　　You have to crack it open and when you do, you find an intricate and complicated system of gears designed to make this machine function.

　　The force of one Newton gives the mass of one kilogram an acceleration of one meter per second.

The positive value tells us that this distance is above the point from which the stone was thrown.

Marie believed that the emission of these rays was an atomic property of uranium.

Dozens of households might share a single entrance, and although the old residences have running water, few people have private bathrooms, so public toilets play a major role in local life.

The lines between internet communication and business communication are being blurred, with millennials finding it difficult to switch between the two styles and identifying which one is appropriate.

四、表语

表语在连系动词后面，主要说明主语的特征或状态。连系动词主要包括 be、感官动词（feel/look/sound/taste/smell）与表示变化或不变的词（get/turn/go/become/keep/stay/remain 等）。一般由名词、代词、形容词、非谓语动词、介词短语或从句充当表语。

For every job, though, the No. 1 thing we look for is general cognitive ability, and it's not I. Q.

The workout stations are perfect for the ultimate hutong sport: hanging around in the street with the neighbors.

The deep sea is the most hostile environment on Earth.

It is imperative that we keep pushing the limits of our ocean.

Back then, Beijing's early fifteenth-century layout was still intact, and it was unique among major world capitals: an ancient city virtually untouched by modernity or war.

Like many Beijing people I knew, Wang Zhaoxin was practical, good-humored, and unsentimental.

Pierre was a brilliant researcher himself and had invented several instruments for measuring magnetic fields and electricity.

It could signal an angry meeting or a passionate meeting but add a coffee cup, a big smiley face or an angry face and it becomes clear what's really going on.

In fact, I was on the same research vessel, just before the filming of the squid, making a documentary that would later become the Shark Week program Alien Sharks of the Deep.

五、定语

在句中修饰名词或代词的成分叫定语。用作定语的主要是形容词、代词、数词、名词、动词不定式、介词短语或从句等。形容词、代词、数词、名词等作定语时，通常放在被修饰的词前面。动词不定式、介词短语、从句等作定语时，则放在被修饰的词之后。

Then she stated a revolutionary hypothesis; Marie believed that the emission of these rays was an atomic property of uranium.

New protocols for separating the pitchblende into its chemical components had to be devised.

He always contributed more than his share to a W. C. Club barbecue, and he was always the last to leave.

It wasn't the brick and tiles and wood that mattered; it was the way that people interacted with their environment.

He showed me the place where he was born.

In June 1903, Marie was the first woman in Europe to earn a doctorate in physics.

Although we did not get to film the giant squid or observe any species new to science, we did manage to film an important and often overlooked part of the ocean life cycle.

This is an active-device-imposed relationship.

六、状语

状语是句子的重要修饰成分，用于说明动作发生的地点、时间、原因、目的、结果、条件、方向、程度、方式和伴随状况等情况。作状语的一般是副词、介词短语、非谓语动词或从句。状语一般放在句末，也可放在句首或句中。

On July the 4th in 1934, she died of a plastic anemia, a blood disease that is often caused by too much exposure to radiation.

There was no reason for such people to feel threatened by the initial incursions of modernity—if anything, such elements tended to draw out the hutong spirit, because residents immediately found creative ways to incorporate a

McDonald's or an Olympic toilet into their routines.

In 1911, after Pierre's death, Marie was awarded a second Nobel Prize in Chemistry for her discovery of the elements polonium and radium.

And now there was no doubt who had been the true chairman, because the W. C. Club died as soon as he left the hutong.

For years, Good Old Wang had predicted demolition, and in September of 2005, when his apartment building was finally torn down, he moved out without complaint.

In fact, I was on the same research vessel, just before the filming of the squid, making a documentary that would later become the Shark Week program Alien Sharks of the Deep.

This is critically important for us this century.

Unlike the coelacanth, which was thought to have gone extinct, we have known for centuries that giant squid have existed in our oceans' depths.

Little by little, various components of the ore were tested. The Curies found that two of the chemical components, one containing mostly bismuth and another containing mostly barium, were strongly radioactive.

＊注：本节例句主要摘自 New Progressive College English Integrated Course 4。

第三节　标点的用法

英语写作中，常会用到的标点符号包括句号（Full stop）、逗号（Comma）、冒号（Colon）、分号（Semicolon）、感叹号（Exclamation mark）、引号（Quotation mark）、问号（Question mark）、省略号（Ellipsis）等。

一、句号

句号（Full stop）主要用于当一句话完全结束时，表示语意的完结。另外，句号也可以用于英文单词的缩写，如 B. C. /No. /Mrs. /P. S. /Aug. 等。如：

New manufacturing technologies have generated feverish excitement about what some see as a Third Industrial Revolution.

That is, until 2012, when Drs. Edith Widder, Steve O'Shea and Tsunemi Kobodera filmed the elusive and mysterious giant in its natural deep-sea habitat for the first time—a landmark moment in ocean exploration and an example of how technology and ingenuity can overcome the monumental challenges we face in exploring the deep.

And now there was no doubt who had been the true chairman, because the W. C. Club died as soon as he left the hutong.

二、逗号

英语逗号（Comma）与汉语句号相比，承担更多的语法功能，其中包括：

a. 用于分隔并列的词汇，如：

The building had running water, infrared-automated flush toilets, and signs in Chinese, English, and Braille.

For the next 18 years she watched the street people starving, sick, homeless, living and dying in the dirty city streets.

Job-reducing technological innovations will affect education, healthcare, government and even transportation.

At the exercise stations, people can spin giant wheels with their hands, push big levers that offer no resistance, and swing on pendulums like children at a park.

b. 与并列连词共同连接并列分句，如：

Obviously, this is not the first time the world has faced such problems, and the past can help serve as a model for resolving them.

Child labor was abolished throughout the developed world, working hours and conditions became more humane, and a social safety net was put in place to protect vulnerable workers and stabilize the macro economy.

The nominating committee objected to including a woman as a Nobel Laureate, but Pierre insisted that the original research was Marie's.

c. 当短语作为状语放在句首时，一般要用逗号与句子隔开，如：

In 1898, she coined the term "radioactive" to describe materials that had this effect.

Not long after I moved into Little Jue'er, Beijing stepped up its campaign to host the 2008 Games.

In fact, I was on the same research vessel.

d. 隔开插入语，如：

Governments, too, are shedding labor—particularly governments burdened by high deficits and debts.

In November of that year the Curies, together with Henri Becquerel, were named winners of the Nobel Prize in Physics for their contributions to the understanding of atomic structure.

e. 在复合句中，逗号常用来隔开主句与从句，如隔开非限制性定语从句与主句，隔开状语从句与主句，如：

When World War I broke out in 1914, she suspended her studies and organized a fleet of portable X-ray machines for doctors on the front.

Emoticons and emojis are arguably more meaningful than slang and shorthand, which can be too easily misunderstood.

三、冒号

冒号（Colon）主要用于解释、说明后面的内容，或引出较长的正式引语。如：

In order to master English, students should be proficient in five areas: listening, speaking, reading, writing and translating.

The workout stations are perfect for the ultimate hutong sport: hanging around in the street with the neighbors.

Recent technological advances have three biases: they tend to be capital-intensive; skill-intensive; and labor-saving.

China's leader Mao Zedong set up a drug discovery project, known as 523, for the date it was launched: 23 May 1967.

In Obama's most famous speech, he said: Together, we resolved that a great nation must care for the vulnerable, and protect its people from life's worst hazards and misfortune. .

But while the means will change, our purpose endures: a nation that rewards the effort and determination of every single American.

As a mark of the esteem in which it held the tiny nun, the Indian government had given Mother Teresa its highest honor: a state funeral.

But that was just the icing on the cake: "I feel more reward when I see so many patients cured."

四、分号

分号（Semicolon）主要用于连接并列句，与句号相比，用分号连接的并列句关系更加紧密。另外，分号还用于分隔已有逗号的并列成分，以避免歧义。此外，当用逗号可能表达不清或短语过长时，也可用分号。例如：

To stop resistance from spreading further doctors now only use artemisinin in combination with another antimalarial; it is harder for the parasite to evolve resistance to two drugs simultaneously.

Recent technological advances have three biases: they tend to be capital-intensive (thus favoring those who already have financial resources); skill-intensive (thus favoring those who already have a high level of technical proficiency); and labor-saving (thus reducing the total number of unskilled and semi-skilled jobs in the economy).

AI is not in one or two hands; it's in 1 billion or 2 billion hands.

The essence of the hutong had more to do with spirit than structure: it wasn't the brick and tiles and wood that mattered; it was the way that people interacted with their environment.

In the nineteenth century the compound had belonged to a Manchu prince; in the 1940s, Chiang Kai-shek used it as his Beijing office.

五、感叹号

感叹号（Exclamation mark）主要用于表达感叹、命令与惊讶的语气。如：

What a nice day!
How moving the movie is!
Shut up!

六、引号

引号（Quotation Marks）用于引出直接引语、标示标题、强调或引起读者注意等用法，如：

"Humans know much less about the deep oceans than we know about the surface of the Moon and Mars. That's why I want to develop the facility for ocean scientists to reach the deep seas," says Prof. Cui Weicheng.

"The first is definitely the scientists who are interested in studying deep-sea science and technology. The second group is offshore companies and oil companies. The last one is tourists and adventurers who want to go down themselves to have a look at what's going on there," he says.

During the 1950s, sixties and seventies the village's population swelled as one of Chairman Mao's rural production teams was set up and educated "sent-down youth" began arriving from the cities to learn about the hardships of country life.

As China transformed into the "factory of the world" and millions set off for the cities, the exodus began.

In October, senior Communist Party leaders said they were "determined" to protect "traditional and historic villages" from abandonment and demolition.

"Enjoy the good city life: build a new rural community," reads one propaganda poster.

七、问号

问号（Question mark）用在直接问句中，用于表达疑问、反问、难以置信等语气。

"What can you do? Everyone is moving down. The living conditions are better down there," said Mr Qiao.

"See?" says Houng, pointing at a little watch tower atop a hill. "That tower was already there in 1974; seeing it meant you were nearly on the Hong Kong side."

Should you cross this line to get the job?

The question: is it bragging or relevant to add, say, that you're an ultra-marathon runner or that you've summited Mount Qomolangma?

Plays sports? There's a high chance of being sociable and competitive.

But what are the skills employers want and how much do they differ between the two nations? That is the question Dr. Troy Heffernan, a senior lecturer in marketing at the University of Plymouth, set out to answer through his involvement in one of 13 partnerships between institutions in the UK and China.

Style and trend pieces wondered: Are they wildly inappropriate? Are they offensive? What if you just use one?

Language is, of course, ever-evolving. So now that the exclamation mark has become mostly accepted, what's next for English?

But why are people using emoticons or emoji in the workplace? The answer is that they're useful.

八、省略号

省略号（Ellipsis）可用于表达直接引语中的省略、语气的犹豫和迟疑，如：

The Zen master says, "No...Tuhao, can I become your friend?"

"Writing has become more idiosyncratic and unique," says Parreira, "creating new breeds of writers—those that specialise in short form and those that focus on long form...it's rare to find writers that can excel in both."

In 1953, on the heels of a discovery of a second coelacanth specimen in the Comoros Islands off Madagascar's coast, J. L. B. Smith, the man who described the species, wrote in The Times of London: "We have in the past assumed that we have mastery not only of the land but of the sea...We have not. Life goes on there just as it did from the beginning. Man's influence is as yet but a passing shadow. This discovery means that we may find other fishlike creatures, supposedly extinct but still living in the sea."

*注：本节例句主要摘自 New Progressive College English Integrated Course 4

第四节　英语句子的规范化

第一、二节中讲到了句子的基本句型知识，学习者在掌握此部分知识基础上，在实际写作练习中，将对基本句型进行扩展以丰富句子的表达力，正如树木的主干生枝长叶从而枝繁叶茂。如：

基本句：Mother Teresa received honors.

扩展句：In recognition of her tireless efforts on behalf of the world's needy and unwanted, Mother Teresa received numerous honors during her lifetime, none as prestigious as the Nobel Peace Prize, granted by the Norwegian Nobel Committee in 1979.

在扩展句式过程中，一定要保持句子写作的规范性。规范的英语句子表达是写好作文的基础。在各类英语水平测试的写作评分标准中均对句子写作的规范性提出要求，要求表达准确、清楚，语句通顺、连贯性好，基本无语言错误。因此，表达规范的句子一般具有以下几个特点：合乎语法规则、语意完整统一、句子连贯一致、表达清晰简练与句式多样化。

一、合乎语法规则

合乎语法规则是英语句子写作的最基本要求。句子结构的准确性首先是语法结构的准确，即所写的句子结构合乎语法规则。初学者容易受汉语句式的影响，但英汉句式表达差异很大。因此，在写作中要注意遵循语法规则，如句子的主要成分、词的性数格、主谓一致、动词的时态语态等规范问题。初学者在写英语句子时常常出现下列问题。

（一）主语中的问题

马秉义（1995）曾对英汉主语差异作了深入探讨，指出了两者之间存在的不同之处。主要体现在以下几方面。

1. 英汉主语概念不同

英汉句子结构的不同，会导致初学者在写句子时出现错误。如汉语中"今天晚上特别冷"中偏正短语"今天晚上"做主语，但在英语中，"今天晚上"要作为时间状语出现，即"It is very cold tonight"，主语则是"it"。因此，汉英主语差异常常会是初学者混淆并出现错误。如（下文中 I 代表 Incorrect，C 代表 Correct）：

a. I：The ability of writing, I think I am the best in my class.
C：I think I am the best in my class as far as the ability of writing is concerned.

b. I：If factory wants to carry machines, automobiles are necessary.
C：If machines are carried in the factory, automobiles are needed.

c. I：She feels the study of students is very busy.
C：She feels students are very busy with the study.

d. I：Some large instruments parts use plastics may be reduced in the weight.
C：The weight of large instruments parts may be reduced by using plastics.

e. I：We wear shoes are made of leather.
C：The shoes we wear are made of leather.

f. I：This program can use not only to calculate...
C：This program can be used not only to calculate...

g. I：Women like the activities which need pay more attention.
C：Women like the activities which need paying more attention.

h. I：Her speech didn't confine to learning methods.

   C：Her speech wasn't confined to learning methods.
 i. I：I want to say about is the teaching methods.
   C：What I want to say is the teaching methods.

2. 无生物主语

 a. I：Is your work busy?
   C：Are you busy with your work?
 b. I：His name is called Jack.
   C：He is called Jack.
 c. I：Her illness was restored.
   C：She was restored to health.
 d. I：She has recovered to health.
   C：She has recovered from her illness.
 e. I：His English speaks good.
   C：He speaks good English.
 f. I：His heart is kind.
   C：He is kind-hearted.
 g. I：My exam was not pass.
   C：I failed in the exam.
 h. I：The holiday was free and happy.
   C：I was free and happy in the vacation.
 i. I：Now people's life don't leave smart phones away.
   C：Now people cannot do without smart phones in their lives.

3. 状性主语

  汉语中用地名、时间、工具作主语很普遍，因为它们实际上是被看作句子的话题。因此即使是状语成分，也可放在主语的位置上。谓语对它们进行说明解释判断，汉语语法称之为状性主语。而英语一般没有状性主语。（蔡基刚，2003）

 a. I：There is my home.
   C：My home is there.
 b. I：There were holding a sports meeting.
   C：They were holding a sports meeting there.
 c. I：That day blows lightly wind.
   C：It blows lightly that day.
   C：There was a light wind that day.

4. 主谓搭配

英语是一种注重主语的语言，英语中的主谓结构语法限制非常严格。而在汉语中主语和谓语间的语法关系与其说是一种是施事和动作关系，不如说是话题和说明的关系。（赵元任，1979）汉语是一种注重主题的语言，这样主语和动词的语法关系就不那么重要了。（王敏，2014）

a. I：It is sure that she will come.
   C：It is certain that she will come.

b. I：If you are convenient...
   C：If it is convenient to you...

5. 主语的省略

汉语造句是意合法，常要承前省略，而英语是形合，要求句子结构完整，每句都有主语。由于汉语大多数句子是主题结构，并非主谓结构，因此只要句子意思表达清楚了，逻辑主语有没有就不是很重要了。而英语作为主谓结构，句子没有主语就不成句子。（蔡基刚，2001）

a. I：And the dry kernels are put into a mill which squeezes out their oil content. Then put into bottle and tins for marketing.
   C：And the dry kernels are put into a mill which squeezes out their oil content. Then people put the oil into bottle and tins for marketing.

b. I：Too easy or too difficult is not good for us.
   C：The books which are too easy or too difficult are not good for us.

c. I：Some people like to watch TV, no matter what program always see it through.
   C：Some people like to watch TV, and no matter what program they always see it through.

（二）谓语的问题

汉语谓语无人称和数的变化，英语谓语有人称和数的变化。在一个汉语句子中，主语无论是第几人称，还是单数、复数，其谓语的形态都不变。而在英语中，句子的谓语则要根据人称和数的变化而变化。汉语谓语本身不表示时间概念，而英语谓语动词本身体现时间概念，有时态的复杂变化。在汉语中，谓语动词发生的时间往往通过添加不同时间概念的词或以动词排列的先后顺序来体现；而英语中，除了在句中有表示时间的状语外，谓语动词发生的时间概念还通过它本身的时态变化来体现，这是英语句子里谓语成分最突出的特点。汉语谓语的范围非常宽泛，可用来充当谓语的成分也多种多样，因而汉语主谓搭配的形式也复杂多变。英语的谓语则只能由动词来充当，但英语中有些助动词可直接作谓语，还有些助动词可与实义动词一起构成谓语，这也是汉语中没有的。（陶振英等，1999）

1. 动词的词性

英语的动词包括及物动词与不及物动词。英语中及物动词必有宾语，没有宾语则是不完整的，不及物动词则不需要宾语。

a. I：The old people had to worry their own health condition.

C：The old people had to worry about their own health condition.

b. I：Before long my dream came to realize.

C：Before long my dream came true.

C：Before long my dream was realized.

c. I：She serves for the players.

C：She serves the players.

2. 状态动词和动作动词

英语中的动词可分为动作动词和状态动词。动作动词用于描述动作，常用于一般时态和进行时态，而状态动词用于描述状态，常用于完成时，一般不用于进行时态。

a. I：She has come there for two years.

C：She has been there for two years.

C：She came there two years ago.

b. I：She always doesn't sleep until late at night.

C：She always doesn't go to sleep until late at night.

c. I：On New Year's Eve we slept very late.

C：On New Year's Eve we stayed up very late.

d. I：I knew him when I was working in the factory.

C：I made his acquaintance when I was working in the factory.

3. 动词形式

英语中动词谓语的时态是十分讲究的，不同的时态是由不同的动词形式表现出来的，而汉语则通过加词来完成。另外，词语的搭配对动词的形式也有要求。例如：

a. I：Edison invent more than a thousand things.

C：Edison invented more than a thousand things.

b. I：He always studied hard and learn from others.

C：He always studied hard and learned from others.

c. I：She did not wanted to go with me.

　　　　C：She did not want to go with me.
d.　I：She must teaches other girls.
　　　　C：She must teach other girls.
e.　I：I hope visiting Beijing again.
　　　　C：I hope to visit Beijing again.
f.　I：I'd rather staying where I am.
　　　　C：I'd rather stay where I am.

4. 主谓一致

主谓一致，即谓语动词在人称和数上必须和主语一致。

a.　I：Statistics are a branch of mathematics.
　　　　C：Statistics is a branch of mathematics.
b.　I：The variety of pictures at this exhibition please me.
　　　　C：The variety of pictures at this exhibition pleases me.

二、语意完整统一

　　首先，句子的完整统一性，是指一个句子应该语意完整、结构合理，用完整的结构来表达完整的意思，英文句型比较多且每种句型都有各自的固定模式。中国学生由于受母语的影响，往往用写中文句子的习惯，去写英文句子，必然发生句子不完整的错误。例如：

a.　I：There are many kinds of new novels are very interesting.
　　　　C：There are many kinds of new novels which are very interesting.
b.　I：Although it was late, but she went on working.
　　　　C：Although it was late, she went on working.
c.　I：The climate of Israel is somewhat like southern California.
　　　　C：The climate of Israel is somewhat like that of southern California.
d.　I：December is the coldest time of the year, and my birthday comes in this month.
　　　　C：I was born in the coldest month of the year, December.
e.　I：Hong Kong is great and cosmopolitan, with fine universities and ultramodern architecture, I hope to go there in summer holiday.
　　　　C：Hong Kong is great and cosmopolitan, with fine universities and ultramodern architecture, and I hope to go there in summer holiday.
f.　I：English is a language, language is something used to communicate with other people.

C：English is a language which is used to communicate with other people.

g.　I：A good English class is the all students can speak.

　　C：A good English class is one in which all the students can speak.

其次，句子的完整统一性，是指一个句子应具有一个统一的、完整的思想。若一个句子包含多个彼此并非紧密相关的意思，这种句子就与完整统一性原则相违背。例如：

　　a. Brought up by her aunt in the south of China, she was considered a promising girl and she liked singing very much.

此句包含的三层意思"she was brought up by her aunt in the south of China""she was considered a promising girl"与"she liked singing very much"各成独立整体，语意并不相关，这样的句子就没有遵守完整统一性原则。修改如下：

Brought up by her aunt who was a famous singer, she liked singing very much and was considered a promising girl.

　　b. Brought up by his uncle, who was fierce in nature, the boy was aggressive.

此句中包含的三层意思"He was brought up by his uncle""His uncle was fierce in nature"与"The boy was aggressive"成因果关系，关系密切，因此符合完整统一性原则。

三、句子连贯一致

句子的连贯性与一致性，要求句中内容语意关联，词与词组的表达始终不偏离中心思想，使句意能够准确、清楚、流畅地得到表达。而学生在英语写作中，句子经常不能表达一个完整的意思，缺乏连贯性与一致性。违反连贯一致性的句子，主要有以下几种情况：

（一）平行结构的使用

平行结构的使用能够使表达更加清晰有力，但也要求表达的内容应是并列的思想，且在使用时需要用相同的语法形式。例如：

a.　I：He wants to go, to pursue and success.

　　C：He wants to go, to pursue and to succeed.

b.　I：The young man is kind, active and loved by all.

　　C：The young man is kind, active and lovable.

c.　I：Both Mary went marketing, and her mother did the cooking.

C：Mary went marketing, and her mother did the cooking.

（二）代词的指代关系

代词主要用来代替上文中出现过的名词、动词、形容词或数量词，如 we、they、who、these 等，是简化叙述和衔接前后的手段。代词通常会显示出人称、格和数的区别。但在学生习作中，常常出现代词的指代关系不清楚不明确的问题，一个代词有可能有多个指代的东西，或者代词指代的内容在前文并未出现过。如：

a. I：To do that, it must find a place where it can keep fairly warm, and it must be a place where its enemies cannot find it.

C：To do that, the bat must find a place where it can keep fairly warm, and there its enemies cannot find it.

b. I：The old lady asked her sister whether her daughter was in her room.

C：The old lady asked her sister, "Is my daughter in your room?"

c. I：My friend teach me how to learn it.

C：My friend teach me how to learn Philosophy.

d. I：He was knocked down by a bicycle, but it was not serious.

C：He was knocked down by a bicycle but was not seriously hurt.

（三）指代的跨度

代词常用来指代上文中较靠近且关系明确的名词。若前面出现了若干名词，中间又有大量其他信息，然后再出现指代前面某个名词的代词，就会出现大跨度指代现象，这种情况下，大跨度指代会导致代词指代不明，需要读者从头再次阅读、依据语义推断代词的指代指向。这种现象应避免。如：

I：The book, which was complex and full of technical terms that could not be easily understood, was on a table, among many things such as a series of books, a vase, a smart phone, pencils and other objects. She picked it out and sat down to read it.

C：The book, which was complex and full of technical terms that could not be easily understood, was on a table, among many things such as a series of books, a vase, a smart phone, pencils and other objects. She picked the book out and sat down to read it.

（四）非谓语动词的逻辑主语

非谓语动词的逻辑主语应与句子的主语一致，若不一致，应在非谓语动词前加逻辑主语构成复合结构,以表明该动作的发出者,避免混淆。

a. I:Do you mind opening the window?

C:Do you mind my opening the window?

b. I:He suggests going there.

C:He suggests our going there.

c. I:To catch the early train, everything is ready.

C:To catch the early train, we've got everything ready.

d. I:Looking from the top of the hill, the village is beautiful.

C:Looking from the top of the hill, one can see a beautiful village.

C:Seen from the top of the hill, the village is beautiful.

四、表达清晰简练

英语句子的表达应清晰简练,减少不必要的重复,句式也应更加简洁,不应为了写长句子而添加冗余信息。简洁精炼往往能使句子更富有表现力。例如:

a. I:In China, Some cities are seriously polluted, and some cities are being polluted.

C:In China, Some cities are seriously polluted, some being polluted.

b. I:Perhaps the most interesting person I have met is an interesting American teacher of English who teaches at Peking University in Beijing. Although I last met this man years ago, I have not forgotten his special qualities. First of all, I was impressed by his devotion to teaching. Because his lectures were always well prepared and clearly delivered, students swarmed into his classroom, fitting the classroom to capacity. (https://www.koolearn.com/)

C:Perhaps the most interesting person I have met is an American teacher of English at Peking University. Although I last met this man years ago, I have not forgotten his special qualities. First of all, I was impressed by his devotion to teaching. Because his lectures were always well prepared and clearly delivered, students fit the classroom to capacity.

五、句式多样化

句子形式多样是好文章的基本要求。同一语意可以通过不同句型来表达，写作中交错使用长句、短句、简单句、复合句、并列句、疑问句等，达到形式与内容的统一，会使人觉得内容丰富，语言生动有力。

（一）简单句型中的语序、词汇转换

a. Hainan is a garden city, with one of the most delightful climates in the world.

A garden city, with one of the most delightful climates in the world, is Hainan.

Hainan, a garden city, has one of the most delightful climates in the world.

b. He knew English very well.

He had a good command of English.

He had a good knowledge of English.

（二）主动句与被动句的转换

a. The journalist wrote the event up for the newspaper.

The event was written up for the newspaper by the journalist.

b. The American people elected Donald John Trump their President in November, 2016.

Donald John Trump was elected the American President in November, 2016.

（三）简单句与复合句的转换

a. We are unable to observe them alive in their deep sea home. We have understood very little about how they live, where they live and how they behave.

Unable to observe them alive in their deep sea home, we have understood very little about how they live, where they live and how they behave.

b. The building, which was painted a garish red, didn't find a buyer for six months.

The building, painted a garish red, did not find a buyer for six months.

The garishly red building did not find a buyer for six months.

（四）简单句与并列句的转换

Most metals are good conductors, and silver is the best.

Most metals are good conductors, silver being the best.

Most metals are good conductors, with silver in the lead.

篇章的写作中，应尽量做到句式多样化，能够增强语言表达力。如下面段落：

I live in a modern three-story building, but it's surrounded by the single-story homes of brick, wood, and tile that are characteristic of hutong. （用but连接并列句，用that引导定语从句）These structures stand behind walls of gray brick, and often a visitor to old Beijing is impressed by the sense of division: wall after wall, gray brick upon gray brick. （并列句）But actually a hutong neighborhood is most distinguished by connections and movement. （简单句）Dozens of households might share a single entrance, and although the old residences have running water, few people have private bathrooms, so public toilets play a major role in local life. （包含并列句、让步状语从句与结果状语从句）In a hutong, much is communal, including the alley itself. （简单句）Even in winter, residents bundle up and sit in the road, chatting with their neighbors. （现在分词作状语）Street vendors pass through regularly, because the hutong are too small for supermarkets. （原因状语从句）（New Progressive College English Integrated Course 4）

第五节 写作常用规范句型

考研写作训练的办法之一，就是模拟和套用规范的英语句型。尤其在写作开始阶段，写作就是学会模拟套用，即模拟套用在写作中频繁使用的句型，而不是自己创造。

二语习得过程是一种潜意识获得"可理解输入"的过程，且"可理解输入"是习得的唯一来源（Krashen, 1985）。同年，Swain提出了输出假设理论，她认为要想提高二语学习者语言的流利度与准确性，不仅需要可理解性输入，而且需要可理解性输出，后者是二语习得过程的重要环节。学习写作是一个输入与输出相结合的过程。尤其是对于初学者，在写作刚刚起步的时候往往"巧妇难为无米之炊"，应先不断学习规范的常用句式，理解、模仿和套用常用句型，才能不断提高自身写作水平。本节主要介绍写作中常用的句式与表述不同内容时的常用写作句型。

一、写作中常用句式

同样的内容可以用不同的句式表达，以下九种句式易学易用，而且在写作时常常会用到。（注：该部分例句主要出自 New Progressive College English Integrated Course 4）

（一）主谓宾和主系表

Most people don't like the heavy traffic during the evening rush hour.

Smart phones can also help children of all ages with homework.

A foreign language is a tool for communication in life.

The problem is very difficult to all of us.

For the past five years, I've lived about a mile north of the Forbidden City in an apartment building off a tiny alleyway in downtown Beijing.

The deep sea is the most hostile environment on Earth.

（二）并列句和主从复合句

并列句是指用 and、but、or 等并列连词连接两个或两个完整结构分句的句子。并列句中的分句通常用逗号加并列连词或用分号连接。主从复合句是由主句和用从属连词连接的从句构成。

All of these types of findings fit together in a jigsaw puzzle that, as it reaches completion, reveals to us how people fit into the picture and how we can best manage, conserve and protect the oceans for our own benefit.

There are no doubt countless discoveries to be made under the surface of the sea, whether they are species we know to exist but have yet to observe in their own habitat, species new to science or those species thought long extinct.

Healthy oceans can help ease the increasing burden our population is placing on this planet, but we need to be able to explore, observe and learn about the oceans in their entirety in order to protect and conserve them effectively.

（三）It 引导的句型

当句子的主语是动词不定式、动名词或主语从句时，常常把 it 放在句首作形式主语。当句子的真正宾语是动词不定式、动名词或从句时，习惯上把它们放在补语后面，而 it 作形式宾语。有时为了强调句子中的某一部分，常常会用强调句型"It + be + 被强调的部分 + that/who..."，被强调的部分可以是主语、宾语、状语等。

It is imperative that we keep pushing the limits of our ocean.

It is important for us to master a foreign language.

It is he who made great contribution to the celebration party.

Because of his disability, Chu was licensed to drive a small motorized cart, which made it easy for him to transport skewers of mutton through the hutong.

It's the ability to process on the fly.

It's the ability to pull together disparate bits of information.

It's rare to find writers that can excel in both.

It is only natural that they are influenced by it and respond in the same way.

It's therefore best for those entering the workforce to assume nothing and communicate formally with older coworkers and clients.

It's still now difficult to imagine senior executives using LOL and ROFL when signing a deal.

It wasn't too long ago that the exclamation mark was a point of etiquette contention in the world of email and the workplace.

It's for this reason that the happy-face emoji dominates.

(四) That 引导的句型

That 可引导主语、宾语、表语、同位语、定语等从句。

The biggest problem about all electronic communication is that it's toneless.

Along with the usefulness of emoticons and emoji in clarifying tone in emails, another partial explanation for the rise of emoji at work is that digital work communication now incorporates casual communication as well.

Stewart Butterfield, the CEO and co-founder of Slack, says that one of the aims of the tool was let people feel comfortable with these casual interactions online.

That might sound a little lofty, but we believe there is a widespread feeling that people are meant to check a lot of stuff at the door when they arrive at work.

Register is the idea that there are different kinds of language that we use in different situations.

(五) What 引导的句型

what 可引导主语、宾语、表语等从句。

What's critical to be an effective leader in this environment is you have to be willing to relinquish power.

What we care about is, when faced with a problem and you're a member of a team, do you, at the appropriate time, step in and lead.

What we've seen is that the people who are the most successful here, who we want to hire, will have a fierce position.

You can't understand what the problem is by just looking.

Mr. Cao, a driver for the Xinhua news service, discussed what was happening in the papers.

（六）There be 句型

After a while, there was so much furniture, and so many people there every night, that Wang Zhaoxin declared the formation of the "W. C. Julebu": the W. C. Club.

And now there was no doubt who had been the true chairman, because the W. C. Club died as soon as he left the hutong.

There's no doubt that the consumption of abbreviated digital content is having a huge effect on language.

There's little room to worry about grammar in 140 characters, goes the argument, and besides, conforming to the rules of engagement in the Twitter-sphere is far more important than old grammatical rules.

And there is huge value in that.

There are five hiring attributes we have across the company.

（七）被动句型

The plan was especially supported by those who wished to have more chance to speak English.

I live in a modern three-story building, but it's surrounded by the single-story homes of brick, wood, and tile that are characteristic of hutong.

Rigid measures are being taken to control air pollution.

But actually a hutong neighborhood is most distinguished by connections and movement.

The question is far from being solved.

The machines are scattered throughout old parts of the city, tucked into narrow alleyways.

The coal-fired grill was attended to by a handicapped man named Chu.

Because of his disability, Chu was licensed to drive a small motorized cart, which made it easy for him to transport skewers of mutton through the hutong.

（八）比较句型

We have better maps of the surface of Mars than we do of our own planet's sea floor.

He always contributed more than his share to a W. C. Club barbecue, and he was always the last to leave.

The essence of the hutong had more to do with spirit than structure: it wasn't the brick and tiles and wood that mattered.

But nobody appreciates the exercise stations more than hutong residents.

Together, they found that two ores, chalcolite and pitchblende, were much more radioactive than pure uranium.

Emoticons and emojis are arguably more meaningful than slang and shorthand, which can be too easily misunderstood.

Those that use a basic form of ELF online can understand each other far easier than native English speakers.

There's little room to worry about grammar in 140 characters, goes the argument, and besides, conforming to the rules of engagement in the Twitter-sphere is far more important than old grammatical rules.

（九）虚拟语气句型

（1）用 should + 动词原形表示：在 Suggest, recommend, demand, propose, request, desire, insist 等动词后面的宾语从句用虚拟语气；It is desired, important, suggested, requested, ordered, proposed, necessary, essential 等后边的主语从句用虚拟语气：suggestion, motion, proposal, order, recommendation, plan 等词后面的表语从句用虚拟语气。

（2）通过词形变化来表示：在虚拟条件句、wish、It is time that 等句型中使用虚拟语气。

It is very important that you (should) be here on time.

My suggestion is that we (should) cooperate with the other group.

If it had not rained so hard yesterday we could have played football.

Practice

下列四个段落表达的主题与内容相同，但使用了不同的句式。结合以上所学内容，尝试分析下列段落中使用了哪些句式。

Paragraph One

As is depicted in the above picture, an American girl is amused with appreciation of the Chinese national costumes. Wearing typically Chinese costume, the girl looks very beautiful. From her happy smile, we may draw a conclusion that she has accepted what is part and parcel of a foreign tradition as international. The picture clearly reveals Chinese culture is being internationally accepted little by little.

Paragraph Two

It can be observed in the picture that an American girl is amused with appreciation of the richly-decorative Chinese national costumes. From her happy smile, we may come to a conclusion that she has accepted what is part and parcel of a foreign tradition as international. What impresses us most is that the girl wearing Chinese national costumes is a foreigner rather than a Chinese. As is symbolically revealed in the pictures, Chinese culture is being internationally accepted little by little.

Paragraph Three

The picture depicts an American girl in traditional Chinese costumes. Wearing typically Chinese costume, the girl looks very beautiful with a sweet smile on her face. Obviously, we can deduce from the picture that national culture have no boundary and may be appreciated and shared by people from other cultural background.

Paragraph Four

The picture depicts an American girl who looks so comfortable in the beautifully decorated Chinese national costumes. It can be seen that she accepted what is part and parcel of a foreign culture. As is indicated, a national culture has to keep its own features in order to be regarded as an integral ingredient of the international community.

二、不同内容的表述方法

(一) 概括图画内容的表达方法

a. It goes without saying that drawings aim at revealing a common and serious problem in the world: how to protect the ocean resources.

b. Let's take a closer look at the two pictures. The one on the left shows the state before..., whereas the one on the right illustrates the situation afterwards.

c. As described/portrayed/illustrated/shown in the picture, many people nowadays like to go to fitness centers to keep their bodies in shape.

(二) 概述图表内容的表达方法

a. The graph shows that the incidence of violent crime has in fact dropped in most US cities over the past decade.

b. As we can see from the chart, divorce increased phenomenally up until about 2010, but has since remained at a fairly constant level.

c. The sales figures for A amount to the combined sales figures for B and C. The profits over the past five years add up to an incredible 1.2 billion dollars.

d. The figures fluctuate between 1000 and 1100 units per year.

　　The sales are expected to go up and down over the next few months.

e. The number of pandas in the reserve suddenly rose to over 400.

f. The birth rate decreased steadily after World War II.

　　The number of users rose smoothly throughout the decade.

g. Computer use is forecast to shoot up in China in the coming decade.

　　Housing prices soar when there is a sudden increase in demand.

h. There was a slump（下降）in production between 1980 and 1985.

i. The number of Internet users should climb from 20 million in 2004 to 50 million in 2008.

j. The number of road accidents is expected to decrease from 50,000 in 2005 to 40,000 in 2007.

　　Unless the situation changes, there will be a decline from 20 in 2006 to 12 in 2010.

k. January will witness the launch of two new products, which should increase revenue dramatically.

l. The population will remain stable thanks to the one-child policy.

m. The percentage of young people attending university reached a peak of 47% in 2003.

n. The number of people who could not read hit its lowest point in 2003.

o. The number of Internet users is on the rise/increase at the moment.

p. Book sales are on the decline nowadays.

（三）揭示图画含义的表达方法

a. What does the author really want to tell us? In my opinion, his real implication is that everyone has to deal with lots of difficulties in their life experiences.

b. The purpose of the pictures is to warn us that due attention has to be paid to the pollution.

c. The idea conveyed by the cartoon is apparent that the finishing point is just a new starting point.

d. I cannot help relating these drawings to reality. They clearly show…

（四）举例论证的表达方法

a. A case in point is Beijing, which has a pedestrian（步行）shopping street.

b. The list of such examples can go on and on./Examples like these can form a long list.

c. Take my teacher as an example.

d. Numerous examples can be given easily. But these will suffice.

e. Another case in point is the misleading packaging used on many products.

f. This is also true in the case of Beijing, which has many restrictions on cars.

It is the same with other countries, which have huge debts.

The same thing goes for other cities in America.

The same sort of thing happens in developed countries, though not as often.

In this case, Beijing can also serve as a good example.

g. Perhaps the most striking instance happened to me when I was a child at primary school.

（五）原因分析的表达方法

a. A number of factors can account for the increase in deaths from heart disease.

b. Another important factor is the availability of the Wifi.

c. Finally, the creation of more jobs is responsible for the change/increase/decrease/growth.

d. Why does this phenomenon appear? I think there are several possible reasons for this situation.

（六）提出观点的表达方法

a. It is generally accepted/universally acknowledged that vehicles are a major source of air pollution.

b. There is an assumption that modern life exerts a lot of pressure upon people.

c. Everybody agrees that smart phones have become a necessity for most people, with the development of information technology and reduced price of communication products.

d. Nowadays it has become fashionable for the young people to mimic their idols' hair and dressing styles.

e. As every college student/everybody would agree, employment pressure has become their biggest problem.

（七）建议措施的表达方法

a. It is high time that parents, educators and the government made concerted efforts to put an end to this situation.

b. The best way to solve this problem I think is to give young people opportunities to do things independently.

c. It is imperative that rigid measures should be taken to end poverty worldwide.

d. These are not the only three measures we can take. But it should be noted that we need to take strong action to eliminate the air pollution.

e. Only in this way can we overcome this difficulty, and we will have a bright future.

◆ **Practice**

结合以上所学内容,尝试分析下面考研真题范文中使用了哪些表达方法。

1. 2012 年考研英语一写作真题

Directions: write an essay of 160 – 200 words based on the following drawing. In your essay you should

(1) describe the drawing briefly

(2) explain its intended meaning, and

(3) give your comments

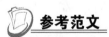

参考范文

In the above picture, we can see an interesting scene: a bottle is knocked over with the liquid inside splitting out, and two men respond to it in totally different ways. One is expressing his disappointment for the loss of half of the liquid while the other feels thankful for the remaining half with a smile on his face. Obviously, the drawer wants to tell us that different people may have different outlooks on various difficulties in life.

When faced with obstacles in life, the pessimistic person always focuses on the negative side and exaggerates the worst situation, while the optimistic one always look on the bright side of life. The pessimistic person chooses to give up quickly and then broods over their loss or failure, which in turn will throw their life in the vicious circle. On the contrary, the optimistic person, who always bears hope in mind, will never flinch and will summon up courage to find the way to conquer the obstacles. Therefore, the way people perceive difficulties will determine their way to cope with them.

From the above discussion, we come to know that if people want to succeed in this highly competitive society, they should try to develop an optimistic perception toward life. Moreover, the government, mass media and schools should take the responsibly to awaken people to the significance of optimism. Only in these ways can people achieve more rapid progress and greater success in their life.

（范文选自新东方在线 http://kaoyan.koolearn.com/20161117/967073.html）

2. 2015 年考研英语一写作真题

Directions: Write an essay of 160 – 200 words based on the following picture. in your essay, you should

（1）describe the pictures briefly,

（2）interpret its intended meaning, and

（3）give your comments.

手机时代的聚会

参考范文

A group of friends, boys or girls, are having a dinner party while each one of them is checking messages in their mobile phones without saying a word to one another, leaving the dishes untouched. We are informed that this is a gathering in the era of mobile phone.

The above picture unveils a common social phenomenon and the symbolic meaning of the photo is the effect of the mobile phone on people's way of life. Undoubtedly, the phone provides us with considerable convenience, making many things possible which are beyond our dreams. As a communication tool, the phone makes us closer than ever before by providing immediate communication. Meanwhile, there are negative effects on our personal life. As is shown in the picture, people are imprisoned in their own world! They choose contacting online rather than communicating face to face.

Accordingly, enjoying the convenience provided by the phones, we should bear in mind that human beings are social beings who need real interpersonal interactions! Joint efforts are needed to ensure people to have face-to-face communication! I believe a harmonious relationship between friends is awaiting us if we set aside our mobile phones and enjoy the untouched meal!

（范文选自新东方在线 http://kaoyan.koolearn.com/20161118/967162_2.html）

3. 2013 考研英语二作文真题

Directions: Write an essay based on the following chart. In your writing, you should

(1) interpret the chart, and

(2) give your comments.

You should write about 150 words.

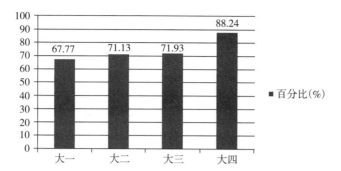

参考范文

What can be seen from the chart is the proportion change of students having part-time jobs during the four years' college study. The proportion increases slightly from the first year to the third year, however, the fourth year has witnessed a dramatic increase, surging to 88.24%.

There is no denying the fact that this trend is very pervasive in current colleges and, to some extent, quite proper. It is not difficult to come up with some possible factors accounting for this trend. To begin with, the major jobs of freshman and sophomore are to study, and to lay a solid foundation for their future work. What's more, when students are going to step out of school and enter into society, they have to master lots of practical skills, for example, how to deal with challenges outside, so they have to take part in some part-time jobs. Apparently, doing part time job has many advantages. On the one hand, students can learn how to get along well with others and know the society more profoundly. On the other hand, to take a part-time job provides students with a valuable opportunity to put what they have learned from books into practice and make some money, which helps to reduce their families' financial burden.

Due to the analysis above, this trend will continue for quite a while in the future. And it should be pointed out that study is the major task for college students though work experience is valuable. Students have to strike a balance between study and part-time job.

（范文选自新东方在线 http：//kaoyan.koolearn.com/20151209/882516.html）

I. Translation

A. Translate the following sentences into English

1. 一批数据叫数据集,(而)单个观测结果叫数据点。

2. 计算机是一种装置,该装置接收一系列含有信息的电脉冲。

3. 计算机工作起来比人类大脑中的神经细胞要快很多倍。

4. 漂在水面上的软木塞没有随波流走。相反,它随波上下浮动。

5. 一个力不仅有大小,而且有方向。

6. 聚合物是一种高分子的物质,其大小远远超出迄今所提到的各种化合物。

7. 港口是船只停泊处,有各种必要的终端设备以加速客货流通。

8. 动力反应堆不需要空气,因为在铀堆中产生的热室核裂变而不是燃烧的结果。

9. 机械系统控制办公室有另一个仪表板,将清楚地显示楼内的任何险情。

10. 已经建立了特殊基金资助这些国家使用新的化学品和新技术。

B. Translate the sentences into Chinese

1. The main spindle bearing are designed for a constant preload that does not vary while the machine is in operation.

2. To obtain the best performance and ensure years of trouble free use, please read this instruction manual carefully.

3. Network module hardware installation guide

4. Operation and maintenance of any arc welding equipment involves potential hazards.

5. If the machine is not allowed to stop operation for the required time, the thermal over-load device will be started.

6. Be sure to install the unit on a perpendicular wall that is not subject to vibration.

7. The type CY15 oil pumping machine is of simple and compact construction.

8. It is reliable in usage, convenient in maintenance and able to work under very bad conditions.

9. Motor puller is provided with taper sleeve so as to be easy in installing and dismounting it.

10. The motor shaft and main shaft should be in correct alignment so as to avoid vibration and hot bearings.

(练习选材自：https：//wenku.baidu.com/view/2f45e3a2e43a580216fc700abb68a98271feac2d.html

II. Reading Comprehension

Directions：In this section, you are going to read a passage with ten statements attached to it. Each statement contains information given in one of the paragraphs. Identify the paragraph from which the information is derived. You may choose a paragraph more than once.

Passage one

Media Selection for Advertisements

A) After determining the target audience for a product or service, advertising agencies must select the appropriate media for the advertisement. We discuss here the major types of media used in advertising. We focus our attention on seven types of advertising: television, newspapers, radio, magazines, out – of – home, Internet, and direct mail.

Television

B) Television is an attractive medium for advertising because it delivers mass audiences to advertisers. When you consider that nearly three out of four Americans have seen the game show Who Wants to Be a Millionaire? you can understand the power of television to communicate with a large audience. When advertisers create a brand, for example, they want to impress consumers with the brand and its image. Television provides an ideal vehicle for this type of communication. But television is an expensive medium, and not all advertisers can afford to use it. Television's influence on advertising is fourfold. First, narrow casting means that television channels are seen by an increasingly narrow segment of the audience. The Golf Channel, for instance is watched by people who play golf. Home and Garden Television is seen by those interested in household improvement projects. Thus, audiences are smaller and more homogeneous（具有共同特点的）than they have been in the past. Second, there is an increase in the number of television channels available to viewers, and thus, advertisers. This has also resulted in an increase in the sheer number of advertisements to which audiences are exposed. Third, digital recording devices allow audience members more control over which commercials they watch. Fourth, control over programming is being passed from the networks to local cable operator sand satellite programmers.

Newspaper?

C) After television, the medium attracting the next largest annual ad revenue is newspapers. The New York Times, which reaches a national audience, accounts for $1 billion in ad revenue annually, it has increased its national circulation（发行量）by 40% and is now available for home delivery in 168 cities. Locally, newspapers are the largest advertising medium. Newspapers are a less expensive advertising medium than television and provide a way for advertisers to communicate a longer, more detailed message to their audience than they can through 48 hours, meaning newspapers are also a quick way of getting the massage out. Newspapers are often the most important form of news for a local community, and they develop a high degree of loyalty from local reader.

Radio

D) Advertising on radio continues to grow Radio is often used in conjunction with outdoor bill-boards (广告牌) and the Internet to reach even more customers than television. Advertisers are likely to use radio because it is a less expensive medium than television, which means advertisers can afford to repeal their ads often. Internet companies are also turning 10 radio advertising. Radio provides a way for advertisers to communicate with audience members a tall times of the day. Consumers listen to radio on their way to school or work, at work, on the way home, and in the evening hours. Two major changes—satellite and Internet radio—will force radio advertisers to adapt their methods. Both of these radio forms allow listeners to tune in stations that are more distant than the local stations they could receive in the past. As a result, radio will increasingly attracttargetaudiences who live many miles apart.

Magazines

E) Newsweeklies, women's titles, and business magazines have all seen increases in advertising because they attract the high-end market, magazines are popular with advertisers because of the narrow market that they deliver. A broadcast medium such as network television attracts all types of audience members, but magazine audiences are more homogeneous, if you read sports illustrated, for example, you have much in common with the magazine's other readers. Advertisers see magazines as an efficient way of reaching target audience members.

F) Advertiser using the print media-magazines and newspapers-will need to adapt to two main changes. First, the internet will bring larger audiences to local newspapers, these second. Advertisers will have to understand how to use an increasing number of magazines for their target audiences. Although some magazines will maintain national audiences, a large number of magazines will entertain narrower audiences.

Out-of-home advertising

G) Out-of-home advertising. Also called place-based advertising, has become an increasingly effective way of reaching consumers, who are more active than ever before. Many consumers today do not sit at home and watch television. Using billboards, newsstands, and bus shelters for advertising is an effective way of reaching these on-the-go consumers. More consumers travel longer distances to and from work, which also makes out-of-home advertising effective, technology has changed the nature of the billboard business, making it a more effective medium than in the past. Using digital printing, billboard companies can print a billboard in 2 hours, compared with 6 days previously. This allows advertisers more variety in the types of messages they create because they can change their messages more quickly.

Internet

H) As consumers become more comfortable with online shopping, advertisers will seek to reach this market As consumers get more of their news and information from the Internet, the ability of television and radio to get the word out to consumers will decrease. The challenge to Internet advertisers Is to create ads that audience members remember. Internet advertising will play a more prominent role in organizations' advertising in the near future. Internet audiences tend to be quite homogeneous, but small. Advertisers will have to adjust their methods to reach these audiences and will have to adapt their persuasivestrategies to the online medium as well.

Direct mail

I) A final advertising medium is direct mail, which uses mailings to consumers to communicate a client's message Direct mail includes newsletters. postcards and special promotions. Direct mail is an effective way to build relationships with consumers. For many businesses direct mails the most effective from of advertising.

1. Television is an attractive advertising medium in that it has large audiences.

2. Internet advertisers will have to adjust their methods to reach audiences that tend to be quite homogeneous, but small.

3. Direct mail is an effective form of advertising for businesses to develop relationship with consumers.

4. This passage discusses how advertisers select the appropriate for advertisements.

5. With the increase in the number of TV channels the number of TV viewers has increased.

Passage two
Can Digital Textbooks Truly Replace the Print Kind?

A) The shortcomings of traditional print edition textbooks are obvious: For starters they're heavy, with the average physics textbook weighing 3.6 pounds. They're also expensive, especially when you factor in the average college student's limited budget, typically costing hundreds of dollars every semester. But the worst part is that print versions of textbooks are constantly undergoing revisions. Many professors require that their students use only the latest versions in the classroom, essentially rendering older texts unusable. For students, it means they're basically stuck with a four pound paperweight that they can't sell back.

B) Which is why digital textbooks, if they live up to their promise, could help ease many of these shortcomings. But till now, they've been something like a mirage (幻影) in the distance, more like a hazy (模糊的) dream than an actual reality. Imagine the promise: Carrying all your textbooks in a 1.3 pound iPad? It sounds almost too good to be true. But there are a few pilot schools already making the transition (过渡) over to digital books. Universities like Cornell and Brown have jumped on board. And one medical program at the University of California, Irvine, gave their entire class iPads with which to download textbooks just last year.

C) But not all were eager to jump aboard. "People were tired of using the iPad textbook besides using it for reading," says Kalpit Shah, who will be going into his second year at Irvine's medical program this fall. "They weren't using it as a source of communication because they couldn't read or write in it. So a third of the people in my program were using the iPad in class to take notes, the other third were using laptops and the last third were using paper and pencil." The reason it hasn't caught on yet he tells me, is that the functionality of e-edition textbooks is incredibly limited, and some students just aren't motivated to learn new study behavior.

D) But a new application called Inkling might change all that. The company just released an updated version last week, and it'll be utilized in over 50 undergraduate and graduate classrooms this coming school year. "Digital textbooks are not going to catch on," says Inkling CEO Matt MacInnis as he's giving me a demo (演示) over coffee. "What I mean by that is the current perspective of the digital textbook is it's an exact copy of the print book. There's Course Smart, etc., these guys who take an image of the page and put it on a screen. If that's how we're defining digital textbooks, there's no of that becoming a mainstream product".

E) He calls Inkling a platform for publishers to build rich multimedia content from the ground up, with a heavy emphasis on real-world functionality. The traditional textbook merely serves as a skeleton. At first glance Inkling is an impressive experience. After swiping (触击) into the iPad app (应用软件), which you can get for free here, he opens up a few different types of textbooks.

F) Up first chapters is a chemistry book. The boot time is pretty fast, and he navigates through (浏览) a few before swiping into a fully rendered 3D molecule that can be spun around to view its various blocks. "Publishers give us all of the source media, artwork, videos," he says, "We help them think through how to actually build something for this platform." Next he pulls a music composition textbook, complete with playable demos. It's a learning experience that attacks you from multiple sensory directions. It's clear why this would be something a music major would love.

G) But the most exciting part about Inkling, to me, is its notation (批注) system. Here's how it works: When you purchase a used print book, it comes with its previous owner's highlights and notes in the margins. It uses the reading (how much experience you trust of someone who already went through the class to help improve your each notation is obviously up to you). But with Inkling, you can highlight a piece of content and make notes. Here's where things get interesting, though: If a particularly important passage is highlighted by multiple Inkling users, that information is stored on the cloud and is available for anyone reading the same textbook to come across. That means users have access to notes from not only their classmates and Face-book friends, but anyone who purchased the book across the country. The best comments are then sorted democratically by a voting system, that your social learning experience is shared with the best and brightest thinkers. As a can even chime in (插话) on discussions. They'll be able to answer the questions of students who are in their class directly via the interactive book.

H) Of course, Inkling addresses several of the other shortcomings in traditional print as well. Textbook versions are constantly updated, motivating publishers by minimizing production costs (the big ones like McGraw-Hill are already on board). Furthermore, students will be able to purchase sections of the text instead of buying the whole thing, with individual chapters costing as little as $2.99.

I) There are, however, challenges. "It takes efforts to build each book," MacInnis tells me. And it's clear why. Each interactive textbook is a media-heavy experience built from the ground up, and you can tell that it takes a respectable amount of manpower to put together each one.

J) For now the app is also iPad-exclusive, hardware away for free, for other and though a few of these educational institutions are giving students who don't have such a luxury it's an added layer of cost—and an expensive one at that.

K) But this much is clear: The traditional textbook model is and has been broken for quite some time. Whether digitally interactive ones like Inkling actually take off or not remains to be seen, and we probably won't have a definite answer for the next few years. However, the solution to any problem begins with a step in a direction. And at least for now, that hazy mirage in the distance? A little more tangible (可触摸的), a little less of a dream.

6. The problem with Course Smarts current digital textbooks is that they are no more than print versions put on a screen.

7. Digital textbooks haven't fixed all the shortcomings of print books.

8. One of the challenges to build an interactive digital textbook from the ground up is that it takes a great deal of manpower to put together each one.

9. Some students still use paper and pencil because they find it troublesome to take notes with an iPad.

10. According to the author, whether digital textbooks will catch on is still unclear.

11. Inkling's notation system is very exciting because one can share his learning experience with the best and brightest thinkers.

12. The biggest problem with traditional print textbooks is that they are not reused once a new edition comes out.

13. One additional advantage of the interactive digital textbook is that professors can give prompt feedback to students' homework.

14. One problem for students to replace traditional textbooks with interactive digital ones is the high cost of the hardware.

15. Matt MacInnis describes the updated version of Inkling as a platform for building multimedia content.

第三章

英语段落的写作

美文赏析

Of Studies
论读书

——Francis Bacon（王佐良译）

Studies serve for delight, for ornament, and for ability. Their chief use for delight, is in privateness and retiring; for ornament, is in discourse; and for ability, is in the judgment and disposition of business.

读书足以怡情，足以博彩，足以长才。其怡情也，最见于独处幽居之时；其博彩也，最见于高谈阔论之中；其长才也，最见于处世判事之际。

For expert men can execute, and perhaps judge of particulars, one by one; but the general counsels, and the plots and marshalling of affairs, come best from those that are learned. To spend too much time in studies is sloth; to use them too much for ornament, is affectation; to make judgement wholly by their rules, is the humour of a scholar.

练达之士虽能分别处理细事或一一判别枝节，然纵观统筹、全局策划，则舍好学深思者莫属。读书费时过多易惰，文采藻饰太盛则矫，全凭条文断事乃学究故态。

第三章 英语段落的写作

They perfect nature, and are perfected by experience: for natural abilities are like natural plants, that need proyning (pruning) by study; and studies themselves do give forth directions too much at large, except they be bounded in by experience.

读书补天然之不足,经验又补读书之不足,盖天生才干犹如自然花草,读书然后知如何修剪移接,而书中所示,如不以经验范之,则又大而无当。

Crafty men contemn studies, simple men admire them, and wise men use them; for they teach not their own use; but that is a wisdom without them, and above them, won by observation.

有一技之长者鄙读书,无知者羡读书,唯明智之士用读书,然书并不以用处告人,用书之智不在书中,而在书外,全凭观察得之。

Read not to contradict and confute; nor to believe and take for granted; nor to find talk and discourse; but to weigh and consider.

读书时不可存心诘难读者,不可尽信书上所言,亦不可只为寻章摘句,而应推敲细思。

Some books are to be tasted, others to be swallowed, and some few to be chewed and digested; that is, some books are to be read only in parts; others to be read, but not curiously; and some few to be read wholly, and with diligence and attention. Some books also may be read by deputy, and extracts made of them by others; but that would be only in the less important arguments, and the meaner sort of books; else distilled books are, like common distilled waters, flashy things.

书有可浅尝者,有可吞食者,少数则须咀嚼消化。换言之,有只须读其部分者,有只须大体涉猎者,少数则须全读,读时须全神贯注,孜孜不倦。书亦可请人代读,取其所作摘要,但只限题材较次或价值不高者,否则书经提炼犹如水经蒸馏,淡而无味。

Reading makes a full man; conference a ready man; and writing an exact man. And therefore, if a man write little, he had need have a great memory; if he confer little, he had need have a present wit; and if he read little, he had need have much cunning, to seem to know that he doth not.

读书使人充实,讨论使人机智,笔记使人准确。因此不常做笔记者须记忆力特强,不常讨论者须天生聪颖,不常读书者须欺世有术,始能无知而显有知。

Histories make men wise; poets witty; the mathematics subtitle; natural philosophy deep; moral grave; logic and rhetoric able to contend. Abeunt studia in morse.

读史使人明智，读诗使人灵秀，数学使人周密，科学使人深刻，伦理学使人庄重，逻辑修辞之学使人善辩；凡有所学，皆成性格。

Nay there is no stand or impediment in the wit, but may be wrought out by fit studies: like as diseases of the body may have appropriate exercises. Bowling is good for the stone and reins; shooting for the lungs and breast; gentle walking for the stomach; riding for the head; and the like. So if a man's wit be wandering, let him study the mathematics; for in demonstrations, if his wit be called away never so little, he must begin again. If his wit be not apt to distinguish or find differences, let him study the schoolmen; for they are cymini sectors. If he be not apt to beat over matters, and to call up one thing to prove and illustrate another, let him study the lawyers' cases. So every defect of the mind may have a special receipt.

人之才智但有滞碍，无不可读适当之书使之顺畅，一如身体百病，皆可借相宜之运动除之。滚球利睾肾，射箭利胸肺，慢步利肠胃，骑术利头脑，诸如此类。如智力不集中，可令读数学，盖演题需全神贯注，稍有分散即须重演；如不能辨异，可令读经院哲学，盖是辈皆吹毛求疵之人；如不善求同，不善以一物阐证另一物，可令读律师之案卷。如此头脑中凡有缺陷，皆有特效可医。

▶ **赏析：**

弗兰西斯·培根撰写的随笔因透彻精辟、语言独到而享誉世界。《论读书》中，段落结构规整，每段表达一个观点，并进行充分论述，观点之间环环相扣，充分说明了读书的三种功用，即：怡情、博彩和长才。"怡情"使人即使独处也不失生活的情趣，"博彩"使人善于言辩或烘托气氛，"长才"则使人圆观周览，于待人、接物、进业，更加精熟完满。其次，文章谈如何读书。书有好坏优劣：开卷未必有益，因此需区别对待：有可浅尝者，有可吞食者，多数只需大体浏览，少数则须认真阅读、仔细消化。最后，书犹镜子，可以映照出多种人生样态，狡黠者鄙读书，无知者羡读书，唯有明智者读书，既能入乎其中，又能出乎其外，将立身处世、做人之道与书本中传递出来的人生智慧和经验结合起来，修饰剪裁，去留取舍,全在一心,所谓"用书之智不在书中,而在书外,全凭观察得之"。第四,是说书如良药,可以疗治各种心智缺陷。不同书籍,各有专能,史使人明智,诗使人灵秀,科学使人深刻,逻辑使人善辩,所以,读书也应因人而异,正如治病理当对症下药。

第一节 段落的构成

写好段落是篇章写作的关键环节。一篇文章可由几个自然段组成。各段落均应为文章的中心思想服务,形成一个有机的整体。好的段落应该意思完整、语义连贯、完全体现文章主旨中心,同时又是层次分明、结构严谨、逻辑关系合理的。

一个段落,总是有一个主题句,它体现段落的中心思想和观点(central idea),然后,伴随若干个扩展句,来支持和发展中心思想和观点。最后,有一个结尾句(有时没有),概括和归纳全段内容。也就是说,一个段落由三部分组成:

(1) 主题句(topic sentence):点出段落的主题。
(2) 扩展句(developing sentence):说明和支持主题。
(3) 结尾句(concluding sentence):概括和归纳全段内容。

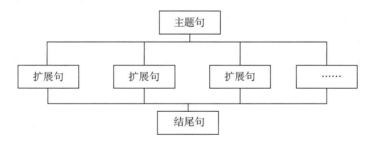

请仔细阅读下面的段落,并体会段落的构成。

例1:

Economic status of women is clearly of utmost importance. (topic sentence) In achieving women's equality to men, it is imperative that women should be economically independent. Without this economic base, a woman no matter where she is from—a rich or a developing country—cannot enjoy equal right to men. This is because the economic and political power often go hand in hand. (developing sentences) Without economic independence, women's equality is just an empty dream. (concluding sentence)

例2：

Slavery in the United States existed almost unchanged for 250 years. (topic sentence) During this time, most slaves were not allowed to marry or to raise families. Usually they were not allowed to learn to read. It was very dangerous for a slave to travel, since even free Negroes could be kidnapped and sold at any time. (developing sentences) Under these conditions, it was almost impossible for them to organize to help each other. (concluding sentence)

例3：

Now, my hearing of tones is, quite frankly, appalling. (topic sentence) Tell me one word in 4 different tones which then makes 4 different words and I just don't get it at all, they all sound the same to me. On the other hand, write it down in pinyin so I can see the tones and I am not ever going to forget. Unfortunately, the tones are generally not taught in this manner; tones are just said at me over and over again and I still can't hear the difference. (concluding sentence) (Mandarin Madness: The Tones)

例4：

What adulthood means in a society is an ocean fed by too many rivers to count. (topic sentence) It can be legislated, but not completely. Science can advance understanding of maturity, but it can't get us all the way there. Social norms change, people choose not to perform traditional roles, or are forced to take them on way too soon. You can track the trends, but trends have little bearing on what one person wants and values. Society can only define a life stage so far; individuals still have to do a lot of the defining themselves. Adulthood altogether is an impressionist painting—if you stand far enough away, you can see a blurry picture, but if you press your nose to it, it's millions of tiny strokes. (developing sentences) Imperfect, irregular, but clearly part of a greater whole. (concluding sentence) (When Are You Really an Adult?, Julie Beck)

例5：

Magic Bands, tech-studded wristbands available to every visitor to the Magic Kingdom, feature a long-range radio that can transmit more than 40 feet in every direction. (topic sentence) The hostess, on her modified iPhone, received a signal when the family was just a few paces away. Tanner family inbound! The kitchen also queued up: Two French onion soups, two roast beef sandwiches! When they sat down, a radio receiver in the table picked up the signals from their Magic Bands and triangulated their location using another receiver in the ceiling. (developing sentences) And it all worked seamlessly, like magic. (concluding sentence) (Disney's $1 Billion Bet on a Magical Wristband, Cliff Kuang, p125)

例6:

Does the truth still matter? (topic sentence) Though political figures often tell whoppers, it is incontrovertible that there is such a thing as the truth. The president's taunts have prompted long-overdue if uncomfortable and unwelcome reflection in our newsroom and others. But it has also prompted all of us to be more humble, more careful and more dedicated than ever to the basic elements of our craft: to marshal facts, produce stories and pay little mind to criticism, whether from left or right. (developing sentences) To show, by our work, that the truth still matters. (concluding sentence) (纽约时报中文网)

例7:

Many parents do not seem to know how to keep a good relationship with their children. (topic sentence) They do not know what activities to do or what topics to talk about with their children. Here are a few useful tips. Having a family trip sometimes is a wonderful way for all family members to bond together. And you and your children can do fun things together, such as playing football or watching their favorite show. Besides, a very good activity to bond with your young children is storytelling! You can tell them the stories you heard from your parents or stories about your childhood. (developing sentences) All these ways will contribute to a better relationship with your children. (concluding sentence) (新视野大学英语读写教程第三版, p43)

My working holiday changed my perspective on life. (topic sentence) It helped me to grow personally, have fun professionally and realise that I can do and be anything I desire. It allowed me to realise that from now on, I will always follow my heart and do what makes me happy. Whether that is living in another country again, settling in Australia or living the nomad life, I am not sure. (developing sentences) (How My Working Holiday Changed Me, Hayley)

由上面段落可以看出，段落通常由若干个围绕一个观点扩展的句子组成。主题句用以表达观点，扩展句用以支撑观点，总结句进行归纳总结。段落中的所有句子均应服务于中心观点，中心内容一致，前后衔接，而不应该把内容互不关联的句子堆砌在一起，使内容支离破碎。

一、段落的主题句

一篇文章有中心意思，也就是题目。而每个段落则有段落主题，段落主题是为文章中心思想服务的。每个段落只能有一个主题（central idea），它用一个句子加以表达，所以称为主题句。主题提出后需要很多结构严谨的句子来支持和说明，称为扩展句。最后得出一个结论，并用一个结尾句表达。

阅读下面两组段落，并分析每组两个段落表达效果的异同。

第一组：

Paragraph A：

I passed the history test I'd been reading. Then I found out I got an A on my English term paper. My afternoon classes had been canceled. So I went to the river to relax. That evening I saw one of the best movies I'd ever seen, and I didn't pay a penny to see it. And for the first night in weeks, I slept sweetly.

Paragraph B：

Yesterday was my best day of the semester. I passed the history test I'd been reading. Then I found out I got an A on my English term paper. My afternoon classes had been canceled. So I went to the river to relax. That evening I saw one of the best movies I'd ever seen, and I didn't pay a penny to see it. And for the first night in weeks, I slept sweetly.

第二组：

Paragraph A：

We have history books recording past events, geography books dealing with the earth, mathematics books focusing on space and numbers, language books studying the means of communication and literary books reflecting social problems.

Paragraph B：

There are various books with different contents in our library. We have history books recording past events, geography books dealing with the earth, mathematics books focusing on space and numbers, language books studying the means of communication and literary books reflecting social problems.

从以上两组段落看出，Paragraph A 与 Paragraph B 的区别在于 B 段有主题句，而 A 段没有。没有主题句的段落，会使读者不易找到整个段落的中心思想，使段落表达成为细节的罗列，而无提纲挈领的中心思想，可读性不强。B 段中添加了段落的主题句，每段开门见山点出中心思想，简明扼要地表达段落的主要内容，使读者对段落内容一眼明了，继而用多个扩展句进行有效支撑说明，大大加强了说服力。因此，段落中的中心句至关重要。

二、主题句的写作

主题句是段落中最重要的句子。主题句应为一个完整且简明扼要的句子，用以概括、叙述和说明该段的主题。主题句一般位于段首，也可置于段尾或段中，初学写作者最好将主题句放在段首，这样较易掌握和构思。

主题句位于段首，即段落的第一句便是主题句。段落开头便开门见山地提出问题，后面的扩展句围绕主题句加以说明、支持、补充和解释。例如：

Learning English at college is different from learning English at the middle school. In the middle school, the students are more dependent and passive. But college students must solve most of the problems by themselves. They will have to consult the dictionaries and reference books by themselves and prepare their lessons.

主题句位于段尾，即主题句在段落最后总结全段的内容，给读者以深刻的印象，是写作中的一种演绎方法。例如：

Similarly, in order to write successful answers to essay questions on history or anthropology examinations, a student must arrange the relevant facts and opinions according to some accepted pattern of paragraph structure. And certainly when a student writes a book report for English, or a critiques for politics studies, or a term paper for sociology, style and organization are often as important as content. Clearly, the ability to write well organized, concise paragraphs and essays is essential to a student's success in almost all university courses.

主题句位于段中，即主题句出现在段落中部起承上启下的作用，这类主题句多起转折作用，一般由"but, however, yet, anyhow, nevertheless"等词连接，主要观点位于转折词后面，用于引起下文。例如：

What we teach ourselves sometimes indeed in more useful than what we learn from others. Some great men had little or no schooling. But these great men probably studied harder by themselves than most boys do in school. The greatest minds do not necessarily of those who have never been able to distinguish themselves at school, have been very successful in life later. It has been said that

Wellington and Napoleon were both dull boys at school, and so were Newton and Albert Einstein.

有时，也会无主题句，个别段落的主题思想通过文章内容来提示，这种方法能促使读者阅读文章内容时进行思考和分析，但初学写作者不宜采用这种方法。例如：

There came a breeze, then a gust of wind, and the wind became stronger. It rattled the windows, turned up the fallen leaves, bent down the trees. Distant rumbling thunder was heard and came nearer and nearer. Large drops of rain began to fall. Flashes of lightening lit up the sky. Thunder roared overhead. Now the rain poured down.

三、如何写好主题句

（一）主题句要概括

主题句的表述不要太空泛，要概括一定内容，将段落内容限定到一定范围内，否则扩展句将难以说明和支持它，例如：

Sentence A：English language is very important.

Sentence B：English language is very important in our daily life.

Sentence A 的表述过于空泛，未将内容限定在一定范围内，缺乏论证的着力点；Sentence B 则限定了论证的范围，将 English language is very important 限定在 daily life 范围内，便于写作者在范围内选材充分说明与支持主题句。

Sentence C：The Olympic Games are exciting.

Sentence D：In the Olympic Games the football teams from many countries compete intensely.

同样，Sentence D 与 sentence C 相比，限定了写作论证的范围，便于学习者聚焦主题。

（二）主题句要简洁

主题句的撰写，应尽量使用简单句或简洁明了的句子，例如：

Sentence A：Collecting stamps is her hobby.

Sentence B：She likes collecting stamps which is her hobby.

Sentence C：I enjoyed watching *Gone with the wind* very much.

Sentence D：*Gone with the wind* was a good film which I enjoyed watching very much.

上列两组主题句的表述中，Sentence B 和 Sentence D 分别与 Sentence A

和 Sentence B 的表达内容一致,但在句式的运用上稍嫌啰唆,从句只是对主句内容的重复,不够简练。在此种情况下,选择使用简单句更加简洁明快。

(三) 主题句要完整

主题句应该做到句子完整和表达的主题思想完整,例如:

Sentence A: How to write a composition.

Sentence B: How to write a composition is not an easy thing to talk about.

Sentence C: If the weather was fine.

Sentence D: If it was fine, we would have had a good time.

Sentence A 和 Sentence C 不是完整的句子,不能作为主题句。

(四) 主题句要有关键词

写好主题句中的关键词,关键词是直接表达主题的词汇,它决定段落的内容和展开的方法,引导整个段落的发展,例如:

There are several ways to boil the water.

The task can be finished in three steps.

There is a new method to reduce the cost.

Fake and inferior goods can do lots of harms to us.

There are many means of getting information in the current era "The Information Age."

Newspaper has several advantages over radio and TV.

People have different opinions about the laid-off problem.

Modernization will bring a number of benefits to the people of China.

上列句子均可以作为段落的主题句,每句中均含有关键词,分别为 several ways、three steps、a new method、do lots of harms、many means、several advantages、different opinions 与 a number of benefits。一方面作者以关键词为着力点展开论述,另一方面便于读者快速获取主要信息,对段落内容进行有效预测。

例如下面的段落主题句以 many means 为关键词,整个段落写作围绕该关键词展开,可运用排序法、举例法等方式进行论证说明。

There are many means of getting information which enable us to keep up with what is going on in the world. (topic sentence) First, we read newspaper and magazines. For example, the typical daily newspaper contains articles about local, regional, national and international news, as well as business news, sports news, weather reports, and other features in which we are very interested. Second, we listen to the news on the radio and watch it on television. In addition, some TV stations offer early morning news, late night news and weekly news program. (developing sentences) No doubt, there still many other means of getting information which we need and want. (concluding sentence)

四、段落的扩展句

扩展句是围绕主题句展开，对主题句进行支持、说明和阐述句子。扩展句应紧扣主题句中的关键词而展开，是段落的主体部分，句子与句子之间逻辑清楚，上下转承结合得当，简明扼要，重点突出。一般来说，每个自然段除了主题句与结尾句之外，还应包含若干个扩展句。所以，写好了扩展句便基本上完成一个自然段落。

英语写作初学者的写作中往往出现的一个问题是文章中缺乏足够的具体信息支撑观点。写作时，一旦确定了主题和关键词，作者便应按照自己的思路来组织段落中的句子，写好扩展句的关键是不能偏离主题句的中心思想，不能出现新的分歧，必须紧紧围绕主题句中心内容一步步展开。句子之间要具有连贯性，就必须由一系列的逻辑关系构成，例如：并列关系、因果关系、递进关系、转折关系、解释关系、概括关系、顺序关系、让步关系、对照比较关系、转换关系，等等，这些逻辑关系一方面需要句子的内容上有此衔接关系，另外可选用相关的过渡词（transitional words）来明确标识。过渡词在句子与句子之间、段落与段落之间起到承上启下的作用，使句子或段落之间的衔接自然、连贯，逻辑合理，结构严谨，因此极为重要。

例如下面段落中，作者在扩展段落时除了句子与句子内容紧密关联，而且用了 also、besides、for instance、nonetheless、and 等过渡词来连接上下文，同时，用代词代替上句的名词，上下文环环相扣，语意连贯。

Faced with the US' excessive scrutiny and baseless accusations, the Confucius Institute should illustrate with hard facts that it is not involved in any infiltration activities on US campuses or elsewhere. It should also gain the world's understanding and trust by showing the results of its programs and their contribution to the overall well-being of people around the world. Besides, the Confucius Institute needs to be more careful with its overall arrangement and management. For instance, it has partnered with universities that already have their own departments of Chinese language and literature, resulting in unnecessary competition and complication. Besides many Confucius Institutes are concentrated in a certain region, which may prompt local residents to doubt the intention of the organization, not to mention the waste of resources. Nonetheless, the Confucius Institute's future will remain promising as long as it sticks to its guiding principle of helping foreigners learn the Chinese language and culture. And hopefully, the clouds gathering over Confucius Institutes will soon dissipate. (from Confucius Institute victim of US policy shift, Chinadaily)

请认真阅读下面各段落，重点关注每个段落中扩展句之间语意的衔接与过渡词的使用。

Paragraph A:

Kazakhstan, immediately after the collapse of the USSR, took a sharp start to the development of a market economy. And, unlike most states of the post-Soviet space, Astana did not conduct experiments with the gradual transformation of the economy. Therefore, 25 years after gaining sovereignty, this country is considered one of the most liberal for business throughout the former Soviet union. (Kazakhstan improves business conditions, by Zhao Yanjun, Chinadaily)

Paragraph B:

China invested more than 1.76 trillion yuan ($253.2 billion) in research and development last year; in comparison the US federal government invested $118.3 billion in R&D, which shows China's longing for innovations. But China should do more to evaluate the efficiency of its investment and the returns it has made on it. Meanwhile, the number of corruption cases involving officials and researchers embezzling research funds that have been exposed in recent years indicate many people treat the government's research funding as a cash cow to fatten their private pockets. (Strict oversight over use of funds to get real results, China Daily)

Paragraph C:

This value, or in Chinese President Xi Jinping's words, the "spirit of a community" that was widely commended by all sides, offered the APEC meetings a great success and furthered its institutional progress and contribution to the regional economy and trade. However, Trumpist unilateralism and protectionism have put sand in the wheels of APEC by wearing and tearing its original spirit of "Decision by Consensus". In addition, there is another piece of bad news that during the meeting, the U. S. Vice President Mike Pence claimed that the U. S. would join Australia in developing a naval base in PNG, as "an apparent move to curb China's growing influence" to help "protect sovereignty and maritime rights in the Pacific islands." However, as the local media of PNG and international commentators pointed out, the "Pacific Rim" does not need an arms race in any form, but the re-building of the spirit of "Decision by Consensus" in an era of deteriorating unilateralism and protectionism. (Unilateralism and Protectionism are wearing-and-tearing the APEC platform, CGTN)

Paragraph D:

In a sign that the all-around cooperative partnership between China and Singapore has progressed with the times, Premier Li Keqiang started a five-day official visit to the Southeast Asian country with a meeting with his Singaporean counterpart on Monday. His visit, during which he is also scheduled to attend the 33rd ASEAN Summit and related meetings, caps off a year of engagement between both countries, which have enjoyed friendly relations for decades. Although small in size, Singapore has played an indispensable role in China's reform and opening-up, by generously sharing its development experience with Chinese leaders as China transitioned from a centrally planned economy to a market economy. And over the years, Singapore has helped train hundreds of thousands of Chinese officials in public administration and economic management. (China, Singapore to advance bilateral, regional relations: China Daily editorial, China Daily)

以上各段落中,作者用过渡词来表明上下句之间的关系,使语句表达更加流畅。例如,在写作中常用来表达时间先后关系的过渡词包括 first, second, in the first place, since then, thereafter, therefore, lately, later, meanwhile, at last 等词。常用来表达空间关系的过渡词包括 before, behind, below, between, beyond, farther, in front of, near to, next to, over, under, up, close to 等。

下面以 2002 年考研英语作文第一段的写作为例:

Directions:

Study the following picture carefully and write an essay entitled "Cultures-National and International". In the essay you should

1) describe the picture and interpret its meaning, and

2) give your comment on the phenomenon.

You should write about 200 words neatly on ANSWER SHEET 2. (20

points)

Cultures—National and International

As is shown by the picture, we can see an American girl who is wearing a suit of tradition Chinese costume. With a smile on her face, she looks beautiful and the traditional Chinese costume fits well on her. Studying further, we will obtain more meanings. In the first place, the traditional Chinese costume stands for our national culture. In the second place, the case of the American girl, who comes from a totally different culture, but appears to be satisfied with the traditional Chinese costume, is of universal significance. What the picture implies is that the Chinese national culture, which is characterized by our national spirit, has been accepted by the international society.

An American Girl in Traditional Chinese Costume

译文：如图所示，我们可以看到一个身穿中国传统服装的美国女孩。她微笑着，看起来很漂亮，中国传统服装也很适合她。进一步看这幅图，我们了解到更多含义。首先，中国传统服装代表着我们国家的文化。第二，这个女孩的例子是有世界意义的。她来自完全不同的文化，却很喜欢中国服装，这幅图画表达的是我们以自己的民族精神为特征的中国文化，已经被国际社会所接受。

五、扩展句写作的注意事项

（一）扩展句围绕主题展开

扩展句的作用是用来说明、支持主题句的观点，要避免写出与主题不相关的句子。例如：

There are several ways to improve our English writing skills and keeping a diary in English is surely one of them. Compared with other forms of writing, it is shorter and takes less time. My mother advised me to write diary when I was very young. It can help us cultivate the habit of thinking in English. If we can keep this practice, we will gradually learn how to express ourselves in English.

该段落的第一句是本段的主题句,主要提出 keeping a diary 是一种提升英语写作的有效方式。该断的扩展句应围绕写日记的有效性展开论述。其中,My mother advised me to write diary when I was very young 虽字面上也出现了 to write diary,但未提及有效性,对段落的中心思想并未起到支持作用,因此,建议将该句删除。

(二)扩展句的句式多样化

扩展句往往包括若干个句子,建议混合使用简单句、并列句、复合句等多种句式。如果段落中都是一种结构的句子,虽然都能支持主题句,但内容仍读起来单调。句式有变化,文章读起来才有活力,令人回味。例如下面的段落,主题句使用了主从复合句,扩展句混合使用了并列句、主从复合句与用分词作状语的简单句。

There are also many quite, private things that I enjoy doing.(主从复合句)I would spend a whole day reading a book, and I sometime stay up late at night reading a good novel.(并列句)When I am tired of physical activities, I may find a good movies or a light TV program very entertaining.(主从复合句)In short, I like to do many different kinds of things, depending on the mood I am in and the kind of people I am in and the kind of people I am around.(简单句,分词短语作状语)

六、总结句的写作

总结句一般放在段落结尾其概括和总结作用,往往是对主题句的再现,或是对扩展句的要点进行总结。阅读下面两个段落,体会段尾划线句子对整段内容的概括作用。

The interest is natural, as African countries and Afghanistan are all China's good friends and partners. We are all developing countries, used to be colonized and bullied by external powers. We all share the common mission of embracing peace and development, and are jointly building the Belt and Road Initiative, facing unprecedented challenges such as hegemonism, power politics, protectionism and unilateralism and etc. <u>Therefore, every step of China-Africa cooperation will resonate with Afghan friends.</u> (Liu Jinsong, Enlightenment for China-Afghanistan Cooperation from China-Africa Cooperation)

参考译文:

第三章　英语段落的写作

这种兴趣是很自然的，因为非洲国家和阿富汗都是中国的好朋友、好伙伴，非洲国家、阿富汗以及中国都是发展中国家，都曾有被外部列强殖民、欺凌的遭遇，都面临和平与发展的共同使命，都在共建"一带一路"，都在迎接前所未有的挑战例如霸权主义、强权政治、保护主义和单边主义等。因此，中非合作的每一脚步，都会引起阿富汗朋友的共鸣。

During the Summit, China decided to launch eight major initiatives in close collaboration with African countries in the next three years and beyond. Some of these initiatives are already being implemented, and some of them are of reference significance for the China-Afghanistan cooperation. These includes: Implementing of the industrial promotion plan, encouraging Chinese companies to increase investment in Africa, building and upgrading a number of economic and trade cooperation zones in Africa, carrying out agricultural assistance programs; Implementing infrastructure connectivity projects, opening more direct flights between China and Africa; Implementing trade facilitation activities, increasing imports from Africa, particularly non-resource products and setting up relevant mechanisms to promote e-commerce cooperation; Undertaking aiding projects on green development, and ecological and environmental protection in Africa, strengthening exchanges and cooperation with Africa on climate change, ocean, desertification prevention and control, and wildlife protection; Setting up Luban Workshops in Africa to provide vocational training for young Africans, carrying out tailored programs to train 1,000 high-caliber Africans; Upgrading medical and health aid programs for Africa, particularly flagship projects such as the headquarters of the African Center for Disease Control and Prevention and China-Africa Friendship Hospitals, training more medical specialists for Africa; Implementing people-to-people exchange programs, establishing China-Africa Joint Research and Exchange Center and China-Africa Media Cooperation Network; Setting up a China-Africa Peace and Security Fund, continuing to provide military aid to the Africa Union, launching security assistance programs to advance China-Africa cooperation in the fields of law and order, UN peacekeeping missions, fighting piracy and combating terrorism. <u>All of the above mentioned eight major initiatives are the result of deep consultations and strategic coordination between China and Africa. The initiatives worth studying for the Afghan friends, and use it for reference in promoting China-Afghanistan cooperation.</u> (Liu Jinsong, Enlightenment for China-Afghanistan Cooperation from China-Africa Cooperation)

参考译文：

在这次北京峰会上，中国决定未来3年和今后一段时间在非洲重点实施"八大行动"。这些行动有些中非之间已经在做，有些对未来中非合作具有借鉴意义。例如：实施产业促进行动，鼓励中国企业扩大对非投资，在非洲新建和升级一批经贸合作区，实施农业援助项目；实施一批设施联通项目，开通更多中非直航；实施贸易便利行动，中国扩大进口非洲商品特别是非资源类产品，推动中非电子商务合作；为非洲实施绿色发展和生态环保援助项目，重点加强在应对气候变化、海洋合作、荒漠化防治、野生动物和植物保护等方面交流合作；在非洲设立"鲁班工坊"，向非洲青年提供职业技能培训，支持设立旨在推动青年创新创业的中非创业合作中心，为非洲培训1000名精英人才；实施健康卫生行动计划，重点援建非洲疾控中心总部、中非友好医院等旗舰项目，为非洲培养更多专科医生；实施人文交流计划，决定设立中国非洲研究中心，打造中非媒体合作网络；决定设立中非和平安全合作基金，继续向非洲联盟提供无偿军事援助，在社会治安、联合国维和、打击海盗、反恐等领域实施安全援助项目。上述八大行动，都是中国与非洲国家深度磋商和战略对接的结果，值得阿富汗朋友研究，并在推进中阿合作时加以参考。

第二节　段落的组织

很多初学写作者，在撰写段落时总苦于无从落笔，在寥寥几笔陈述观点后便无话可说。究其原因，一方面是掌握的语料不够充分，另一方面，对于段落如何组织了解较少，无法展开思路，也就无法做到逻辑清晰。段落的组织，应以保持段落的整体性和连贯性为前提，采取恰当的方法来排列句子。要层次分明、条理清晰地围绕段落中心展开段落，可以采取以下方法。

一、时间顺序或空间顺序

按照时间和空间的顺序来组织段落是最为常用的方法。两种方法可单独使用，亦可混合使用。例如：

（一）按时间顺序

We tried a lot to get Tom out of the well. First, we made a rope by linking our belts together. Then we lowered it to Tom, telling him to grasp the end. After he had hold the end of the rope, we began to pull him slowly, out of the well. During his ascent, no one dared speak a word. Finally, we could grasp his arms, and we pulled him out.

时间顺序法常用的标识词包括 now, at present, recently, after, afterwards, after that, after a while, in a few days, at first, at the beginning (of sth.), to begin with, to start with, later, next, finally, immediately, soon, suddenly, at that moment, as soon as, from now on, from then on, gradually, at the same time, till, not…until…, before, after, when, while, as, during 等。

（二）按空间顺序

The doors to their rustic, cozy teahouse in Maming village open just half an hour later. Located at a 30-minute drive from the ancient water town of Wuzhen, Maming village is the polar opposite of the famed tourist destination. There are hardly any crowds here. The old houses are not as well maintained. There are no bright colorful lights that flank the walkways. At the end of the street is a bridge that leads to a temple. According to local folklore, the village was named Maming because during the Qing Dynasty, Emperor Qianlong's horse neighed three times as he made his way to the temple. (Xing Yi, Wuzhen villages offer authentic rural experience, China Daily, 2017.12)

空间顺序法常用的标识词包括 beyond, above, under, nearby, outside, in here, across, close to, on (to) the left (right), ahead of, in front of, above, across, from, adjacent to, against, around, at the bottom, before, behind, below, beneath, between, beyond, close at hand, close to down, far, farther, in the center of, in the distance, in the middle of, nearby, near to, on the opposite side, opposite to, on top of, over, under, up 等。

二、定义法

当段落的主题阐述"是什么"时，便可用定义法。定义法是用一段话来解释说明某事物的性质和特征、结构、用途、行为、原理、来源等。例如：

What is upwelling? Upwelling is a process in which deep, cold water rises toward the surface. Winds blowing across the ocean surface push water away. Water then rises up from beneath the surface to replace the water that was pushed away. This process is known as "upwelling." Upwelling occurs in the open ocean and along coastlines. The reverse process, called "downwelling," also occurs when wind causes surface water to build up along a coastline and the surface water eventually sinks toward the bottom. (https：//oceanservice.noaa.gov/)

定义法常用的标识词包括 what is..., to be defined as, to refer to, the definition of...is, to be used to describe, in a very real sense, in a limited sense, this is, this means, be explained, state that, in other words, namely 等。

三、因果法

段落的写作可以根据主题内容，采用原因分析法或影响分析法来展开，即因果法。例如：

According to an estimation by financial information platform Wind Info, based on bond trading data, the issuance of local government bonds may have dropped to 46 billion yuan in November from 256 billion yuan a month earlier. The reason was that the quota for local government bond issuance this year was almost used up by October, showed by data from the Ministry of Finance. The ministry has yet to report November's local government debt data.

本段的第一句提出"have dropped"这一现象，扩展句用"The reason was that"作为标识解释原因，说明主题句中现象出现的原因。

因果法常用的标识词包括 because, since, as, seeing that, the reason why..., because of, on account of, due to, so, thus, hence, therefore, accordingly, consequently, so that, as a result of, in consequence of, result in, result from, lead to, owing to, to have an effect on, for the reason 等。

四、比较与对比法

当段落的主题要指出两件以上事物的相同或不同之处时，可采用比较或对比的方法。用此法展开段落时，主要是将两个或两个以上的事物的共同点或不同点进行比较，从而显示出各自的特点。"比较法"阐述相似之处，"对比法"阐述不同之处。例如：

Television and newspaper are all very important news media. However, there are great differences between them as sources of news. (topic sentence) Television presents a colorful world in front of us. First, it shows us what is happening throughout the world. Second, it presents us world famous scenic spots and wonders. Third, it entertains us with colorful sports, music and other TV programs. On the other hand, the newspaper has the advantages of a different kind of convenience. The reader does not have to remain sitting before a TV set but can read news at his leisure and enjoy special stories. (developing sentence) So, TV has the advantage of immediate and dramatic effect, while newspaper is far less costly and more convenient. (concluding sentence)

该段主题句中关键词"great differences"确定了中心思想，段落内容应围绕 differences 展开论述，因此采用对比法。本段中首先用 first、second 与 third 作为标识词阐明 television 的三个特点，继而使用 on the other hand 作为标识词列出 newspaper 的特点，进行 television 与 newspaper 不同之处的整体对比。

Alfred Nobel, the Swedish inventor and industrialist, was a man of many contrasts. He was a son of a bankrupt, but became a millionaire; a scientist with a love of literature, an industrialist who managed to remain an idealist. He made a fortune but lived a simple life, and although cheerful in company he was often sad in private. A love of mankind, he never had a wife or family to love him; a patriotic son of his native land, he died alone on foreign soil. World famous for his works, he was never personally well known, for throughout his life he avoided publicity, but since his death his name has brought fame and glory to others.

该段主题句中关键词"a man of many contrasts"确定了中心思想，因此采用对比法展开段落。但与前一段整体特点进行对比不同的是，该段是分层次进行对比，词汇的使用充分体现了诺贝尔传奇人生中的矛盾冲突，如 bankrupt 与 millionaire、a scientist 与 a love of literature、an industrialist 与 an idealist、made a fortune 与 a simple life、cheerful in company 与 sad in private、a love of mankind, he never had a wife or family to love him 等内容充分体现了诺贝尔人生的 many contrasts，段落对比处也用到 but、although 等标识词。

由上述两个例子可以看出，比较和对比法一般采用两种方法来组织：

(1) 对两项或多项事物的异同之处整体进行比较对照，句子排列顺序为：A1, A2, A3; B1, B2, B3; …

(2) 对两项或多项事物的异同之处逐点进行比较对照，句子排列顺序为：A1, B1; A2, B2; A3, B3; …

下列段落实例中，Paragraph A 采用比较法对二者的相似之处进行比较，比较的顺序为逐点进行比较，即 A1, B1; A2, B2。Paragraph B 采用对比法对传统新闻报道和新闻杂志报道的不同之处进行了分析，采用 A1, A2; B1, B2; …的方法进行整体对比。Paragraph C 采用对比法对二者的不同之处进行比较，对比的顺序为逐点进行，即 A1，B1；A2，B2。

Paragraph A：

Paragraph and Essay

Despite their obvious differences in length, the paragraph and the essay are quite similar structurally. For example, the paragraph is introduced by either a topic sentence or a topic introducer followed by a topic sentence. In the essay the first paragraph provides introductory material and establishes the topic sentence. Similarly, the body of an essay consists of a number of paragraphs that expand and support the ideas presented in the introductory paragraph. Finally, a terminator—whether a restatement, conclusion, or observation—ends the paragraph. The essay, too, has a device which brings its ideas to a logically and psychologically satisfying completion: the concluding paragraph. Although exceptions to these generalizations may be observed in modern creative writing, most well written expository paragraphs and essays are comparable in structure.

Paragraph B：

There is an essential difference between a news story, as understood by a newspaperman or a wire-service writer, and the newsmagazine story. The chief purpose of the conventional news story is to tell what happened. It starts with the most important information and continues into increasingly inconsequential details, not only because the reader may not read beyond the first paragraph but because an editor working on galley proofs a few minutes before press time likes to be able to cut feely from the end of the story. A newsmagazine is very different. It is written to be read consecutively from beginning to end, and each of its stories is designed, following the critical theories of Edgar Allen Poe, to create one emotional effect. The news, what happened that week, may be told in the beginning, the middle, or the end; for the purpose is not to throw information at the reader but to reduce him into reading the whole story, and into accepting the dramatic (and often political) point being made.

Paragraph C：

Railways and Automobile Roads

Some people say that railways are more important than automobile roads. But in my opinion, automobile roads and railways complement each other. Railways do not touch small places, while automobile roads can be constructed to reach every place, even villages situated in remote corners of the country. Railways are constructed only for the trains, but roads will prove equally useful for bicycles, carriages and other kinds of vehicles. The cost of building automobile roads is also such lower than that of building railways.

比较和对比法常用的标识词包括 like, likewise, unlike, similarly, in the same way, on the other hand, compared with, by comparison, in contrast to, on the contrary, but, despite, yet, instead, while, whereas, however, nevertheless, although, even though, conversely, different from, equally important, in spite of, instead, in the same manner, still 等。

五、举例法

在确定段落的主题后,以举例的方法展开段落是最简洁方便的方法。一般段落的主题比较抽象概括,用举例的方法进行具体的阐述和论证,从而强化和突出主题句的中心思想和观点,并使之得到进一步验证。例如:

Paragraph A:

For many years, human society develops with the advance of science and technology, and the development of science and technology has brought about many changes in people's life (topic sentence). For instance, the invention of television and the space rocket has opened a new era for mankind. By the use of TV people can hear the sound and learn the invention of the spaceship and the rocket. The dream of man's landing on the moon has come true. For another example, the use of modern communication means such as mobile telephone, fax, e-mail etc. have brought great convenience to us. If one has a mobile telephone, he can talk to whom he wants almost everywhere, on his way to the office, in a bus or in a train. He doesn't have to try hard to find a public phone box or wait patiently for it. (developing sentence) So the life we are living now is more civilized than that of our forefathers. (concluding sentence)

该段落主题句中关键词"many changes"指明了本段写作的范畴。科技给人类生活带来的变化表现在很多领域,此处以列举法最为方便可行。本段通过列举生活中的具体变化事例,如电视、通信等方面给人们带来生活的便捷,使读者感同身受,切实体会到科技带来的变化。本段运用了标识词 for instance 与 for another example。

Paragraph B:

Tourism is becoming an increasingly important industry in China, and our country benefits a lot from it (topic sentence). For instance, the tourism industry is a large source of foreign exchange. This means more income for the country. It also means more employment. For another instance, the tourism can help to promote the understanding and friendship among the people of different cultures. As Francis Bacon said, "Travel in the younger sort is a part of education; in the elder, a part of experience." (developing sentence) Therefore, the tourism gives us a chance to widen our intellectual horizons, and people of different cultures can learn from each other. (concluding sentence)

该段落主题句中关键词"benefits a lot"指明了本段写作的范畴。旅游业给我国带来的好处以 income、employment 和 understanding and friendship 诸方面为例,支撑论点。本段运用了标识词 for instance 与 for another instance。

Paragraph C:

In many countries cigarette smoking is restricted in many ways. For example, in Britain, cigarettes are not allowed to be advertised on TV or radio; the American government requires manufacturers to print the warning that smoking is dangerous to health on every package of cigarettes; in our country a regulation is being drafted banning the sale of tobacco products to people under eighteen. There is no doubt that the world-wide anti-smoking campaigns will make more and more people be aware of the danger of smoking and become conscious fighters for cleaner air.

该段落主题句中关键词"in many ways"指明了本段写作的范畴。吸烟被以各种方式加以限制,围绕这一中心思想,本段通过标识词 for example 体现了香烟广告、警告标志等方面的例子,说明吸烟所受的限制,例子之间用分号隔开。

举例法常用的标识词包括 for example, for instance, for one thing, for another, to illustrate, one example is, a case in point, as an illustration, incidentally 等。

六、排序法

为了支持和说明主题句所体现的中心思想和观点,扩展句把要阐述的内容按其属性的不同,通过排序说明的方式,进行具体阐述说明,从而使主题句的中心思想和观点表达的条理清楚,层次分明,重点突出。例如:

Paragraph A:

Nowadays many people use telephone almost every day. Telephone is the greatest carrier of messages, and has many advantages. (topic sentence) The first thing is the speed and the directness. If you want to get an immediate connection, it is obviously quicker to phone someone rather than to write a letter. If you want information, it is often possible to get it directly by telephone. Another thing is that the telephone can give you a personal feeling. If you want to speak or get in contact with a friend or a relative, you feel much closer to them when you are talking to them on the telephone, whereas in a letter, the words you write down are rather impersonal (developing sentence). So, the telephone is one of the most common means of communication today. People can hardly imagine how they would get on if they didn't have telephones. (concluding sentence)

该段落主题句指出"telephone has many advantages",整段话围绕 advantages 展开。该段运用排序法将电话的好处层层展开论述。用到了 the first thing is、another thing is that 等标识词。

Paragraph B:

Keeping fit is quite important. One should be very careful with one's health in daily life. But what should we do to maintain and enhance our health? (topic sentence) There are many ways which help to build up one's health. Firstly, we should keep a balanced diet, that is to say, we should not have too much intake of animal fat, but more vegetables and fruits. Secondly, if one wants to keep fit, he must give up the habit that damage his health, such as smoking and drinking. Finally, regular physical exercise is essential for a healthy mind and body. In physical exercise, the key point is perseverance. No matter it rains or shines, one must overcome his laziness and continue training. (developing sentence) It is true that health is very important. Without a good health, one can do nothing. (concluding sentence)

该段落主题句为问句,段落要点应围绕回答"what should we do?"展开。扩展句以排序法依次展开,用标识词 firstly、secondly、finally 引出 a balanced diet 与 regular physical exercise 等要点。

排序法常用的标识语包括 first, second, third, finally, in the first (second) place, to begin with, the first thing, besides, moreover, also, in addition to, last but not least 等。

七、综合法

在段落扩展中同时使用几种不同扩展方法,即为综合法。事实上,在多数情况下,段落写作都是各种不同方法的综合应用,很少单纯采用一种方法来展开段落或文章,常见的为两三种方法混合使用。例如:

Paragraph A:

Increasing your vocabulary can help you in a number of ways.(顺序法)You will discover that knowing synonyms, for example,(举例法)will decrease the amount of repetition in your compositions and make them more enjoyable to read. And if a teacher enjoys reading your paper, he may even give you a better grade. Also, an increased vocabulary will make your own reading more enjoyable. You will find it is much easier to follow the ideas in your history textbook or the newspaper when you do not have to continually run to the dictionary to look up unknown word, you will become more eager to read and not as discouraged when you do come across an unknown word.(因果法)As a result, you will read faster and more intelligently, become more knowledgeable, and hence better informed about the world around you. Strange as it may seem, vocabulary study can make you a better person.

段落的第一句为主题句,指出"增加词汇可以使你在多方面受益",然后错综使用顺序法、举例法与因果法说明"这些好处",最后得结论。

Paragraph B:

Several factors may have contributed to the vast increase in the singles' population. To begin with, people on average are getting married at a much later age. In addition, the gradual, yet radical, changes in people's life style, values and views on relationships have led to the exponential increase in the singles' population. For instance, people today are increasingly open to the idea of cohabitation, leading to a significant rise in the number of people opting for live-in relationship. Besides, unlike in the past, single persons are no longer regarded as "weirdoes". The impact of the significant increase in the singles' population on the mainland's economic development would be hard to assess. For example, married couples may be more driven to seek success in work due to the pressure of supporting a family, yet single persons could devote more time and energy to their careers. Also, with the growing singles' population, consumption of single men and women would further increase while family-related consumption could drop in the long term. So contrary to popular analysis, the problem of "leftover" women or men may not pose such a serious challenge to the Chinese mainland's overall economic and social development, because even during historical periods when the sex ratio was not so skewed, there were many unmarried men and women. (Mu Guangzong, Building a more inclusive society for singles, China Daily)

段落在段首句揭示主题"单身人数数量的大幅增长受很多因素影响",继而使用排序法、举例法、对比法与因果法对主题进行了多角度的论证,且使用了明显的标识词,如 to begin with, in addition, besides, also, for instance, for example, yet, so, because 等,因此本段论证使用了综合法。

第三节 段落的模式

大学生的英语写作任务通常包括三个部分。三部分不是指字面上的三段文字,而是从整体写作结构上讲应包括文章的开头、主体和结尾,三个部分各自形成完整的段落,相互衔接,相互补充,形成一个有机的整体,其中的每一个段落又有段落总起句,拓展句和段落总结句。不同文体的文章分别遵循不同的写作布局、涉及不同的内容,但可提炼出具有共性的段落,如观点段、描述段、说明段等。各种文体有其不同的段落排列组合规律,具有共性写作特点的段落在不同的文体中出现的位置不同。本节的内容主要是帮助学习者归纳出段落具有共性的写作模式。下面以大学英语四六级与考研作文常见题型文字命题作文和图表命题作文为例,来说明段落排列组合的规律并探索段落写作的模式。

一、篇章中的段落题材

(一) 图表命题作文

图表命题作文,通常要求根据题目给出的图画或图表进行描述,继而对图画图表反映的现象进行分析,最后表达个人对此现象的态度。因此,图画图表作文中的段落一般会涉及描述段、说明段、观点段。如下面的一篇考研作文:

Directions: Write an essay of 160 – 200 words based on the following drawing. In your essay, you should first describe the drawing, interpret its meaning, and give your comment on it.

You should write neatly on ANSWER SHEET2. (20 points)

Outline:

1. write out the messages conveyed by the cartoon
2. give your comments

如此承诺

各行各业兴承诺

欢迎监督不推托

原本皆为分内事

何须高唱"文明歌"

　　The boastful promise the hen is giving would make people neither cry nor laugh. People cannot help asking what duty the hen should do and what particular eggs she would lay. It is clear that the hen is deliberately mystifying those who are interested in the eggs she lays.

　　Unfortunately, in our society, many enterprises try to fool consumers in much the same way that the hen does. With empty promise, they advertise products of poor quality, sometimes even fake commodities, with a view to promoting sales. And other profiteers try hard to follow their example. As a result, battles of false promise-making become more and more severe in the commercial warfare, causing greater and greater harm to society.

　　Mendacious promises not only undermine the trust between the producers and customers, but also pollute the social ethos, the loss of which is fatal to our society. So it is high time we took measures to have the deceitful and pretentious promises uprooted by way of exposure, punishment and education.

　　本篇文章涵盖了描述图画、举例说明、观点论证三方面内容，可按照段落的主要内容将其称之为描述段、说明段与观点段。三部分依次排列组合，构成了切合题意、有机衔接、论证充分的篇章。

（二）文字命题作文

文字命题作文，通常为考生提供题目与简明的写作提纲，要求考生紧扣题目主题，并依据提纲提示的思路和要点展开段落。

Directions：For this part, you are allowed 30 minutes to write a short essay on The Telephone based on the outline below. You should write at least 120 words but no more than 180 words.

Outline：

(1) the telephone is a useful tool

(2) how to use it

(3) the improvement of its use

 范文

  The telephone is an efficient means of communication, which enables people to talk with each other over long distances. If you are overseas and your family is left behind, you may miss them now and then. Besides fishing out their photos, you can dial a long distance call and send your love to them. For business with another company, the telephone is the most convenient means for you to turn to. It saves much of your travel.

  It is easy to learn how to use a telephone. First, take the receiver off the hook. Then listen for the dial tone. You can begin to dial the number you want when you hear a long steady signal. If you hear a rapid series of very short tones after dialing, the phone is "busy." Each town has special emergency numbers for the fire department and police station, which are often listed in the front of the telephone directory.

  People have made much improvement in telephone. For example, they can record telephone talks on tapes, use a radio telephone on a moving car or see the speaker by using the vision telephone.

本篇文章涵盖了观点论证（第一段对重要性进行了正面论证）、说明（用排序法说明用法）、观点论证三方面内容，可按照段落的主要内容将其称之为议论段、说明段与观点段。三部分依次排列组合，构成了切合题意、有机衔接的篇章。

由上面例证可以看出，无论是文字命题作文还是图表命题作文，作文题材都是由相关段落体裁的写作与组合构成的。文字命题必然有观点、有现象要论述，那就必然要用议论段和说明段。图表作文题必然有图表、图画，那就必然要用描述段描述图表的内容并揭示解释寓意和问题，其后要阐述现象、观点和揭示问题就必然要用说明段；最后则使用议论段表达作者自己的观点、建议、方法或态度（结尾段）。

二、不同题材段落的写作模式

篇章是各种题材段落的有机组合。写作无定法，但对于初学者，分析佳作的写作特点、探索各种题材段落的写作规律与内在逻辑、归纳写作模式是掌握写作规范、提高写作水平的有效途径。初学者接触的段落写作题材主要包括叙述段、说明段与议论段。每种段落的写作、不同题材的组织有其模式可遵循，归纳段落写作的模式不是要在写作时生搬硬套，而是要通过分析段落的写作模式来体会句型的错综使用和由此体现的层次感，并能够灵活运用。

（一）叙述段

叙述段主要起记叙、描述的作用，主要出现在记叙文、图表（图画）作文的描述部分与文字命题的现象、背景描述部分。因此，叙述段主要包括描述图表段与描述背景段。

1. 描述图表段

描述图表段通常出现在图表作文里的第一段，也就是提纲要点的第一点"Describe the picture"。考研写作与四六级写作多次出现图表图画作文，并在提纲要点的第一点明确提出要描述图画内容。在描述图画时一般要遵循的逻辑顺序为：

第一步，描述图中主要信息（按照一定顺序）；第二步，将图中的寓意提炼成全文的观点。

当学习者在理顺这一写作逻辑顺序后，要进行遣词造句，使用起描述作用、概括观点的相应句式与相关词汇。如在描述图画时，常常使用 As is depicted in the pictures 的句式，其中 depict 可以用其他词汇如 show 来替换，picture 也会依据题干展现方式用 pie chart、cartoon 等词进行替换。下面通过分析 2003 年与 2004 年考研英语作文来分析描述段的常用写作模式。

例 1：

Directions: Write an essay of 160 – 200 words based on the following drawing. In your essay, you should first describe the drawing, interpret its meaning, and give your comment on it.

You should write neatly on ANSWER SHEET 2. (20 points)
Outline: describe the set of drawings, interpret its meaning

温室花朵经不起风雨

温室花朵经不起风雨

题目要求，本文的写作要首先描述图画并揭示寓意。针对这一要求，可以按照一定的逻辑顺序，先描述图画，从第一幅画描述到第二幅画，然后再揭示图画寓意。范文如下：

> As is depicted in the pictures, a flower in a greenhouse is destroyed when exposed to a storm. ［图画内容总概括］In the first picture, the flower is shown to be healthy and strong while it is covered from any harm outside. ［描述图画一的内容］However, in the second picture, as the protection is removed, the flower soon dies in the real weather of heavy rains and high winds. ［描述图画二的内容］It is safe to draw the conclusion that what seems to be a strong life is actually weak, all due to excessive protection and care. ［揭示图画寓意］

该描述段切题且逻辑清晰，先对图画内容进行总的概括，然后先后描述图画一与图画二的内容，继而揭示图画的寓意。标识词与典型句型的使用使段落层次分明，使读者一眼明了。

例2：

Directions: Write an essay of 160 – 200 words based on the following drawing. In your essay, you should first describe the drawing, interpret its meaning, and give your comment on it.

You should write neatly on ANSWER SHEET2. (20 points)

Outline: describe the drawing

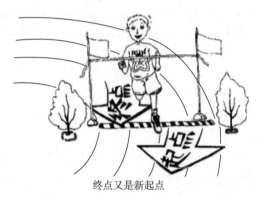

终点又是新起点

通过审题了解到题目要求，本文要首先描述图画。针对这一要求，可以按照一定的逻辑顺序，先描述图中的主要信息，再通过描述细节反映主题，然后揭示图画寓意。范文如下：

> As is depicted in the drawing, the runner reaches the finishing line and starts towards a new goal again. [图画内容总概括] Although sweating heavily, he does not stop and continue to run forwards. [进一步具体阐述图画内容] As is revealed, we in real life should not stop at the achievement we have made. [揭示寓意，折射生活中的含义] It is safe to draw the conclusion that our life is a course that requires constant pursuit of greater goals. [对寓意进一步解释]

该描述段先对图画内容进行总的概括，然后给出图画的具体信息，继而揭示图画的寓意。本段共四句话，句与句之间层层递进，逻辑层次清晰，分别使用了相应的标识词与典型句型。

基于上面两个例子的分析，我们可以概括出描述图表段的写作模式，即描述图表段的常用语型、常用词汇与写作逻辑顺序。初学者可以借鉴下列段落的写作模式来增强作文的层次感。

模式一：(1) From the picture/graph/ chart/ table, /pie/ bar), we know that (图表内容总概括). (2) On one hand, the left/ first picture tells us that (图表一/部分图表的内容). (3) On the other hand, (the right/ second) picture informs us that (图二/表二/另一部分图表的内容). (4) It can easily be seen that (揭示寓意).

模式二：(1) As is shown/ described/ depicted in the cartoon/ picture,

（图表内容总概括）.（2）In the first picture,（描述图表一内容/部分图表的内容）.（3）As is shown in the second drawing/picture,（描述图表二/其余部分图表的内容）.（4）It is safe to draw the conclusion that（揭示寓意）.

模式三：（1）It is shown/depicted/described in the picture that（图表内容总概括）.（2）（进一步阐述图表内容）.（3）As is symbolically revealed in the pictures,（图画的现实意义）.（4）We can say that/ We may draw/ come to a conclusion that / We can see clearly that（对寓意进行归纳）.

2. 描述背景段

描述背景段往往在文字命题题型中出现，主要用于陈述话题背景或描述现象。如下列考研真题：

Direction：Write an essay of 120 – 150 words with the title *The Hope Project*. Your composition should be based on the outline below and should start with the opening sentence "Education plays a very important role in the modernization of our country."

Outline：

（1）present situation

（2）necessity of the project

（3）my suggestion

该题目要求首先以给出句子作为段首句来描述现状，继而论证必要性，最后提出个人观点。在现状描述段落中，通过描述细节反映现实，并提出整篇文章的主题。范文如下：

> （1）Education plays a very important role in the modernization of our country.（2）Only good education can enhance people's quality.（3）Yet, the present situation in China is not satisfactory, since many children in the remote poor areas cannot go to school or have to drop out.（4）Therefore, a plan called Hope Project is carried out to support the dropouts.

如上述范文，描述背景段往往采用的叙述层次为：首先给出起始句，继而扩展进一步介绍起始句，并展现现状积极的方面或指出现状的不足，最后引出全文中心或提出主题句。基于此范例的分析，我们可以概括出描述背景段的写作模式。初学者可以借鉴下列段落的写作模式来增强作文的层次感。

描述背景段模式：（1）主题句（视提纲内容而定）；（2）扩展句：

Only…can/ With…；（3）转折句：Yet/ However, the present situation…（提出现状的不足）；（4）段落总结句：Therefore/ So/ Thus（提出主题句的必要性）。

（二）说明段

说明段一般处在作文的中间段，属于文章的主体段落，因为无论是文字命题还是图表命题作文，第一段描述了图表内容揭示了寓意，或描述了问题的背景或现状，第二段必然要对第一段提出的观点、寓意即问题进行阐述、说明和分析，故说明段是文章的主体段落。

1. 举例说明段

举例说明段就是指主要以举例的说明方法来阐述主体论点。如前面讲解"描述段"时选用的第二个例子，在篇章的第一部分描述现象之后，第二部分应对于此主题进行说明，可采用举例说明的方式进行写作，如下段：

> The truth also applies to our life. There are many examples proving that every success is a result of unremitting endeavor.（观点句）Take the space flight project of our country as a typical example. Since we first launched our rocket into the sky, our scientists have been working on the project to send human being to the outer space, which resulted in the accomplished flight of ShenZhou V spaceship last year.（阐述第一个例子）That would be day dreaming if we just dwell on the achievements in rockets we made and do not move on to spaceship research.（进一步具体阐述例子或从反面阐述）Another case in point is that today we participate the test for Master degree with the purpose of furthering our tomorrow's studies. Entering post graduate education is not the eventual aim, but a new beginning of a longer journey.（引出并阐述第二个例子）Therefore, only if we persevere to work hard and keep doing what we really want to do and like to do, can we be successful persons.

该段落主要是通过举例来说明主题，说明层次分明，先是由段落主题句表达段落总体思想，然后阐述第一个例子，接着进一步说明第一个例子，然后引出并说明第二个例子，最后用段落总结句进行中心思想的归纳。因此，当进行举例说明时，可使用以下段落写作模式：

模式一：（1）There are many examples found to prove that（主题句）.

(2) Take...as a typical example. / The first example is that（阐述第一个例子，可再加扩展句进一步阐述）. (3) The second example is that/ In addition/ Moreover/ Another case in point is that（第二个例子的内容，可再加扩展句进一步阐述）. (4) Therefore, only...can...（段落总结句）.

模式二：(1) 主题 can be best/ well illustrated in / explained by（例子）. (2)（阐述例子）. (3)（扩展句进一步阐述例子）. (4)（段落总结句，进一步总结观点句的必要性和重要性）.

2. 原因说明段

原因说明段是指该段主要是从几个方面的原因来解释主题相关现象。下面通过考研英语作文来分析原因说明段的常用写作模式。题目要求如下：

Directions：You should describe the picture and interpret its meaning, and give your comment on the phenomenon.

本文在首先描述图画并揭示寓意之后，对出现该现象的原因进行分析，便于作者在最后部分表达观点。篇章的写作提纲包括三点：describe the picture and interpret its meaning; show the reasons of the phenomenon; give your comment on the phenomenon. 其中原因分析段可借鉴下列写法：

Culture—National and International

There are many reasons explaining why a trend of internationalization in national cultures is emerging in recent years.（段首提出段落主题句）The first reason is no other than the globalization in economy, which provides more opportunities for people to promote mutual understanding than ever before.（阐述第一个原因）The second reason is that more and more people have gradually realized a national culture must acquire global recognition before it thrives in today's world.（阐述第二个原因）The third reason is that the desire of every ethnic group to live with each other in harmony also plays an important role.（阐述第三个原因）

该段先进行总的概括表明要说明的主题，然后阐述三点原因，为使段落层次分明，作者使用了标识词与典型句型。该段落写作模式亦可用于其他主题的原因说明。

模式一：(1) There are many reasons responsible for this phenomenon/ case/instance and the following are the typical ones. (2) The first reason is that

（原因一）.（3）The second reason is that（原因二）.（4）The third reason is that/ A case in point is that（原因三）.

模式二：（1）There are many reasons to explain/explaining the effect/phenomenon/case/instance.（2）The most contributing one is/ the main reason is no other than（原因一）.（3）What is more（原因二）.（4）（原因三）also play a role in this case.

3. 说明性议论段

说明性议论段既不是通过实例来说明问题，也不是从几个方面的原因来解释问题，而是从几个层面上来阐述段落的主题。如下面的考研真题：

Directions：Write an essay of 160 – 200 words based on the following drawing. In your essay, you should first describe the drawing the interpret its meaning, and give your comment on it.

Outline：Deduce the purpose of the drawer.

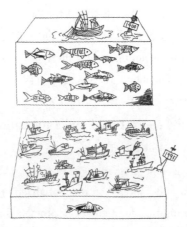

该题目在首先描述图画并揭示寓意之后，要求对出现该现象进行分析，可采取下列写法：

> Judging from the pictures, we can clearly infer that the drawer's intention is to warn people of the worst consequence if fishing activities don't follow the sustainable development pattern.（根据提纲写出段落主题句，阐述作图人的意图，提出问题）For one thing, the population growth of fishing is controlled by natural laws. It is true that if we disturb that law we should send nature into disorder. With the situation of fishing, if we fish so excessively we could have disturbed the continuity of fish

> growth. （扩展句，阐述第一个层面）For another, if we don't respect the law of nature, we will be punished someday. That is because we human beings are part of nature. If we don't control the sharp increase in fishing, many fishes will become extinct. （扩展句，阐述第二个层面）As a result, the ecological balance will be disturbed in the sea and natural disasters will happen soon. （总结句）

该段在表述段落主题句后，分两个层面对该现象进行说明，分别用标识词 for one thing、for another 厘清句与句之间的逻辑关系，段落层次分明。分层次进行问题说明时可采用以下段落模式：

（1）主题句（视作文提纲内容而定）.（2）For one thing/First of all/Firstly 第一个层面的扩展句.（3）扩展句 For another/Besides/Moreover/In addition/Secondly 第二个层面的扩展句.（4）Thus/As a result/Therefore/Finally 总结句.

（三）议论段

1. 个人观点段

作文题中一般要求在最后部分表达作者自己的想法、观点、建议、方法或态度，作为结尾段。结合大学生经常接触的四六级作文和考研作文的规律性和该段内容的特点，我们将此段称为个人观点段。如前面讲解"描述段"时选用的第二个例子，篇章写作包括三个部分：（1）describe the drawing and interpret its meaning；（2）give examples to support your view；（3）give your suggestions. 在描述图画、举例说明之后，在最后部分作者应对此现象提出个人的看法，可采用下面的写作方式：

> In order to improve the situation, I think we need to take some positive measures. （段落主题句）For one thing, people should always learn to keep up with the change of the time. （阐述第一个建议）For another, we should always keep in mind the dangers of being satisfied and refusing to move ahead. （阐述第二个建议）Thus, we could be driven with the desire to achieve one goal after another. （段落总结句）

该段在表述段落主题句后，分两个层面提出建议，并分别用标识词 for one thing、for another 连接句子，突出段落层次。表述个人观点的段落可采用以下段落模式：

模式一：(1) Considering all these reasons/ Confronted with such a problem, I think we need to take some positive measures. (2) On the one hand, 方法/建议一. (3) On the other hand, it is necessary for us to 方法/建议二. (4) Thus, 总结自己的观点/建议/态度.

模式二：(1) To sum up the above argument/ Confronted with such an issue/ a problem, we should find several solutions to it. (2) On the on hand, we should 方法/建议一. (3) On the other hand 方法/建议二. (4) Only in this way, can 解决问题或重申主题.

模式三：(1) As far as I am concerned/ In my opinion, the proper attitude towards/ suggestion for 主题 is that 概括观点/态度/建议. (2) For one thing 方法/建议一. (3) For another, 方法/建议二. (4) Therefore/ Thus/ Only in this way, can 段落总结句.

2. 正反论证段

写作中，通过正反对比来得出结论能够加强说服力，正反论证段是初学写作者常常用到的方法。如下面命题：

Directions: your composition should bewritten with the title *Good Health* based on the outline below and should with the given sentence: "The desire for health is universal"

Outline:

(1) Importance of good health

(2) Ways to keep fit

(3) My own practices.

依据题目要求，第一段应对 good health 的重要性进行论证，此时可采用正反论证法，请阅读下面例文并体会写作模式：

> The desire for good health is universal. (主题句) On the one hand, people with good health can do work with high spirit and their progress in work in turn contributes to their health and happiness. (扩展句，从正面论证) On the other hand, a sick person, is usually interested in nothing around him and then he misses many opportunities to become successful. (扩展句，从反面论证) Therefore, keeping good conditions very important. (段落总结句)

该段落首先阐述段落主题句，又使用标识词 on the one hand 与 on the other hand 体现正面论证与反面论证，通过对比，最后进行观点总结。正反论证段落可采用以下段落模式：

（1）主题句（视作文提纲内容而定）．（2）On the one hand/ Firstly, if/Only...can...（正面论证扩展句）．（3）On the other hand/ In contrast/ Secondly, if/Otherwise...（反面论证扩展句）．（4）So/ Therefore/Thus...（段落总结句）．

三、段落模式的有机组合

篇章的写作中离不开叙述、说明、议论等段落的写作。篇章是段落的有机组合，不同题材写作中包含共性的段落，以大学生常见的四六级考研题型为例，文字命题作文常常用描述段进行现象的描述，用正反论证段论证话题的重要性与必要性，用说明段说明分析该问题，用议论段表达个人观点；图表作文题一般要用描述段描述图表的内容并揭示解释寓意，用说明段分析问题、影响或原因，用议论段表达作者自己的观点、建议、方法或态度。不同篇章中的共性段落要依据题目的要求进行有机排列组合。下面以本节第一部分"篇章中的段落题材"中考研题为例，使用前面已讲解过的各种段落模式来进行篇章的写作。题目的提纲可以列为以下三个部分：

（1）Describe the cartoon and interpret the meaning of the picture.

（2）Give examples.

（3）Provide some solutions.

分析该提纲，第一段为描述段，第二段为举例说明段，第三段为个人观点段，我们可运用本节第一部分"不同题材段落的写作模式"所提供的相关段落模式，依据提纲要求将段落进行有机排列组合进行篇章的写作。段落模式运用如下列范文：

> It is described in the picture that a hen make a promise that her eggs include things that an egg should have. In the picture, the hen grasp a bulletin with words like this: "I promise my egg have no angles and ridges. My egg include shell, yolk and egg white." As is symbolically revealed in the picture, just like the hen, some people deliberately make commitments within their responsibilities. We can clearly say that it is very ridiculous and unnecessary to make such commitments. （描述图画段）
>
> There are many examples found to prove that it is very absurd to make promises within responsibility. Take one commitment in hospitals as

a typical example. Doctors often promise they will give timely treatment to patients. It is universally acknowledged that it is doctor's responsibility to give patients timely treatment. People will realize how idle, unnecessary and ridiculous such a commitment is. In addition, manufacturers guarantee to turn out products of good quality; commercial enterprises swear to provide genuine commodities and enthusiastic services; administration departments assure to perform their task effectively and fairly without taking any bribes. But they all forget one thing: what they promise to people is their duties. Therefore, only by being honest and shouldering their own responsibility, can companies win people's respect and survive in the fierce competition. （举例说明段）

In order to improve the situation, we should find several solutions. For one thing, our government must supervise every institution and organization to clearly identify their duties before they make commitments. For another, we should always keep in mind people are respected by what they did rather than what they said. Only in this way, can we eliminate the phenomenon of such "promises." （个人观点段）

Exercises

1. There should be topic sentence in every paragraph, which would be at the beginning, in the middle or at the end of the paragraph. Please find out the topic sentence for each paragraph and write it on the line below the paragraph.

(1) It was the best of times, it was the worst of times; it was the age of wisdom, it was the age of foolishness; it was the epoch of belief, it was the epoch of incredulity; it was the season of light, it was the season of darkness; it was the spring of hope, it was the winter of despair; we had everything before us, we had nothing before us; we were all going direct to Heaven, we were all going direct the other way.

（From A Tale of Two Cities by Charles Dickens, 1859）

The topic sentence: _____

(2) "But people are not born as a failure," he said. "A man can be destroyed but not defeated." I am sorry that I killed the fish though, he

thought. Now the bad time is coming and I do not even have the harpoon. The dentuso is cruel and able and strong and intelligent. But I was more intelligent than he was. Perhaps not, he thought. Perhaps I was only better armed.

(From The Old Man and Sea by Ernest Miller Hemingway, 1952)

The topic sentence: _____

(3) We are busy all day, like swarms of flies without souls, noisy, restless, unable to hear the voices of the soul. As time goes by, childhood away, we grew up, years away a lot of memories, once have also eroded the bottom of the childish innocence, we regardless of the shackles of mind, indulge in the world buckish, focus on the beneficial principle, we have lost themselves.

(From The little prince by Antoine de Saint - Exupéry, 1979)

The topic sentence: _____

(4) If God had gifted me with some beauty and much wealth, I should have made it as hard for you to leave me, as it is now for me to leave you. I am not talking to you now through the medium of custom, conventionalities, nor even of mortal flesh: it is my spirit that addresses your spirit; just as if both had passed through the grave, and we stood at God's feet, equal — as we are!

(From Jane Eyre by Charlotte Brontë, 1847)

The topic sentence: _____

(5) Shakespeare is above all writers, at least above all modern writers, the poet of nature; the poet that holds up to his readers a faithful mirror of manners and of life. His characters are not modified by the customs of particular places, unpractised by the rest of the world; by the peculiarities of studies or professions, which can operate but upon small numbers; or by the accidents of transient fashions or temporary opinions: they are the genuine progeny of common humanity, such as the world will always supply, and observation will always find. His persons act and speak by the influence of those general passions and principles by which all minds are agitated, and the whole system of life is continued in motion. In the writings of other poets a character is too often an individual; in those of Shakespeare it is commonly a species.

(From Shakespeare, Sammuel Johnson, 1765)

The topic sentence: _____

2. Paragraph Writing. (1) and (2) are from the writing tasks in previous entrance examinations for post-graduate. (3) to (7) are from the Writing part in

"New Progressive College English: Integrated Course 2" by Li Yinhua etc.

(1) Directions: Write a paragraph based on the following drawing. In the paragraph, you are required to describe the picture briefly and interpret its meaning.

图一：把崇拜写在脸上　　图二：花300元做个"小贝头"

(2) Write a paragraph about what we can do in our daily life with regard to green, sustainable living.

a. Write a paragraph of no less than 130 words.

b. Begin your writing with a topic sentence which clearly states the main idea of the paragraph, for example: It is possible to live a green, sustainable life.

c. List the small things we can do to make it happen.

(3) Suppose you are a close friend of the Elliott family. Write a letter of condolence to Pauline on the death of Frank.

a. Write a letter of about 130 words.

b. Include the basic structure and components of a letter of condolence.

(4) Read the following topic sentence carefully and then develop it into a paragraph.

a. Write a paragraph of no less than 130 words.

b. Topic sentence: Friendship is often compared to a flower.

c. Make sure you explain clearly why friendship can be compared to a flower and how it can be protected from blows.

(5) Suppose you were Yilu Zhao in a Shanghai senior high school, write an application letter to Yale University.

a. Have you written no less than 130 words for the main body of your letter?

b. Have you stated clearly why you want to attend Yale University's Directed Studies program?

c. Have you explained what you can bring to the Directed Studies program and to Yale?

d. Is your letter free of grammatical and spelling errors?

e. Do you use standard letter format and commonly accepted fonts?

f. Have you tried your best to use the new words?

(6) Write a paragraph about Howard Hughes and his Spruce Goose, using the following criteria for evaluation.

a. You must write a passage of no less than 130 words.

b. The passage may begin with Howard Hughes was an American entrepreneur and an aviation pioneer.

c. It should focus on Hughes's construction of the Spruce Goose.

d. It should tell about the fate (命运) and significance (意义) of the Spruce Goose.

e. It should bring out the point that Howard Hughes was an aviation pioneer.

(7) Write a paragraph about the possible benefits of bringing the maker movement into the classroom, where you, as a student, can learn to build something of your own.

a. Write a paragraph of no less than 130 words.

b. Begin with a topic sentence which clearly states the main idea of the paragraph. For example: There are many benefits of bringing the maker movement into the classroom.

c. Support the topic sentence with possible benefits that can be derived from the practice.

第四章

英语篇章的写作

美文赏析

I Have a Dream

by Martin Luther King, Jr.

Five score years ago, a great American, in whose symbolic shadow we stand today, signed the Emancipation Proclamation. This momentous decree came as a great beacon light of hope to millions of Negro slaves who had been seared in the flames of withering injustice. It came as a joyous daybreak to end the long night of bad captivity.

But one hundred years later, the Negro still is not free. One hundred years later, the life of the Negro is still sadly crippled by the manacles of segregation and the chains of discrimination. One hundred years later, the Negro lives on a lonely island of poverty in the midst of a vast ocean of material prosperity. One hundred years later, the Negro is still languished in the corners of American society and finds himself an exile in his own land. So we've come here today to dramatize a shameful condition.

I am not unmindful that some of you have come here out of great trials and tribulations. Some of you have come fresh from narrow jail cells. Some of you have come from areas where your quest for freedom left you battered by the storms of persecution and staggered by the winds of police brutality. You have been the veterans of creative suffering. Continue to work with the faith that unearned suffering is redemptive.

Go back to Mississippi, go back to Alabama, go back to South Carolina, go back to Georgia, go back to Louisiana, go back to the slums and ghettos of our northern cities, knowing that somehow this situation can and will be changed. Let us not wallow in the valley of despair.

I say to you today, my friends, so even though we face the difficulties of today and tomorrow, I still have a dream. It is a dream deeply rooted in the American dream.

I have a dream that one day this nation will rise up, live up to the true meaning of its creed: "We hold these truths to be self-evident; that all men are created equal."

I have a dream that one day on the red hills of Georgia the sons of former slaves and the sons of former slave-owners will be able to sit down together at the table of brotherhood.

I have a dream that one day even the state of Mississippi, a state sweltering with the heat of injustice, sweltering with the heat of oppression, will be transformed into an oasis of freedom and justice.

I have a dream that my four children will one day live in a nation where they will not be judged by the color if their skin but by the content of their character.

I have a dream today.

I have a dream that one day down in Alabama with its governor having his lips dripping with the words of interposition and nullification, one day right down in Alabama little black boys and black girls will be able to join hands with little white boys and white girls as sisters and brothers.

I have a dream today.

I have a dream that one day every valley shall be exalted, every hill and mountain shall be made low, the rough places will be made plain, and the crooked places will be made straight, and the glory of the Lord shall be revealed, and all flesh shall see it together.

This is our hope. This is the faith that I go back to the South with. With this faith we will be able to hew out of the mountain of despair a stone of hope. With this faith we will be able to transform the jangling discords of our nation into a beautiful symphony of brotherhood. With this faith we will be able to work together, to pray together, to struggle together, to go to jail together, to stand up for freedom together, knowing that we will be free one day.

This will be the day when all of God's children will be able to sing with new meaning.

My country, 'tis of thee,
Sweet land of liberty,
Of thee I sing:
Land where my fathers died,
Land of the pilgrims' pride,
From every mountainside
Let freedom ring.

And if America is to be a great nation this must become true. So let freedom ring from the prodigious hilltops of New Hampshire.

Let freedom ring from the mighty mountains of New York!

Let freedom ring from the heightening Alleghenies of Pennsylvania!

Let freedom ring from the snowcapped Rockies of Colorado!

Let freedom ring from the curvaceous slops of California!

But not only that; let freedom ring from Stone Mountain of Georgia!

Let freedom ring from Lookout Mountain of Tennessee!

Let freedom ring from every hill and molehill of Mississippi!

From every mountainside, let freedom ring!

When we let freedom ring, when we let it ring from every village and every hamlet, from every state and every city, we will be able to speed up that day when all of God's children, black men and white men, Jews and Gentiles, Protestants and Catholics, will be able to join hands and sing in the words of the old Negro spiritual, "Free at last! free at last! Thank God almighty, we are free at last!"

▶ 赏析：

1963年8月28日，马丁·路德·金在华盛顿林肯纪念堂前向25万人发表演讲《我有一个梦想》，表达了对黑人和白人一样享有平等和自由权利的期待，使人倍受鼓舞，激发了美国黑人追求自由和幸福的信心和勇气。该篇演讲自发表以来，就被世人广为传诵，被誉为 20 世纪最著名的演说之一。本篇演说词不仅仅是一篇言辞恳切、慷慨激昂、具有极强号召力的演说，也是一篇文笔优美、逻辑严密、极富感染力的美文。几十年过去了，人们读起此文，仿佛亲临现场，依旧能够感受现场掌声雷动、情感共鸣的情景。

马丁·路德·金正是在演讲中借助语言的恰当使用达到了这一效果。语言的表达力与感召力取决于演讲的主题以及词汇的选择和句式的组织。演讲中，作者运用了大量正式、高级词汇包括很多双词素词汇与多词素词汇，如 momentous、injustice、segregation、discrimination、languished、unmindful、tribulations、persecution、brotherhood、interposition、nullification、symphony、heightening、curvaceous 等词，这些词汇的使用体现了马丁·路德·金演讲的正式性与严肃性，阐明了其庄重的政治追求使听众们信服。在该篇演讲中，句式的运用多样化，有短句、长句，有简单句、复合句，有陈述句、祈使句。文中最短的句子由 4 个词构成、最长句由 77 个词组成，并单独成段，另外 50 词以上的句子出现了两处。有很多简单句语气果断干脆，也有包含时间状语从句、定语从句的复合句将民众的理想娓娓道来。文章多处出现感叹句，强烈的语气表达了作者坚定的决心、实现梦想的紧迫感与对美好未来的期待。该篇演讲词通篇饱含热情，语势节奏分明，既有对当前形势的分析，也有对平等与自由的热切期盼，体现了作者的果敢与坚定，感染力强，具有极高的语言艺术欣赏价值。

第一节　英语写作的谋篇布局

篇章由段落组成，涉及不同的文体和不同的写作方法。谋篇布局大多要遵循相对固定的结构模式，文章的篇章结构大多可以寻找到一定的规律。认真分析题目的要求，搞清写作的层次，通过每个独立的自然段落体现层次内容，再通过内在与外在的连接体现层次关系，文章主旨、文章脉络和逻辑结构就能够实现了。掌握篇章结构的写作规律后，能够对文章框架心里有数，做到写作切题布局合理。

一、英语作文的布局

从《大学英语教学指南》（教育部，2017）与各类考试作文的命题特点和写作要求来看，初学者写作文时内容分为三部分是最佳选择。英语作文的布局分为三部分，包括开头、主体与结尾，能够做到结构完整、论证透彻、字数达标。

文章的第一部分为引言段，主要是破题开篇，列举现象、说明图表图画内容，字数不宜过多，防止喧宾夺主。第二部分为主体部分，展开说明、讨论主题，通常要求联系实际，进行举例分析，或说明原因、理由或后果。最后一部分进行收尾，通常是要进行总结，提出个人的看法或提出解决问题的办法、措施、建议等。以往年的考研及四六级考试真题为例，题型与主题逐年变化，但是内容始终是三个部分。如：

A. 1996 年考研真题：提纲作文

Directions：

［A］Title：GOOD HEALTH

［B］Time limit：40 minutes

［C］Word limit：120 – 150 words（not including the given opening sentence）

［D］Your composition should be based on the OUTLINE below and should start with the given opening sentence："The desire for good health is universal."

OUTLINE：

1. Importance of good health

2. Ways to keep fit

3. My own practices

提纲作文本身就给了三点提纲，这样就要求考生必须按照提纲规定的内容和指导的思路，完成三段式作文，否则就会不切题或遗漏要写的内容，影响到作文得分。

GOOD HEALTH

The desire for good health is universal. Wherever you are and whatever you do, staying healthy is always important. With the improvement of our living standards, people are attaching more and more importance to their health. We students can't keep the high study efficiency without good health. The same thing is true with workers, scientists and doctors.

In my opinion, good diet and exercises are two major ways to keep healthy. The food we eat every day must be rational and should include meat, vegetables, eggs, and fruit. It is important to drink water every day and not to get addicted to drinking coffee or some other soft drinks. Exercising every day is also essential for us to stay healthy. We can ride bicycles, play tennis or swim. Of course, we don't need to exhaust ourselves. We should plan our physical exercises according to our actual condition. An hour a day is enough.

　　As a university student, I have much free time to do exercises. I usually play badminton and tennis. But sometimes I am lazy and do not exercise for all kinds of excuses, such as cold weather and exams. I must correct it. I am also careful with my diet. In a way, keeping healthy is not very hard, if you just take it seriously.

（from http://www.kuakao.com/english/zw/25285.html）

B. 2003 年考研真题：图画作文

Directions：

Study the following set of drawings carefully and write an essay in which you should

（1）describe the set of drawings, interpret its meaning, and

（2）point out its implications in our life.

温室花朵经不起风雨

　　依据图画与文字要求，文章第一部分应开篇描述图画、破题点明寓意，按照顺序描述两幅图画，说明温室花朵经不起风雨。第二部分应联系实际，说明这两幅画中反映的我们生活中令人深思的事情。第三部分作为文章的收尾，对教育观念做出评论提出看法。

　　It goes without saying that the drawings aim at revealing a common and serious problem in China: how to educate and cultivate the young.

Let's take a closer look at the drawings. In an ideal condition, the flower blooms. But when moved out of the greenhouse, it perishes under the rain and storm. It is obvious that the flower in greenhouse can't withstand wind and rains.

Nowadays the young generation in China, like the flower in greenhouse, lives under the full protection of their parents. Parents want to show all their love to their children. They give their children all the best things they can afford and do not let their children do anything at home. Self-centeredness and arbitrariness have become a trait of the young generation. Once leaving their parents, many young people cannot make a living on their own. They get lost when stepping into the complex reality and cannot face any hardships and difficulties.

Child education has become one of the most popular topics discussed not only by educational experts, but also by people in all walks of life. The failure of child education does more harm to the development of our society and our civilization than to the children themselves. Thus, it's high time that parents, educators and the government made concerned efforts to put an end to this situation.

C: 2015年6月英语四级作文真题：图画作文

Directions: For this part, you are allowed 30 minutes to write an essay based on the picture below. You should start you essay with a brief description of the picture and then comment on parents' role in their children's growth.

"Good news mom! I was accepted to the college of your choice."

本文第一部分应简要描述图画，指出图画反映问题，第二部分进行现状的原因分析，可进行举例论证，最后一部分提出建议措施。

> The drawing vividly reflects a daughter is chatting with her mother in their house. The eyes sparkling with delight, the daughter tells her mother, "Good news mom! I was accepted to the college of your choice." Obviously, the implication of the portrayal is that the daughter is lack of independence due to her mother's doting care.
>
> The lovely daughter is naturally associated with the only children in our current society; the college of the mother's choice epitomizes parents' doting care and abundant material supplies that can shield the children from the harsh reality. Once the young people begin to seek independence and accept challenges from the real world, they are found too spoiled to be strong enough in the face of difficulties.
>
> Accordingly, it is vital for us to derive positive implications from the thought-provoking drawing. On the one hand, we can frequently use it to enlighten the youth to be more independent in life. On the other hand, parents should be sensible enough to give their children more freedom to deal with troubles and problems.
>
> （from http：//cet4. koolearn. com/20151111/797535. html）

二、写作中的选材与构思

在确定了文章的写作主题后，要开始构思写作的框架与内容了，即在落笔写作之前，要对文章将要涉及的内容以及如何组织这些内容进行思考。

（一）写作的选材

初学写作者往往遇到的问题是，确定主题后寥寥数语便觉得无话可说。这种情况下，我们可以在落笔前广泛搜集写作素材，丰富写作内容。日常练习中，可采用风暴联想法和自我提问法来进行主题选材，能够避免偏离主题或无话可说的问题。

围绕主题广泛搜集写作素材，可首先进行风暴联想，即进行 brain-storming，快速联想与主题相关的内容，然后对这些进行筛选取舍，选取有效内容并进行有机组合，写成文章。具体联想过程中，可以给自己限定三分钟的时间，将想到的所有内容简要地记录下来，如主题 the changes brought by smart phones in our life，在限定时间内我们进行联想，可能会想到的内容包括：online games，convenience brought by Internet，Wechat，e-mail，QQ，MOOC，Parents think it's bad for kids to spend so much time on phones，online reading，bad for eyes，dictionaries，online payment，lack of communication with others，get information，waste time，learn a lot，等诸多内容，然后对这些联想到的内容进行取舍，和主题相关的保留，不能够说明主题的内容舍掉，然后对保留下的内容进行组合，如在这一话题中，changes可以分为两大类，good 和 bad，或者 convenient 和 inconvenient，即根据联想到的有效素材进行文章结构的思考，最终确定文章框架与各部分的内容素材，这就完成了构思选材环节。除了通过风暴联想法来搜索素材以外，我们还可以通过自我提问法来打开思路。围绕主题，借用 what/who/where/when/ why/ how 等疑问词提出问题并一一解答，拓宽看问题的角度，从多个角度打开思路。获得的信息，再结合主题进行取舍，并进行有机组合。

（二）写作的构思

首先，应根据作文命题的类型确定写作的结构，然后再对素材进行有机组合即列出提纲，列出全篇文章的写作思路。列提纲帮助我们有序地组织观点、合理组合材料。列提纲时只需要用词汇或短语等写出框架，便于在落笔写作时围绕提纲思路、时刻紧扣主题进行写作，不至于边写边想而偏离主题。下面结合不同的作文类型，进行构思与写作。

1. 提纲式作文

提纲式作文往往给三点完整的提纲，也就是给出了段落大意。作者应认真审题，分析提纲，并顺着提纲的思路进一步细化每部分的要点内容，围绕主题思考要写几个方面以及用何种段落写作方法进行扩展并选取写作素材。在写作中设计好句型，体现句式变化。例如：

1992 年考研英语作文

Directions：

［A］Title：FOR A BETTER UNDERSTANDING BETWEEN PARENT AND CHILD

［B］Time limit：40 minutes

［C］Word limit：120 – 150 words（not including the given opening sentence）

［D］Your composition should be based on the OUTLINE below and should start with the given opening sentence.

OUTLINE：

1. Present situation: Lack of communication between parent and child
2. Possible reasons:
1) Different likes and dislikes
2) Misunderstanding
3) Others
3. Suggestions:
1) For parents
2) For children

该考题是提纲式作文，已给出三个要点，考生应依据对主题的理解进行构思并选取写作素材，可列提纲如下，并严格按照提纲行文写作。

Para. One: Nowadays there is often a lack of understanding between parent and child

(1) parents' complaint: children's behavior unreasonable

(2) children's complaint: parents too old-fashioned

Para. Two: There are some possible reasons for the present situation

(1) different likes and dislikes lead to having little in common to talk about

(2) Misunderstanding leads to unwilling to communicate with each other

(3) Others: both parent and child are too busy to exchange their ideas with each other

Para. Three: to solve the generation gap problem, both parents and children should make efforts:

For parents: show understanding for the young

For children: show respect for the old

Nowadays there is often a lack of understanding between parent and child. Parents often complain about their children's "unreasonable" behavior, while younger generation usually feels that its style of living is quite different from that of older generation. No one wants to intrude or to be intruded. So, both parent and child have little in common to communicate with each other, and opinions about settling the problem are quite different.

There are some possible reasons for the present situation. Firstly, the two generations have different likes and dislikes. For example, the child likes discos and rock music, or love movies for his entertainment at night, while the parents like peaceful environment and physical exercises. They would like to spend their evenings of life in happiness. This situation leads to having little in common to talk about. Secondly, there often exists misunderstanding between parents and children. The child doesn't know what his parents think and act, while the parents don't understand what their children want to do. They feel that it is uncomfortable to sit face to face with each other talking. Thirdly, with the pace of modern life becoming faster and faster, both parents and child are too busy to have enough time to exchange ideas, even if they find it necessary to communicate.

I think it unfair to say that they are self-centered. This is a generation gap which should be solved by making efforts from parents and children. The children should respect their parents. The old generation, on the other hand, should show understanding for the young. By discovering common interests between two sides, they can interact much better and help each other to deal with their problems.

2. 图画图表作文

图画图表作文的题目往往先给出图表或图画，再给出文字要求。图表作文中往往体现数据变化，首先要掌握全部的信息，通过分析对比得出数字反映的信息，在写作时无须列出全部数字，列出代表性数字反映问题即可。图画作文要求认真读图，描述图画主要内容的同时分析图画所含寓意。图画图表作文的写作中常常要涉及描绘图表图画并揭示寓言、分析原因、联系实际及提出解决方案或建议等内容。

A. 1999 年考研作文

Directions：

[A] Study the following graphs carefully and write an essay in at least 150 words.

[B] Your essay should cover these three points：

1) effect of the country's growing human population on its wildlife

2) possible reason for the effect

3) your suggestion for wildlife protection

可列提纲如下：

Para. One：Describe the two graphs and reveal the effect of the country's growing population on its wildlife.

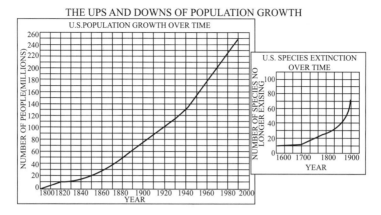

(1) The sharp increase of U. S. population caused the extinction of lots of wildlife species.

(2) The U. S. population expanded quickly.

(3) The number of extinct species also increased greatly.

Para. Two: Possible reasons for the effect

(1) The effect can be explained in two aspects.

(2) More people took more land from wildlife.

(3) More people produced more pollution and endangered wildlife.

Para. Three: Suggestion for wildlife protection

(1) We should take some measures to stop driving wildlife to extinction.

(2) We should increase the protection awareness.

(3) We should set up more nature reserves.

As the two charts show, U. S. population grew rapidly from 1800, but the country's wildlife went extinct sharply during that period. Undoubtedly, it is the expansion of people that had brought an end to many wildlife species.

There are many reasons responsible for the fast extinction of wildlife species, and the following are the typical ones. For one thing, the increasing people were pushing their cities and towns far into the forests, wetland and other places where wildlife once lived. The same species were cut off into small groups which were often hard to survive severe natural conditions. Or, some species were driven to new places, which they couldn't adapt themselves to and died in. For another, human beings brought pollution

> with them wherever they went, setting up plenty of factories. Living in polluted surroundings, some species were forced to die.
>
> There is a great demand for us to take some effective actions to protect wildlife. First, we should make more people aware of the fact and the result. Second, to address the urgent problem, we have to set aside land for more nature reserves, for it's never too late to mend, though some wildlife species is still becoming extinct.

B. 2005 年考研作文

Directions: Write an essay of 160 – 200 words based on the following drawing. In your essay, you should first describe the drawing, then interpret its meaning, and give your comment on it.

养老"足球赛"

该文可列提纲如下:

Para. One: Describe the drawing, and interpret its meaning.

Para. Two: Give some reasons to explain the phenomenon.

Para. Three: Give your comment on it.

在文章写作过程中,我们也可回顾上一章讲述的段落写作模式,来完成每个段落。

第一段属于描述图画段,第二段属于原因说明段,第三段是个人观点段,我们可借用段落模式如下:

Para. One: (1) As is shown/described/depicted in the cartoon/picture,

图表内容总概括。(2) In the first picture，描述图/表一内容（如果是一个图表，则或左或上半部分）。(3) As is shown in the second drawing/picture，描述图/表二内容（如果是一个图表，则右或下半部分）。(4) It is safe to draw the conclusion that 揭示寓意。

Para. Two：(1) There are many reasons responsible for this phenomenon/case/instance and the following are the typical ones. (2) The first reason is that（理由一）. (3) The second reason is that（理由二）. (4) The third reason is that/ A case in point is that（理由三）.

Para. Three：(1) As far as I am concerned/ In my opinion, the proper attitude towards/ suggestion for 主题 is that 我的观点/态度/建议. (2) For one thing 方法/建议一. (3) For another，方法/建议二. (4) Therefore/ Thus/ Only in this way, can 总结句.

篇章写作如下：

As is shown in the cartoon, an aged father huddles up into a ball, looking miserable, helpless while his four children each stand in a different corner of the football field. In the upper part of the cartoon, the elderly son kicks out the father, and the second son is preparing for warding him off. As is shown in the lower part of the cartoon, the other two children are also keeping their goals. It is safe to draw the conclusion that none of the children is willing to take care of their father.

There are many reasons responsible for this phenomenon and the following are the typical ones. The first reason is that many grown-up children view their aged parents as a sheer burden and refuse to shoulder the responsibility of taking care of them. The second reason is that in our society, many people are not fully aware of the fact that supporting parents are within their responsibility. The third reason is that most aged parents are reluctant to take legal measures to protect themselves.

As far as I am concerned, the proper attitude towards supporting parents is that everyone should be kind to his parents and it is the height of virtue in our Chinese culture. First, we owe so much to our parents in that they not only gave us life but also have done so much in bringing us up. Second, we have the duty to pay back their love by making their later years enjoyable and happy. Therefore, it is not reasonable for us to shirk the responsibility of taking care of our parents when they are old.

第二节 大学英语四、六级写作

大学生在进行四、六级备考时,首先要了解《大学英语四、六级考试大纲》的要求。本部分将依据《大学英语四、六级考试大纲》对大学英语四、六级写作进行分析。

一、命题与评分标准

《大学英语四、六级考试大纲》中规定:大学英语四级考试写作部分考试时间为 30 分钟。要求应试者写出一篇不少于 120 个词的短文;写作命题源于日常生活和有关科技、社会文化等方面的一般常识,不涉及知识面过广、专业性太强的内容。

其命题方式有:给出题目,或规定情景,或给出段首句续写,或给出关键词写短文,或看图作文。要求内容切题,文理通顺,表达正确,语篇连贯,无重大语言错误。

大学英语四、六级作文采用总体评分(global scoring)方法,即阅卷人员从内容和语言两个方面对作文进行综合评判。要考虑作文是否切题,是否充分表达思想,也要考虑所用语言是否能清楚而明确地表达思想。阅卷人员根据思想内容和语言表达的总体印象给出奖励分(reward scores),而不是按语言点的错误数目扣分。

大学英语四级考试是 710 分制,作文部分占 15%,满分标准分为 106.5 分。但在阅卷时,还是按照作文满分为 15 分阅卷,然后再换算成标准分,阅卷标准分为五等:2 分、5 分、8 分、11 分和 14 分。

具体评分标准如下:

2 分:条理不清,思路紊乱,语言支离破碎或大部分句子均有错误,且多数为严重错误。

5 分:基本切题,表达思想不够清楚,连贯性差,有较多的严重错误。

8 分:基本切题,有些地方表达思想不够清楚,文字勉强连贯,语言错误相当多,其中有一些是严重错误。

11 分:切题,表达思想清楚,文字连贯,但有少量语言错误。

14 分:切题,表达思想清楚,文字通顺,连贯较好,基本上无语言错误,仅有个别小错。

二、历年真题分析

A. 2018 年 6 月四级（第一套）

Directions: For this part, you are allowed 30 minutes to write a short essay on the importance of reading ability and how to develop it. You should write at least 120 words but no more than 180 words.

范文

The Importance of Reading Ability

Whether in history or in the present day society, reading has always been a hot topic among us human beings. No one can deny the fact that reading is of great importance to the comprehensive development of children and teenagers. The old saying "to open a book is always helpful" clearly shows us how beneficial it is to read a book.

Firstly, reading has become an indispensable part of our lives. We gain new knowledge, directly or indirectly through reading, which will exert profound influence on the way we live, work, play and learn. Secondly, reading can enable many youngsters to get a clear perspective of their career and life plans. Lastly, reading can not only teach us truth, science, literature and philosophy of life, but also cultivate our character and lead us down the road to success.

So how do we develop our ability of reading? As is known to all, "Practice makes perfect." The whole society and schools should encourage teenagers to read more books of great value to broaden their horizons and increase their knowledge. What's more, we teenagers should cultivate the habit of long term and regular reading. Only in this way can we be effective readers.

B. 2018 年 6 月四级（第二套）

Directions: For this part, you are allowed 30 minutes to write a short essay on the importance of writing ability and how to develop it. You should write at least 120 words but no more than 180 words.

The Importance of Writing Ability

Nobody could deny that writing is one of the basic abilities for men. Put it another way, it is unlikely to imagine human civilization without writing ability.

At the top of the list, if we overlook the significance of writing ability, we will suffer a great difficulty in our daily written communication. In addition to what has been mentioned above, it is advisable for us to attach importance to this ability because writing plays a key role in our academic performance. To summarize, writing does carry a positive implication for our life and study.

In view of the great value of writing ability, we should take actions to develop this capability. For my part, initially, we are supposed to keep in mind that reading is the first step of writing, so we should read great books as many as possible, learning from the great works how to write concisely and effectively. Moreover, owing to the fact that practice makes perfect, we should frequently practice writing; for example, we may develop the habit of keeping a diary.

C. 2018 年 6 月四级（第三套）

Directions: For this part, you are allowed 30 minutes to write a short essay on the importance of speaking ability and how to develop it. You should write at least 120 words but no more than 180 words.

The Importance of Speaking Ability

In the present era, speaking ability is increasingly important in both workplace and our daily life. Teamwork is greatly stressed in corporations where good communication among coworkers can more possibly lead to success. Employees with great speaking ability can better cooperate with others and are highly valued. Similarly, in our daily life good speaking ability can earn us more friends.

Good speaking ability lies in extensive reading and attentive listening. Reading extensively can not only enrich our knowledge and vocabulary, but also add flavor to our speech. While through listening attentively to some broadcasts or lectures, we can imitate the speakers' pronunciation and intonation and learn how to attract our audience's attention. Besides, talking with people around us often can certainly improve our speaking ability.

In conclusion, we can develop our speaking ability through reading, listening and constant oral practice. This ability will surely enable us to have a wonderful life and arm us with great edge in this competitive society as well.

D. 2017 年 12 月四级（第一套）

Directions: For this part, you are allowed 30 minutes to write a short essay on how to best handle the relationship between doctors and patients. You should write at lease 120 words but no more than 180 words.

 范文

It's not rare for us to read the news that medical disputes occur to some hospitals. Intense doctor – patient relationship hinders the healthy development of medical care. Then, here comes the question: how to best cope with the doctor – patient relationship?

Some tips are advisable. Patients' trust on doctors comes first. With trust, patients can cooperate well with doctors, ensuring the effect of the treatments. Besides, doctors should be loyal to their occupations. Such work ethics can help doctors win not only patients' support but also good social prestige. Last but not least, mutual understandings are in need. Patients should know clearly that not every disease can be cured. Hostile attitudes can be abandoned only if doctors make efforts to save patients. On the other hand, doctors should be kind enough to their patients even though they lose their tempers or keep asking too many questions and soon. After all, sufferings may lead to patients' abnormal behaviors.

In conclusion, only by adopting the measures above can a harmonious doctor – patient relationship be formed.

E. 2017年12月四级考试（第二套）

Directions: For this part, you are allowed 30 minutes to write a short essay on how to best handle the relationship between teachers and students. You should write at lease 120 words but no more than 180 words.

范文

A doctoral student, it's recently reported that, committed suicide because of the worse relationship with his supervisor, which suggests that worse teacher – student relationship may lead to unhappy end or even a tragedy. Then, here comes a question: how to best deal with the teacher – student relationship?

Some tips are advisable. To begin with, love comes first. Both sides should show their love for each other. It is love that leads to great care. On the one hand, teachers are willing to help students with their study. On the other hand, students make efforts to achieve the best to repay their teachers. What's more, mutual respect and understanding play an indispensable part in such a good relationship. Both sides should communicate with each other, putting their feet in the other side's shoes. Only by doing that can conflicts between them be reduced.

In a word, both teachers and students shoulder the responsibilities to create a harmonious relationship between them, which can benefit both sides, and the education itself as well.

F. 2017年12月四级考试（第三套）

Directions: For this part, you are allowed 30 minutes to write a short essay on how to best handle the relationship between parents and children. You should write at lease 120 words but no more than 180 words.

Youngsters tend to be rebellious while their parents force them to do what they don't want to do. It is generation gap that leads to different notions between parents and children. Such bad parent – children relationship poses threat to children's healthy growth. Then, here comes a question: how to best cope with parent – children relationship?

Some tips are advisable. Mutual trust comes first. Believing in children's abilities, parents support what their children choose to do. And meanwhile, children's trust on parents makes them understand what parents do for them. What's more, keep the lines of communication open with each other. Lack of communication is one of the main causes of conflicts between parents and children. Exchanging ideas can boost mutual understanding, which helps them get on well with each other. Last but not least, love is an indispensable factor for a harmonious parent – children relationship. Out of love, they may forgive each others' mistakes.

In conclusion, only by adopting the measures above can a harmonious parent – children relationship be formed.

G. 2017 年 6 月四级考试（第一套）

Directions: For this part, you are allowed 30 minutes to write an advertisement on your campus website to sell a bicycle you used at college. Your advertisement may include its brand, features, condition and price, and your contact information. You should write at least 120 words but no more than 180 words.

A Used Bicycle for Sale

I currently have a yellow Flying Pigeon bicycle for sale, which I bought last September.

As a used bicycle, thanks to my careful maintenance and its high quality as well, it is still in good condition without any mechanical problems.

> Especially, this bicycle shares the following features: You can change the speed by shifting the gear, which can increase the pleasure of bicycle riding. With a smart lock fixed, it reduces the possibility of being stolen. Its brake works so well that you can avoid being involved in a traffic accident. In addition, the invoice says the frame and seat are covered by a 3-year warranty.
>
> Based on the information above, I think the reasonable price for this used bicycle should be 150 yuan. Anyone who feels interested in it and intends to inquire about the relevant detail can contact Li Ming. My phone number is 13512345678.
>
> Li Ming

H. 2017年6月四级考试（第二套）

Directions: For this part, you are allowed 30 minutes to write an advertisement on your campus website to sell some of the course books you used at college. Your advertisement may include a brief description of their content, their condition and price and your contact information. You should write at least 120 words but no more than 180 words.

 范文

> **Used Course Books for Sale**
>
> Since the graduation is approaching, some of my course books I used at college are for sale here. Some detailed information is as follows:
>
> First of all, those books for sale are about English vocabulary, academic writing and English novels. They are useful and practical, because they can help you enlarge your English vocabulary, and improve your ability to write research articles, and know about western writers and their famous works. With them, you can live a full and meaningful college life. What's more, thanks to my careful maintenance, all those books are kept clean and almost 80% new, without being damaged, which will not affect your proper use of them. In the end, for all those books, I'll give

> you 80% discount of its original price.
> Whoever is interested and intends to know more relevant details can contact me by calling 86543217 or sending e-mails to liming@163.com.
> Li Ming

*注：本节范文赏析出自《大学英语四级考试全真试题及超详解》（竹玛，许文涛）

第三节 研究生入学考试英语写作

一、命题与评分标准

《全国硕士研究生入学统一考试：英语（1）考试大纲（非英语专业）》中要求：写作部分由A、B两节组成，考查考生的书面表达能力。总分30分。

A节：考生根据所给情景写出约100词（标点符号不计算在内）的应用性短文，包括私人和公务信函、备忘录、摘要、报告等。考生在答题卡2上作答。总分10分。

B节：考生根据提示信息写出一篇160~200词的短文（标点符号不计算在内）。提示信息的形式有主题句、写作提纲、规定情景、图、表等。考生在答题卡2上作答。总分20分。

根据大纲中所列提示信息类型可推断研究生入学考试英语写作题型包括提纲式作文、图表图画作文、情景作文与应用文等形式。往年已考查过提纲式作文、图表图画作文与应用文。

提纲式作文为考生提供题目与简要的写作提纲，要求考生依据要点进行写作。往年考查过的提纲式作文及其主题如下：

年份	主题
1991	Where to Live—in the City or the Country?
1992	For a Better Understanding between Parent and Child
1993	Advertisement on TV
1994	On Making Friends

续表

年份	主题
1995	The "Project Hope"
1996	Good Health

图表图画作文是指以漫画或统计表格或是画表皆有为提示信息，并配以文字提示的作文题型，要求考生先阐述图表内容揭示寓意，继而对所提出问题的原因、影响等方面进行分析并表达个人观点。"图画+提纲"形式中的图画通常是漫画，其含义往往反映社会现象，因此考生务必认真审题，正确理解题意。如下列题目：

Directions: Write an essay of 160 – 200 words based on the following drawing. In your essay, you should

1) describe the drawing briefly,

2) explain its intended meaning, and then

3) give your comments.

文化"火锅"，既美味又营养

考研英语大作文满分 20 分，采用通篇分档计分，计分标准如下：

20~17 分：内容切题，包括题中所列三方面的内容；清楚表达其内涵，文字连贯；句式有变化，句子结构和用词正确。文章长度符合要求。

16~13 分：内容切题，包括题中所列三方面的内容；比较清楚地表达其内涵；文字基本连贯；句式有一定变化，句子结构和用词无重大错误。文章长度符合要求。

12~9 分：内容切题，基本包括题中所列三方面的内容；基本清楚地表达其内涵；句子结构和用词有少量错误。文章长度符合要求。

8~5分：内容基本功题，基本包含题中所列三方面的内容；语句可以理解，但有较多的句子结构和词错误。文章长度基本符合要求。

4~1分：基本按要求写作，但只有少数句子可理解。

0分：文不切题，语句混乱、无法理解。

二、历年真题分析

好的作文首先应该做到内容切题，即能够正确理解题目与文字说明或图画图表的要点和信息。在提纲式作文中，有明确的要点说明，一般考生都能够做到内容切题。在图表图画作文中，首先要正确揭示图画寓意，如不认真审题常常会误解题意、不能够正确立意。近年考研命题多采用图画图表作文。做这类题的关键在于把握图画所反映的话题，做到切合题意。另外，考生在备考过程中常常会背诵一些范文，切记不可生搬硬套。如下列真题的写作（例文选自新东方考研写作）。

A：2007年考研作文

Directions：Write an essay of 160－200 words based on the following drawing. In your essay, you should

（1）describe the drawing briefly,

（2）explain its intended meaning, and then

（3）support your view with an example/examples.

习作一：

> As we can see, this cartoon humorously presents two kinds of persons. One of them is quite modest while the other is very proud. Therefore,

we should learn from the former kind and avoid becoming the latter one.

Apparently, the purpose of the picture is to emphasize the importance of keeping modest in our daily life and work. In the face of a little achievement, some people get easily satisfied with themselves and begin to look down upon others. However, they don't realize that there is still much more to purpose. Especially for the students who are so young and have a long way ahead, self-satisfaction is really the least attitude they should take.

Examples of this phenomenon can be found in many situations. For instance, many talented people failed to move on after achieving certain success. Another well-known example is the race between a tortoise and a rabbit. Just due to stupid pride, the rabbit lost the competition which it can win very easily. In a word, we must always be modest so as to make continuous progress.

习作二：

In this drawing, a football-player is try to kick a ball to the net, and also a goal-keeper prevent him to do so. We see that in the player's mind is appearing a scene in which the keeper become so a big man and covering the net completely, while the latter imagined that he will be a dwarf standing below the broad net. Obviously, both of them lack courage and confidence in the front of risk.

The drawing intended to show us that these two players represent those who often choose to overestimate the difficulties or underestimate their abilities. At last, they can achieve nothing but fail since they exaggerate the dangers.

This sad situation can be showed in the fact that some people lose their chance in the postgraduate entering exams for the MA program. During preparing for the exam, they often feel depressed thinking that they are never good enough. In fact, they will soon realize that it is not as difficult as they think before. In a word, they suffer from lowering

> their abilities. This case really prove that no matter whatever tasks we are confronted, we should never lose our confidence.

解析：两篇习作中，习作一虽然语言规范，句式多样，但是未达到最基本的要求，即偏离了主题，在第一段中表述出习作主题 One of them is quite modest while the other is very proud，显然是没有认真读图审题，因而接下来的写作内容虽然语言表达不错，但是没有切题，因此得分为 0 分；而习作二虽然在语言表达上还有所欠缺，甚至出现了个别语言错误，但做到了认真审题并且写作内容切题误，因此得分远超第一篇，为 12 分。

B. 1997 年考研作文

Directions：

A. Study the following set of pictures carefully and write an essay in no less than 120 words.

B. You essay should cover all the information provided and meet the requirements below：

1. interpret the following pictures，
2. predict the tendency of tobacco consumption and give your reasons.

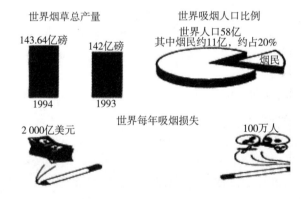

习作一：

> From the picture we can see smoking is harmful to people's health. On one hand, it cause many disease; on the other hand, it costs a lot of money. But today people all over the world still smoke a lot. Some people smoke out of habit. Others enjoy smoking, and find it is good for

their nerves when they are tired. And still others smoke to be sociable: they like offer friends cigarette when doing business with others.

But as we all know doctors have warned people that tobacco is dangerous to the smokers and cause all kinds of illness, including the cancer of lung. Many deaths are caused every year. And the government too are taking measure to prevent people from smoking.

As far as I am concerned, I think smoking is a great evil that should be abolished. I think government should take stranger measures to eventually ban tobacco all together.

习作二：

As is shown in the pie graph, there are 1.1 billion smokers out of the 5.8 billion people in the world, accounting for 20% of the total world population. This causes great harm to us. Financially, it results in the yearly loss of 200 billion US dollars spent on cigarettes. And physically, the poisonous material such as nicotine within tobacco leads to according to official reports, 3 million deaths every year.

Faced with such a problem, people from all walks have tried various measures to cut smoking. The public launch campaigns to appeal to smokers to quit smoking so as to help clear the air. The government pass laws to limit tobacco production, raise tobacco taxes, and prohibit smoking in the public places. And health experts try hard to warn the public, especially the young, of the dangers involved with a view to raising a nation of nonsmokers.

Thanks to the joint efforts, fewer and fewer smokers hesitate to get rid of the bad habit of smoking, hence less and less tobacco consumed in recent years. And the drop of cigarette demand is deeply felt by tobacco companies. That's why the year 1995 saw a decrease of 0.164 billion lbs. in tobacco production as compared with that of 1994. Therefore, we have every reason to look forward to a better future, with a greater decline of tobacco consumption, and a cleaner environment.

解析：习作一内容不切题，套用事先背好的文章，只写到了吸烟有害的一方面。虽然文字流畅，无语言错误，段落衔接自然，但未结合图表反映问题进行写作，不切题，因此得分为 0 分；习作二按照图表写出几个方面，包括世界吸烟人口比例和世界烟草产量及吸烟带来的损失，预测今后的发展趋势，并说明了理由，且语言表达流畅，因此得分为 14 分。

第四节　国际人才英语考试写作

国际人才英语考试（简称国才考试）是近两年才推出的考试，大多数考生对其不太了解，本节主要介绍国才考试的要求与题型。国际人才英语考试（English Test for International Communication，ETIC）是北京外国语大学中国外语测评中心推出的英语沟通能力认证考试体系，旨在为用人单位招聘、选拔人才提供参考依据，尤其是选拔国家急需的具有全球视野、熟练运用外语、通晓国际规则、精通国际谈判的专业人才。"国才考试"包括"国才初级""国才中级""国才高级""国才高端""国才高翻"五大类别，服务于各级各类、各行各业的人才培养与选拔。不同英语水平考生参加不同类别考试，下面重点介绍国才初级考试与国才高级考试。

一、国际人才英语考试（初级）

国际人才英语考试（初级），用于评价、认定考生在日常接待和熟悉的工作场合运用英语开展工作的能力。"国才初级"由口头沟通和书面沟通两部分组成。每部分包括四项任务。考试采用计算机辅助形式。考试时间约 80 分钟。其中，书面沟通部分由浏览材料、分析材料、整理材料和撰写邮件四项任务组成。考试时间约 60 分钟。

书面沟通考试内容与要求

	考试内容	考试时间
任务一	浏览材料	10 分钟
任务二	分析材料	15 分钟
任务三	整理材料	15 分钟
任务四	撰写邮件	20 分钟

在任务一浏览材料部分，考生阅读一篇 300 词左右的说明性材料，为段落选择正确的标题。本任务考查考生归纳段落大意的能力。在任务二分析材料部分，考生阅读三篇共 300 词左右的说明性材料，判别所给信息的出处。本任务考查考生理解关键信息的能力。在任务三整理材料部分，考

生阅读两篇共 300 词左右的说明性材料，选取文中信息填写表格。本任务考查考生理解并呈现关键信息的能力。在任务四撰写邮件部分，考生根据所给话题及要点撰写一封 50 词左右的邮件。本任务考查考生在既定情境下，以特定身份向指定对象说明情况的能力。前三项任务分别考查学生在阅读理解基础上进行语句、段落写作的能力，该部分的写作注意事项可参照本书前三章的内容。第四部分要求撰写邮件，应用文的写作将在第五章进行讲解。（任务四样题如下）

样题 Task 4

You are Jones Cooper, secretary in the Customer Service Development of an international hotel. You are informed that construction work will begin near the hotel and may cause some noises. Write an email to all the guests,

to let them know when construction work will start and finish each day,

to tell them know where the construction work will take place,

to apologize to them for any inconvenience caused.

Write 50 words within 20 minutes.

评分标准

分数档	内容	结构	语言
5分	内容紧扣主题；充分完成任务要求；有丰富的细节支撑，信息准确	条理清晰；衔接自然、行文流畅；格式规范	用词准确；句式灵活；语法正确
4分	内容扣题；完成所有任务要求；有较多细节支撑，信息准确	条理较清晰；衔接较得当、行文较连贯；格式较规范	用词较准确；句式较灵活；有个别语法错误
3分	大部分内容与主题相关（个别内容与主题无关）；基本完成任务要求；有一定细节支撑，大部分信息准确	条理基本清晰；衔接基本得当、行文基本连贯；格式基本规范	用词基本准确；句式有一定变化；有少量语法错误，但基本不影响理解
2分	少部分内容与主题相关；未能完成任务要求，缺失一个内容要点	条理不清晰；衔接手段不足或过度使用、行文不太连贯；格式不规范	用词不准确；句式较单调；语法错误多并影响理解
1分	个别字句与主题相关；未能完成任务要求，缺失两个及以上的内容要点	逻辑混乱	语言错误很多并严重影响理解
0分	作答内容与主题无关或未作答		

例题：Task 4

You are Taylor Wang, working at Supershine Car Wash. Your shop is about to move to a new site. In order to keep its regular customs, the shop will offer a free car-wash service for the first three days after the move. Write an email to your customers:

To tell them when and where you are moving,

To inform them of your offer,

To invite them to come.

Write about 50 words within 20 minutes.

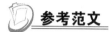 参考范文

Dear customers,

This is to inform you that our Supershine Car Wash will move to No. 101, 7th Avenue next Monday. As a token of appreciation, we will offer a free car-wash service for the first three days after this move. We sincerely invite you to enjoy the service at your earliest convenience.

Yours faithfully,

Taylor Wang

二、国际人才英语考试（高级）

国际人才英语考试（高级），用于评价、认定考生在国际商务交流活动中运用英语开展业务工作的能力。"国才高级"由口头沟通和书面沟通两部分组成。每部分包括三项任务。考试采用计算机辅助形式。考试时间约 105 分钟。书面沟通部分由撰写信函、撰写报告、撰写提案三项任务组成。时间共 90 分钟。

书面沟通考试内容与要求

考 试 内 容		考试时间
任务一	撰写信函	25 分钟
任务二	撰写报告	25 分钟
任务三	撰写提案	40 分钟

在任务一撰写信函部分，考生根据要求撰写一封150词左右的商务信函，内容涉及发出邀请、回应请求、解释进展、征求意见、咨询信息等。本任务考查考生根据给定的商务情境，以特定身份向指定对象描述、解释、说明情况的能力。在任务二撰写报告部分，考生阅读一份商务图表，按要求撰写一份150词左右的报告。本任务考查考生描述、比较、概括图表关键信息的能力。在任务三撰写提案部分，考生根据要求撰写一份300~350词的商务提案，考生需提出并论证某一提议。本任务考查考生根据给定的商务情境，以特定身份向指定对象阐明目的、分析现状、解释需求及进行论证的能力。（样题如下）

Task 1

Your name is Date Matthews. You are Marketing Director for Kando, a furniture manufacturer. Kando wants to start selling in Australia, and is looking for an agency to handle its advertising there. In a business directory, you have seen an entry for the advertising agency N&S, a potential partner. Write a letter to Robbie Johnson, President of N&S.

to introduce your company,

to state why your company wants to start selling in Australia,

to explain your interest in cooperating with N&S.

Write about 150 words within 25 minutes.

You do Not need to write any addresses.

Task 2

The graph on the right shows the exports of the United Stares, Germany, France and Britain to China between 2005 and 2014. Using the information from the graph, write a report describing and comparing the trends of export to China from the four countries.

Write about 150 words within 25 minutes.

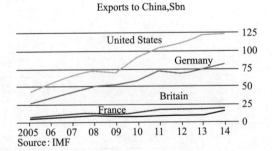

Task 3

You work for a computer manufacturer in China, and your company is considering opening up a new branch in the United States. You are asked to analyse possible problems your company might encounter, and offer your solutions. Write to your CEO a proposal including the following information:

a brief description of the U. S. market,

reasons for setting up a new branch abroad,

problems your company might encounter,

possible solutions to these problems.

Write about 300 words within 40 minutes.

＊注：本节考试信息来源国才官网 http：//etic.claonline.cn/

Exercises

Passage Writing

There are four writing tasks from the CET-4 and Entrance Examination for Postgraduates. Write the passages according to the different requirement.

Task One

Directions: For this part, you are allowed 30 minutes to write an advertisement on your campus website to sell a computer you used at college. Your advertisement may include its brand, specifications/features, condition and price and your contact information. You should write at least 120 words but no more than 180 words.

Task Two

Directions: For this part, you are allowed 30 minutes to write an essay. Suppose you have

two options upon graduation: one is to find a job somewhere and the other to start a business of your own. you are to make a decision. Write an essay to explain the reasons for your decision. You should write write at least 120 words but no more than 180 words.

Task Three

Directions: You are to write an email to James Cook, a newly arrived Australian professor, recommending some tourist attractions in your city. Please give reasons for your recommendation.

You should write neatly on the answer sheet. Do not sign your own name at the end of the email. Use Li Ming instead. Do not write the address.

Task Four

Directions: write an essay of 160 – 200 words based on the following pictures. In your essay, you should

1) describe the pictures briefly

2) interpret the meaning, and

3) give your comments.

有书与读书

第五章

英语应用文写作

美文赏析

Three Days to See
——Helen Keller

All of us have read thrilling stories in which the hero had only a limited and specified time to live. Sometimes it was as long as a year, sometimes as short as 24 hours. But always we were interested in discovering just how the doomed hero chose to spend his last days or his last hours. I speak, of course, of free men who have a choice, not condemned criminals whose sphere of activities is strictly delimited.

Such stories set us thinking, wondering what we should do under similar circumstances. What events, what experiences, what associations should we crowd into those last hours as mortal beings, what regrets?

Sometimes I have thought it would be an excellent rule to live each day as if we should die tomorrow. Such an attitude would emphasize sharply the values of life. We should live each day with gentleness, vigor and a keenness of appreciation which are often lost when time stretches before us in the constant panorama of more days and months and years to come. There are those, of course, who would adopt the Epicurean motto of "Eat, drink, and be merry." But most people would be chastened by the certainty of impending death.

In stories the doomed hero is usually saved at the last minute by some stroke of fortune, but almost always his sense of values is changed. He becomes more appreciative of the meaning of life and its permanent spiritual values. It has often been noted that those who live, or have lived, in the shadow of death bring a mellow sweetness to everything they do.

Most of us, however, take life for granted. We know that one day we must die, but usually we picture that day as far in the future. When we are in buoyant health, death is all but unimaginable. We seldom think of it. The days stretch out in an endless vista. So we go about our petty tasks, hardly aware of our listless attitude toward life.

The same lethargy, I am afraid, characterizes the use of all our faculties and senses. Only the deaf appreciate hearing, only the blind realize the manifold blessings that lie in sight. Particularly does this observation apply to those who have lost sight and hearing in adult life. But those who have never suffered impairment of sight or hearing seldom make the fullest use of these blessed faculties. Their eyes and ears take in all sights and sounds hazily, without concentration and with little appreciation. It is the same old story of not being grateful for what we have until we lose it, of not being conscious of health until we are ill.

I have often thought it would be a blessing if each human being were stricken blind and deaf for a few days at some time during his early adult life. Darkness would make him more appreciative of sight; silence would teach him the joys of sound.

Now and then I have tested my seeing friends to discover what they see. Recently I was visited by a very good friend who had just returned from a long walk in the woods, and I asked her what she had observed. "Nothing in particular," she replied. I might have been incredulous had I not been accustomed to such responses, for long ago I became convinced that the seeing see little.

How was it possible, I asked myself, to walk for an hour through the woods and see nothing worthy of note? I who cannot see find hundreds of things to interest me through mere touch. I feel the delicate symmetry of a leaf. I pass my hands lovingly about the smooth skin of a silver birch, or the rough, shaggy bark of a pine. In spring I touch the branches of trees hopefully in search of a bud, the first sign of awakening Nature after her winter's sleep. I feel the delightful, velvety texture of a flower, and discover its remarkable convolutions; and something of the miracle of Nature is revealed to me. Occasionally, if I am very fortunate, I place my hand gently on a small tree and feel the happy quiver of a bird in full song. I am delighted to have the cool waters of a brook rush through my open fingers. To me a lush carpet of pine needles or spongy grass is more welcome than the most luxurious Persian rug. To me the pageant of seasons is a thrilling and unending drama, the action of which streams through my finger tips.

At times my heart cries out with longing to see all these things. If I can get so much pleasure from mere touch, how much more beauty must be revealed by sight. Yet, those who have eyes apparently see little. The panorama of color and action which fills the world is taken for granted. It is human, perhaps, to appreciate little that which we have and to long for that which we have not, but it is a great pity that in the world of light the gift of sight is used only as a mere convenience rather than as a means of adding fullness to life.

I who am blind can give one hint to those who see—one admonition to those who would make full use of the gift of sight: Use your eyes as if tomorrow you would be stricken blind. And the same method can be applied to the other senses. Hear the music of voices, the song of a bird, the mighty strains of an orchestra, as if you would be stricken deaf tomorrow. Touch each object you want to touch as if tomorrow your tactile sense would fail. Smell the perfume of flowers, taste with relish each morsel, as if tomorrow you could never smell and taste again. Make the most of every sense; glory in all the facets of pleasure and beauty which the world reveals to you through the several means of contact which Nature provides. But of all the senses, I am sure that sight must be the most delightful. (Excerpts)

▶ 赏析：

"Three Days to See"（《假如给我三天光明》）的作者 Helen Keller 是 20 世纪美国著名的盲聋作家、教育家与社会活动家。她幼时因一场疾病丧失了视觉和听觉，后来在莎莉文老师的帮助下，她学会了说话并掌握了五国语言。尽管又聋又盲，她以非凡的毅力面对生活的困难，对人类与自然、生命与生活极度热爱，被《时代周刊》评选为 20 世纪美国十大英雄偶像之一。作品字里行间都体现着她对生命的感恩和对美好生活的向往。文中，海伦想象自己拥有三天的光明去看看这个世界。三天时间，浓缩了作者对光明的强烈渴望，她要去看看老师、亲人和朋友，去看田野与城市、森林与博物馆、白昼与黑夜，她对这个世界充满了感情，热切地对待感受到的一切。

作品以第一人称直抒作者对人类、对自然、对生活的热爱。文章结构工整、语言优美、富含哲理、情感真挚。首先，文章结构工整，逻辑清晰。全文分为三个部分，第一部分以作者的思考、设问作为开篇，第二部分讲述三天光明中看到的内容，第三部分讲作者的感受；第二部分即文章的主体部分按照时间顺序分别讲述了三天的见闻；每一天的所见所闻又分为白天和夜晚。文章各部分排列有序，作者的感情穿插其中，各部分有机衔接，过渡自然。其次，文章的语言叙述朴实、真挚、优美，有对美景的描述、有内心感受的阐发以及人生道理的感叹。作者描述触觉的感受与视觉所见时，将美景描述的生动自然、逼真细腻，像一幅幅美丽的画卷展现在人们面前；对世人的劝诫用词质朴，亲切友善；文中运用了一系列排比句、设问句，启发思考、引发共鸣。另外，文章饱含哲理，文中通过三天的宝贵视觉所见体现了作者对自然与生活的热爱、对人类世界物质和精神世界的关注，启发人们更加珍惜光明、珍爱生命。

第一节　应用文的写作要求

一、应用文的写作要求

在职场、生活实践与各类考试中均对应用文提出了写作要求，学习者应能写不同类型的应用文，如信函、通知、备忘录、报告等。《全国硕士研究生入学统一考试：英语（1）考试大纲》中明确提出，考生应能写不同类型的应用文，包括私人和公务信函、备忘录、报告等，以及一般描述性、叙述性、说明性或议论性的文章。写作时，考生应能：

1）做到语法、拼写、标点正确，用词恰当；
2）遵循文章的特定文体格式；

3）合理组织文章结构，使其内容统一、连贯；

4）根据写作目的和特定作者，恰当选用语域。（指在书面和口语表达中根据不同的交际对象，所采用的话语方式，即正式、一般、非正式的话语。）

在写作的 A 部分要求考生根据所给情景写出约 100 词（标点符号不计算在内）的应用性短文，包括私人和公务信函、备忘录、报告等。共 10 分。

应用文写作的评分要点是能否做到：信息要点的全覆盖、格式的恰当使用、内容的有序以及语言的准确性等方面。

二、应用文的分类与特点

应用文主要包括信函、通知、备忘录、摘要等，即 Letters of invitation、Letters of thanks、Letters of apology、Congratulatory letters、Letters of introduction、Letters of application、Letters of advice、Letters of complaint、Letters of consultation、Letters of recommendation、Notice、Announcement、Resume、Poster、Memo、Report、Abstract 等。每种写作类型有其固定要求，如信函一般都是由写信时间、信内地址、称呼、正文和信尾几个部分组成；摘要包括文章摘要和论文摘要，尤其常用句型，如表示研究目的"In order to…、This paper describes…、The purpose of this study is…"等，表示结论或建议有"The authors suggest/conclude/consider that…"等表达方式。如下述例文：

2005 年考研真题应用文写作：

Directions：Two months ago you got a job as an editor for the magazine Designs & Fashions. But now you find that the work is not what you expected. You decide to quit. Write a letter to your boss, Mr. Wang, telling him your decision, stating your reason（s）, and making an apology.

Write your letter with no less than 100 words. Do not sign your own name at the end of the letter; use "Li Ming" instead. You do not need to write the address. (10 points)

通过认真审题了解到，题目要求写一封信件，因此要嵌套信件格式。题目中给出了要点，在写作时应该做到要点全覆盖。每个要点扩展成句子，并给出具体信息。最后，使用固定表达，表示感谢，期待回信。

Dear Mr. Wang,

　　Please accept my resignation as a editor in the magazine Design &Fashion. After two months of work, I find it is inappropriate for me to take the position as an editor here.

> There are some reasons. First, I have expected the job to be interesting and challenging, but the reality is different. Second, the company is too far from the place I live and it is very inconvenient for me to spend 4 hours on the way. Therefore, I am sorry to say I have decided to quit the job after much consideration.
>
> Thank you very much for offering me the job here. I sincerely hope that you approve of my resignation. I am sorry for any inconvenience caused.
>
> Sincerely,
>
> Li Ming

第二节 书信体应用文写作

一、书信体的写作要求

（一）书信体的结构

1. 称呼

称呼要顶格写，标以逗号，和中文的冒号不同。如"Dear Sir/Madam，""Dear Tom/Lucy，"等。

2. 正文

正文可采用缩进式，即每段开头空四个字母，段落之间不空行。也可采用齐头式，即每段开头不空格，但是各段之间空一行。

3. 结尾与署名

结尾与署名要注意礼貌性，使用如 Yours faithfully、Yours sincerely 等措辞。署名是要依据题目要求署名，一般不要署自己的真名。

（二）书信的语言表达

首先，信件的语言内容表达上要和一般作文一样，做到没有语法错误、用词丰富、句式多样化。另外，按照题目要求，分清是公务信函还是私人信函，注意使用正式文体或非正式文体。要根据要求使用不同的礼貌用语。

（三）要点信息全覆盖

信件写作中，应开门见山交代写信的目的，再从几个方面展开信件的主要内容，各方面应层次分明，最后从交际的角度来结尾，如表示感激、表示歉意等。如：

2008 年考研真题应用文写作

Directions: You have just come back from Canada and found a music CD in your luggage that you forgot to return to Bob, your landlord there. Write him a letter to

1) make an apology, and

2) suggest a solution.

You should write about 100 words. Do not sign your own name at the end of the letter. Use "Li Ming" instead. Do not write the address.

参考范文

> Dear Bob,
>   I am writing to express my apology to you.
>   Several days ago, I borrowed your music CD when I lived in your house. Unfortunately, after I came back from Canada, I found it in my luggage. I am sorry that I was in such a hurry that I forgot to return it to you. I will send it to you as soon as possible. I will compensate for any troubles it may cause.
>   Once again, I feel so sorry for any inconvenience caused. Please accept my apologies.
>
>   Sincerely yours,
>   Li Ming

二、常见书信体应用文

（一）邀请信

邀请信是写信人对收信人表达的邀约，格式与其他信函相同。一般邀请专家参会或邀请朋友参加聚会、来访等。写作中，一般要交代相关信息，如受邀请的人员、邀请的目的、见面地点及时间等内容，并强调邀请收信人而不是别人的原因。如：

> Dear Jane,
>   I am going to have a dinner party at my house on June 10th, 2016 to celebrate my mother's 80-year-old birthday. It is an important occasion for

> our family, and as you are one of our close friends, my parents and I do hope you can come and share our joy.
>
> The party will start at seven o'clock in the evening. There will be a small concert. At around eight o'clock, we will begin to have dinner. And then all the friends will take some photos together.
>
> I know you are busy, but we do hope you can come. My family and I look forward to the pleasure of your company.
>
> Yours affectionately,
Li Ming

邀请信中的常用句式包括：

I am writing to invite you to...

I think it would be a great idea if you could participate in...

Would you please drop me a line to let me know if you can come to...?

My family and I would feel much honored if you could come.

I really hope you can make it.

We would be looking forward to your coming with great pleasure.

I would like to meet you there and please let me know your decision soon.

（二）感谢信

感谢信用以表达对收信人的感谢。感谢信很常用，在收到邀请、受到表扬、接受过帮助等情况下，都应该表示感谢。写作中写明感谢的原因，并要展开说明具体的理由，在信尾要再次表示感谢。如：

> Dear John,
>
> I am writing to show my sincere gratitude for you. During the time I lived in New York, I was under your tender care. I promised myself I would write a letter of thanks as soon as I came back home.
>
> Abundant thanks to you for your patience, expertise and genuine concern. It was you who helped me believe in myself and gave me assurance that I could pass the examination. I would never forget each word you said to me and the things you have done to me. Thank you for understanding and remaining firm with me.
>
> Your help really means a lot to me. My true gratitude is beyond any

words description. Thank you again.

Affectionately,

Li Ming

感谢信中的常用句式包括：

I am writing to express my thanks for...

I would like to convey in this letter my heartfelt thanks to you for...

Thank you so much for the gift you sent me.

Many thanks for all the good things you have done in helping us to...

I would like to take this opportunity to express my great appreciation for your timely help and assistance.

Nothing will be able to erase our wonderful memories, and we will remember them forever.

Thanks again for your kind help.

My true gratitude is beyond any words description.

Please accept my thanks, now and always.

Your help is very much appreciated by each one of us.

（三）道歉信

道歉信主要是向收信人表明歉意，请求对方原谅自己的过失。写道歉信时，首先重述自己的过失，表示歉意。然后解释道歉的具体原因，应尽量详细描述经过，要承认自己的过错并提出弥补过错的具体建议和方法，而非强词夺理为自己的过失开脱。最后再次承认错误，请求收信人的谅解。如：

Dear professor Chen,

I am very sorry that I missed the examination you gave last Monday. I feel badly sorry about it and want you to know what happened.

On my way to school that day, my car ran out of gas, and I had to go to gas station to refuel it. And it was the rush hour in the morning. It took me about one hour to get it done. A copy of the bill is enclosed.

I sincerely hope you can accept my apologies. I would appreciate your allowing me to take a make up examination. I will come to your office during your office hour on Tuesday to discuss this possibility with you. Once

> again, I'm sorry for any inconvenience caused.
>
> Sincerely yours,
> Li Ming

道歉信中的常用句式包括：

Please accept my sincere apology for...

I am indeed very sorry for what I did, but believe I had no intention to insult you.

Please forgive me for a stupid choice of words.

I feel badly sorry about it and want you to know what happened.

Please accept my apologies for my oversight.

Please allow me to say sorry again.

Once again, I'm sorry for any inconvenience caused.

I sincerely hope you can accept my apologies and understand my situation.

（四）祝贺信

祝贺信的使用频率很高。在重要节日如新年、婚礼和生日等，或者亲人朋友晋升、毕业、通过考试时要写祝贺信。祝贺信首先点明要祝贺的事情表达祝贺的心情，继而详述祝贺的事情，最后表达衷心的祝贺之情。如：

> Dear Gary,
>
> I offer my warmest congratulations on your promotion to President of the company. I know you are very talented and you worked very hard. No one could have been more deserving. How exciting it must be for you to realize your ambitions after all those years of hard working. It's been a real encouragement to me to see your efforts rewarded.
>
> Sincere congratulations to you. Your expertise and dedication will bring out the best of everyone on your staff. They're learning from a real professional.
>
> I wish you still further success.
>
> Sincerely yours,
> Li Ming

祝贺信中的常用句式包括：

Congratulations, all of us feel proud of your remarkable achievements!

I am so pleased and happy to hear that...

I write to congratulate you upon...

I offer you my warmest congratulations on your...

We are just as proud as can be of you and send our congratulations.

I wish you still further success!

Please accept our most sincere congratulations and very best wishes for all the good future in the world.

（五）介绍信

介绍信一般是向收信人介绍第三人的情况，并希望得到他的帮助或照顾。介绍信中首先根据介绍目的详细叙述被介绍人的情况，再说明事由，即为何要介绍此人，最后写明希望得到哪些方面的帮助并向收信人致谢。如：

> Dear Mrs. Brown,
>
> I'm writing to introduce to you Miss Zhang, one of my friends. She is presently English teacher and is going to get further education in your city next month.
>
> Since this will be the first time for her to study in a foreign country, she will possibly be faced with many problems, and especially the housing problem. She hopes to obtain your guidance and help in finding a good apartment to live. You are familiar with your city, because you have been there for many years. If you can kindly help find rental quarters for her, I'll be very grateful.
>
> Thanks for your due attention to this letter and hope to receive your reply soon. Many thanks to the trouble you will have to take.
>
> Yours sincerely,
> Li Ming

介绍信中的常用句式包括：

I am writing to introduce Lucy, one of my college classmates.

Please allow me to introduce one of my best friends to you.

I am very glad to have this chance to write to you...

I take pleasure in introducing to you the bearer Mr. Wu.

Thanks for your attention and hope to receive your reply.

It would be appreciated if you can give her some help.

I would be most grateful if you could lend due attention to this letter and contact me at…

In addition, I want to express my sincere thanks for your attention.

（六）申请信

申请信是写信人就职位、学位等向收信人提出请求。在申请信中，首先说明写信的目的，介绍自己以及对所申请的职位或学位等情况的了解以及自己的计划，然后进一步根据要申请的目标介绍自己的相关情况及已取得的成绩，并说明自己为何申请及打算等。最后表示感谢并期待对方优先考虑该申请。如：

> Dear Sir,
>
> I am writing to apply for the position as an English teacher that you recently advertised in Beijing Daily. I take keen interest in the poster because I find that my major and experiences well meet the requirements you stated in the advertisement.
>
> Being interested in English teaching, I pursued my postgraduate study in Shanghai Normal University, and got a Master's Degree in 2013. I was an A student through the three academic years, as can be shown in the enclosed resume and reports. After graduation, I ever taught English in a Shanghai high school. As my wife has been working in Beijing, we want to get together so I venture to apply for the position in your school.
>
> If I were favored with an interview, I would be most grateful. Please contact me at 13512345678. Thank you for your consideration.
>
> Yours sincerely,
> Li Ming

申请信中的常用句式包括：

Your advertised position of English teacher interests me…

I think I am the right person for the job you advertised, because…

I am glad that I feel quite qualified for the position you advertised.

I would like to apply for the vacancy of…

I am writing this letter to recommend myself as a qualified candidate for the job of...

Should you grant me a personal interview, I would be most grateful.

Thanks for considering my application and I am looking forward to your reply.

If you need to know any more about me, please contact me at...

Any favorable consideration of my application would be appreciated.

I have enclosed my resume.

(七) 建议信

建议信是向收信人就某事提出建议。建议信可以是写给个人，也可能是写给某个机构。建议信要写出写信的原因，建议的内容与提出建议的理由。在开头就表明写作意图并简单介绍自己。然后在肯定对方优点的基础上，提出需要改进的地方或针对具体情况提出具体建议。最后对提出的建议进行总结，并注意措辞礼貌。如：

Dear Lucy,

　　I am sorry to hear that you have been ill for days and hope you have got better now. You have worked so hard that you have had no time for exercise. This is harmful for your health. I feel it would be more beneficial to your health if you could take more exercise in future.

　　Exercise can improve your physical condition and refresh the mind. After one hour of exercise every day you can work better. Only when you have a strong body can you keep on working energetically.

　　What I want to say is that exercise is as useful and important as your work. I hope you can take exercise every day after you are recovered. I would be more than happy to see you are healthier and more energetic.

Sincerely yours,
Li Ming

建议信中的常用句式包括：

I would like to suggest that...

I am writing to express my views concerning...

You have asked for my advice with regard to...and I will try to make some suggestions.

If I were you, I would...

I think it would be more beneficial if you could...
I believe you will take my advice into account.
I hope you will find these suggestions helpful.
I will be more than happy to see improvements in this regard.

（八）投诉信

投诉信一般是用来表达不满情绪和提出批评。投诉的目的是要收信人解决问题，所以需要提出解决方案。投诉信中首先表明来信所要投诉的问题，然后说明具体情况，写明投诉的原因、问题的经过和产生的后果。最后提出解决方案。如：

> Dear Sir or Madam,
>
>   I am writing to inform you that I wish to move into a new room next semester. I would like to have a single room, because I find the present sharing arrangement inconvenient.
>
>   I am dissatisfied with my present roommate because of his inconsiderate behavior. For one thing, his friends are constantly visiting him; for another, he regularly makes calls at night. In addition, he often uses my things without asking for my permission. Under such circumstances, I find it difficult to concentrate on my studies, and I am falling behind in my assignments.
>
>   I believe you will agree that the only solution is for me to move into a room of my own, where I will be free from these kinds of distractions. I would be very grateful if you could arrange a single room for me, preferably not in the same building.
>
> Sincerely yours,
Li Ming

投诉信中的常用句式包括：
I am writing to make a complaint about...
I am most reluctant to complain, but...
I would like to draw your attention to the problem...
I wish to express my dissatisfaction/disappointment about...
It would be highly appreciated if you could...
I hope you will give due attention to this matter.

I could not be more satisfied if you can kindly...

I would appreciate it very much if you could...

第三节　其他类型应用文写作

一、便笺

便笺也叫便条，可用于询问、道歉、请假、约会、留言、归还东西等很多事由，较为简便，形式简单，根据事由可分为留言条、请假条等。如：

Oct. 18

Tom,

　　I'm writing to ask you whether you will be at home tomorrow evening, as I wish to see you. Please answer soon.

Peter

Wednesday

Mr. Gao,

　　I'm awfully sorry that I cannot attend the meeting to be held this Friday. I've got a bad cold and the doctor said I must stay in bed for a week. So I'm writing to ask for a leave of five working days. I hope that my request will be given due consideration.

　　Enc. Doctor's Certificate

Frank

3:15 p.m.

Lucy,

　　Lily is now with us. She's going to Beijing tomorrow morning. Would you like to come to meet her this evening? We're going to have dinner at 7 p.m. this evening at my home.

Tom

以上例子在生活中使用频率很高，简单明了，无字数要求。在考试中，往往需要考生结合具体要求写一个便条，如下：

　　Directions: Suppose you and two of your friends have decided to go on a tour to Beijing and you want to invite another friend Lucy to join you. Write a note in about 100 words to her. Do not sign your own name at the end of your letter, using "Li Ming" instead.

Dear Lucy,

　　We have planned a tour to Beijing next Sunday. I wonder if you would like to join us, Lily, Jack and me.

　　Autumn is a good season to travel in Beijing, especially the Forbidden city and the Great Wall. We are going by train in Sunday morning and returning in Monday evening. If you agree to go with us, we plan to book two rooms in the Rujia Hotel which cost about 200 Yuan a night and from which it's only 10 minutes' walk to the Forbidden city.

　　I'm sure we will have a very good time and find the tour rewarding.

Yours,
Li Ming

二、通知

　　通知用来传递信息或分配工作,一般要包含活动的内容、时间和地点。如果是活动,应说明参加的人员范围,如果是讲座或报告,应包含报告人的简介。在写作时,应在首行中间注明 Notice,无称呼语,发通知的日期写在正文的右上方,通知发出者署在正文右下方。如:

　　Directions: Write a notice in about 100 words to inform the students and English teachers of a lecture on American studies.

NOTICE

August 27, 2015

　　We are very honored to invite Prof. John Willis from Yale University to give us a lecture on USA – China relationship in the new era. Prof. John Willis has been teaching American studies for more than 25 years.

　　He has become a leading expert in this field and has published several books and numerous papers. His humorous and thought provoking speech will surely benefit all the audience.

　　The lecture will be given at Yifu Auditorium from 7 to 9 o'clock next Thursday evening. All the teachers and students are welcome to attend this lecture.

English Department

三、启事

启事是一种公告性的应用文,当机构或个人有事情要向人们公开说明或者对大众提出要求时,可以写成启事张贴于公共场所,如遗失启事、招领启事、征稿启事等。如:

Directions: Suppose you carelessly lost a Longman Modern English Dictionary in the reading room. Please write a notice of about 100 words, titled Lost.

Lost

Aug. 18, 2014

I was so careless that I lost a copy of "Longman Modern English Dictionary" when studying in the reading room around 3 o'clock p.m. yesterday. You can find my name "Li Ming" on the cover. The dictionary is the necessity for my study.

If you are the kind finder, could you do me a favor to send it to the office of the Foreign Languages Department or ring me up to fetch it back. I'll be very grateful for your kindness.

Address: Room 1010, Teaching Building A
Tel. No: 010-2483288

Loser,
Li Ming

四、海报

海报是人们日常生活中极为常见的一种招贴形式,多用于电影、戏曲、比赛、文艺演出等活动。海报中通常要写清楚活动的性质,活动的主办单位、时间、地点等内容。海报通常由三部分组成,即标题、正文与落款。海报正文是海报的核心部分,是对海报标题的具体描述。如:

Directions: You are preparing for a friendly Football Match. Write a poster which asks for:

1) the right form of a standard poster
2) write the place and time clearly

You should write about 100 words.

> **POSTER**
>
> Friendly Football Game
>
>   There is going to be a friendly and wonderful Football match between ShanDong Normal University Football Team and our ShanDong University Football Team under the auspices of the the students' union of the University.
>
>   It has been decided that this football match will be held at the Football Field on Sunday, Sep. 23rd, 2016, at 3:00 p.m. It is expected that the competition between the two teams will be keen and severe. All of you are cordially welcome to present the match.
>
> The students' union of ShanDong University.
> Sep. 21st, 2016

Exercises

Passage Writing

1. Directions: You want to invite Mr. Brown to give a lecture on "Australian literature" in your college. Supposed you are the assistant of the English department, write a letter and say:

1) the purpose of the invitation.

2) the time of the lecture.

Your letter should be no less than 100 words. You don't need to write the address. Don't sign your own name at the end of the letter, use Linda instead.

2. Directions: While your family was on vacation, your friend, Lucy looked after your cat, Cathy. Now you came back, write a letter to her to show your gratitude. Your letter should be no less than 100 words. You don't need to write the address. Don't sign your own name at the end of the letter, use Tom instead.

3. Directions: Suppose you cannot attend your brother's graduation ceremony as expected for some reason. Write a letter in about 100 words to make an apology to him. Do not sign your own name at the end of your letter, using Li Ming instead.

4. Directions: Your friend Lucy has got her master's degree. Write a letter to show your congratulations. Your letter should be no less than 100 words. You don't need to write the address. Don't sign your own name at the end of the letter, use

Li Ming instead.

5. Directions: One of your friends Lucy Brown is going to enter Mr. Stone's school after her graduation. Write a letter to Mr. Stone to introduce her. Your letter should be no less than 100 words. You don't need to write the address. Don't sign your own name at the end of the letter, use Li Ming instead.

6. Directions: Suppose your father has come to see you and tonight you will sleep in the room he has booked in a hotel near your university. Write a note in about 100 words to inform your roommate Tom of that. Do not sign your own name at the end of your letter, using "Li Ming" instead.

第六章

数字化时代的英语写作学习

美文赏析

YOUTH

by Samuel Ullman

Youth is not a time of life; it is a state of mind; it is not a matter of rosy cheeks, red lips and supple knees; it is a matter of the will, a quality of the imagination, a vigor of the emotions; it is the freshness of the deep springs of life.

Youth means a temperamental predominance of courage over timidity, of the appetite for adventure over the love of ease. This often exists in a man of sixty  more than a boy of twenty. Nobody grows old merely by a number of years. We grow old by deserting our ideals.

Years may wrinkle the skin, but to give up enthusiasm wrinkles the soul. Worry, fear, self-distrust bows the heart and turns the spirit back to dust.

Whether sixty or sixteen, there is in every human being's heart the lure of wonders, the unfailing child-like appetite of what's next, and the joy of the game of living. In the center of your heart and my heart there is a wireless station; so long as it receives messages of beauty, hope, cheer, courage and power from men and from the Infinite, so long are you young.

When the aerials are down, and your spirit is covered with snows of cynicism and the ice of pessimism, then you've grown old, even at twenty, but as long as your aerials are up, to catch the waves of optimism, there is hope you may die young at eighty.

青　春
王佐良 译

　　青春不是年华，而是心境；青春不是桃面、丹唇、柔膝，而是深沉的意志，恢宏的想象，炙热的感情；青春是生命的深泉在涌流。

　　青春气贯长虹，勇锐盖过怯弱，进取压倒苟安。如此锐气，二十后生而有之，六旬男子则更多见。年岁有加，并非垂老，理想丢弃，方堕暮年。

　　岁月悠悠，衰微只及肌肤；热忱抛却，颓废必致灵魂。忧烦，惶恐，丧失自信，定使心灵扭曲，意气如灰。

　　无论年届花甲，抑或二八芳龄，心中皆有生命之欢乐，奇迹之诱惑，孩童般天真久盛不衰。人人心中皆有一台天线，只要你从天上人间接受美好、希望、欢乐、勇气和力量的信号，你就青春永驻，风华常存。

　　一旦天线下降，锐气便被冰雪覆盖，玩世不恭、自暴自弃油然而生，即使年方二十，实已垂垂老矣；然则只要树起天线，捕捉乐观信号，你就有望在八十高龄告别尘寰时仍觉年轻。

▶ 赏析：

　　Samuel Ullman（塞缪尔·厄尔曼，840—1920），是著名的教育家、社会活动家、作家。散文诗《青春》写于1917年，当时塞缪尔已是77岁高龄，但本文体现了作者对青春的独到见解，作者本人经历亦是这首诗的真实写照，鼓舞了很多人。此诗因麦克阿瑟将军的推崇而广为传颂，将军在指挥太平洋战争期间，时常凝视这首被镶框挂在墙上的诗，用以鞭策、鼓舞自己。日本的松下幸之助也曾把此文作为座右铭。该诗短小精悍，共五个段落，仅248词，但寓意深刻，鼓舞人心。文中运用了排比、对照的手法阐释了青春的含义，进而在第二段描述了青春的特征，青春不为年龄所限，青春受思想的制约。第三段很短，道出了青春皆因 Worry、fear、self-distrust 易逝。第四段中，作者使用隐喻修辞，把如孩童般的那颗探求世界的好奇心比喻成能接收信号的无线电台，只要有儿童般的心境，青春便会永驻。第五段则从反正两方面说明，若天线不再接收信号，锐气消失，青春不再，然而一直保持乐观、探究世界，八十岁时也仍保有青春。

英语写作是衡量英语学习者英语应用能力的一个重要指标。要学好英语，写的重要性怎么强调都不过分（王初明，2004）。国外众多学者也认为写作是评价学习结果最有用的工具（Valenti et al. 2003）。英语写作主要考察学生的输出能力，但有效的输出建立在大量的地道语料输入基础上。在前几章中，编者主要对写作的基础知识与基本规范作了讲解，本章的主要内容是在数字化时代背景下，学习者进行写作训练、提升写作能力的有效途径。英语写作是依赖于大量实践才能提升的技能，需要在教与学过程中探索有效方法，尤其是要利用好现有的数字化平台勤加练习，才能切实解决"耗时低效"的问题，真正提高学生的写作水平。

第一节 数字化学习的理论基础

开展数字化写作学习，有其理据可依。加利福尼亚大学的赫钦斯（Edwin Hutchins）等人于20世纪80年代中后期提出分布式认知（Distributed Cognition）理论。分布式认知是指认知分布于个体内、个体间、媒介、环境、文化、社会和时间等之中。认知不仅仅局限于个体的认知活动，还存在于与学习者个体产生联系的社会、文化与媒介中，即在完成认知活动过程中，学习者可以借助外在环境中的认知资源更新个体认知。分布式认知强调的是认知现象在认知主体和环境间分布的本质。个体、媒介、他人、社会基于某一活动而产生的交互在认知中起着关键作用，认知是通过个体认知内部表征（如个体的记忆）与外部表征（如计算机或纸表征的信息和知识）之间在产生交互活动中传播和发生的，这些交互包括会话、非语言交流、信息形式的转换（如从言语信息转变为键盘输入）、在内外部表征结合的基础上构建新的表征等。在交互活动过程中，媒介、他人、社会与文化等可以被视为学习者大脑的延伸，分布式认知可以为学习者所用，形成智能整合，改变思维方式，拓展认知范围。外部环境，如存储在计算机、互联网中的外部记忆，可以帮助学习者降低认知负荷。基于网络的写作训练充分体现了分布式认知在学习者英语写作学习生成过程中的重要作用。学习不单纯是由教师到学生的知识传递或学习者个体与物质环境互动中的个人认知建构，而是个体与媒介、社会、文化多维互动、共享的过程，在此过程中，学习者从不同维度得到认知训练。人机、师生、生生之间的交互式活动，推动分布式认知建构进程，通过"同化"和"顺应"机制，促进语言知识的内化并建构、更新个体认知结构。因此，由分布式认知推动学习生成，是为数字化背景下的语言学习更为有效的学习方式。

"最近发展区"理论由苏联社会文化历史学派的创始人维果斯基提出。该理论主张：教学时首先要明确学生的发展水平。一种是学生现有的智力水平，即学生自己分析解决问题的水平；二是学生通过成人或集体的帮助才能达到的智力水平。维果斯基将学生现有的智力水平与通过帮助有可能达到的智力水平之间的区域称为"最近发展区"。学生往往借助同伴或教师所搭建的"脚手架"可以达到更高的水平。在英语写作中，同伴反馈即学生在"最近发展区"中相互搭建"脚手架"，从而促进英语水平提高。

元认知策略是有关认知过程的知识，是学习者通过计划、监控以及评估等方法对认知过程进行调整或进行自我管理，它包括事先计划、选择注意、自我管理、自我监控和自我评价等各种具体策略，它是成功地计划、监控和评估学习活动的必要条件，对改善学习效果起着最为关键的作用。（O'Malley &Chamot，1990）元认知策略在英语写作训练过程中起着重要作用，且也有研究证明元认知策略与写作成绩之间有必然联系。学习者的元认知策略在英语写作中起着积极重要的作用。学习者有计划地进行写作训练，有意识地进行阅读输入、习得地道表达、在落笔写作之前认真审题制订写作大纲、根据不同的写作题型采用不同的写作方法、提前规划多样化句式的运用等诸多环节，都体现元认知策略对写作训练的影响，也会直接影响写作能力的提升。

第二节　英语写作数字化平台建设

现代技术的发展为大学英语教学开辟了新的路径，测试、反馈作为教学中的重要环节亦逐渐实现了网络化。计算机自动作文评分在大学英语写作教学中得到了广泛应用。计算机自动作文评分（Automated Essay Scoring）采用统计、自然语言处理以及人工智能等方面的最新成果，依据一定的评分标准对作文进行评分（刘建达，2013）。计算机自动评分系统评分可靠、客观、经济性，可以节省大量人力物力，而且具有人工评分所没有的即时性和互动性（Landauer et. 2003）。

大学英语教学改革顺应《大学英语教学指南（草案）》中"大学英语应大力推进最新信息技术与课程教学的融合，继续发挥现代教育技术，特别是信息技术在外语教学中的重要作用（王守仁，2015）"的要求，将智能写作平台融入大学英语写作教学。批改网是一个用计算机自动批改英语作文的在线系统。就像医生使用CT机一样，老师可以用批改网自动扫描学生作文的各种参数，进而做出更精准更客观的判断和点评。批改网的原理通过对比学生作文和标准语料库之间的距离，并通过一定的算法将之映射成分数和点评，该项技术已获得国内发明专利。批改网认为作文分数重要，但具体的反馈和建议更重要，因为后者使得学生知道如何去修改。（信息来源：https：//www. pigai. org/）。编者所在单位德州学院自 2011 年 12 月起使用批改网辅助教学。截至 2015 年 6 月 15 日，共 48 位教师和 26 763 名学生注册使用批改网，学生总共提交作文 141 761 篇。其中，48 位教师布置作文 522 篇，共收到学生作文 135 846 篇，平均每位老师布置 10.87 篇，平均每篇题目收到作文 260.3 篇。在注册的 26 763 名学生中，有 24 966 名学生提交了老师布置的作文，占注册学生总数 93.28%；学生共提交作文 141 761 篇（其中提交教师布置的作文 135 896 篇，自主提交题库的作文 5 865 篇）；学生共修改作文 597 138 次，平均每篇作文修改 4.212 次；学生作文修改最高纪录为 213 次（XQ－学号 201301801011；教师－LX－作文号 434245）。批改网智能写作平台在写作教学中发挥了积极的推动作用，也大大提高了学生的写作积极性。2015 年，中国高校英语写作教学联盟基于批改网平台发起了"百万同题英文写作活动"。作文题目为"We Are What We Read"，由清华大学命题，规定字数为 300～500 词。2015 年 4 月 16 日至 5 月 31 日活动进行的 46 天中，来自全国 31 个省市地区的 2 792 所学校的老师引用布置题目 17 662 次，共计收到学生作文 1 093 126 篇。德州学院学生广泛参与，共提交作文 8 694 篇，居全国第六位，山东省第二位（数据来源：批改网）。

将以计算机自动作文评分系统为基础的智能写作平台引入教学并推动大学英语教学改革进度，不仅仅是技术层面的问题，更涉及教师层面教学理念的变革。在教师教学任务繁重无法给予学生有效写作反馈的情况下，智能写作平台的出现无疑成为为写作教师减负的利器。

第三节　基于网络的写作训练

在提高英语写作水平过程中，写作反馈起着重要作用。目前，在英语写作教学中，学生作文的反馈形式主要是教师反馈。然而，由于班级规模大，教师反馈给教师带来沉重负担。同时，学生往往看到分数却不清楚写作中的具体问题所在，从而导致其写作水平提高缓慢。因此，在写作训练过程中，网络反馈、同伴反馈与教师反馈都应运用到英语写作学习中，而且实践证明这些途径也确实有效。

一、网络反馈

在学习实践中，网络反馈是最直接最快捷的一种方法。教师将写作任务布置在句酷网上，生成作文号，学习者基于网络完成写作任务。通过实践证明，网络反馈能够有效促进学生写作能力提升。笔者曾做过一个教学实验，在句酷网布置作文，生成作文号432705，选取36位同学在规定时间内提交了作文（见图6-1）。基于智能写作平台写作文本，对36名学生的作文文本进行了文本分析，同时选取学生实施半结构访谈，以了解写作体验。

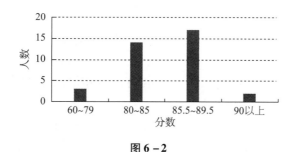

图6-1

研究发现，36位学生在批改网提交并完善修改作文，提交作文总次数为410次，平均修改次数11.3889次/每篇作文，其中，84%的同学对作文进行了至少1次修改，修改次数最多43次（Y同学）。批改网评分显示，写作成绩主要集中在80~90分之间，具体分布情况如图6-2。

图6-2

另外，批改网在平均词长、词汇丰富度、词平均难度、平均句长、从句密度、文章长度、篇章连次数7个维度对学生作文文本进行了分析（见表6-1）。结果表明，学生在写作时重视文章语言的连贯性与结构的完整性，用词也较丰富。

表6-1 学生作文文本分析

网络评分	平均长	词汇丰富度	词平均难度	平均句长	从句密度	文章长度	篇章连词数
75.71	4.3779	5.965118	5.393791	19.940175	1.167531	273.6188	16.680389

同时，提交作文时段分布均匀（见图6-3），在学习时段（上午8：00—12：00；下午13：00—17：00）与业余时段（18：00—次日凌晨7：00），均有学生提交作文，其中，在学习时段提交作文的学生占55.56%，在业余时段提交作文的学生占44.44%，在23：00之后仍有7位学生提交作文，占19.44%。这表明受试学生有兴趣进行网络写作训练，也愿意利用课下时间进行写作，将课上与课下、线下与线上学习相结合。

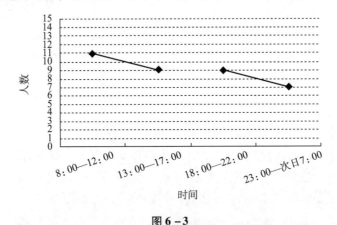

图6-3

在写作过程中，批改网能够就学生的习作问题给出即时反馈，这便大大提高了学习效率，学生可以根据建议进行及时修改，并可反复修改至满意。批改网对于学生习作文本中的语内错误和语际错误均可提出反馈意见。

1. 语内错误

（1）过度概括

当学习者在继续学习目的语的过程中根据已获得的目的语知识，创造出一种不正确的结构的时候，就犯了过度概括的错误。批改网给出修改意见如下：

＊I suggested you to keep a good mood.

修改建议：I suggested that you keep a good mood.

（2）文化迁移

由于对不同文化背景的理解，导致语言使用过程中词语的错用。批改网给出修改意见如下：

＊here is still another example

修改建议：here is yet another example

2. 语际错误

（1）词汇干扰

汉语与英语在词汇表达方面有较大的差异，有些词汇在汉语和英语中基本意思一样，但是内涵、用法和搭配却完全不同。有的同学在只牢记了英语单词的基本意思，却忽视了其用法和搭配，在使用这些词汇时往往是直译。批改网给出修改意见如下：

＊The most fortunate thing is that one falls in love with books at first sight when he can read.

修改建议：The most fortunate thing is that one falls in love with books at first sight when one can read.

（2）语法干扰

英语学习中出现的许多错误，往往是由于汉语语法习惯在学习者的头脑中已经根深蒂固，对英语语法的学习产生了种种干扰。批改网给出修改意见如下：

＊the taste of beauty

修改建议：a taste for beauty

＊it is no denying that

修改建议：there is no denying that

参与的学生认为批改网的评价非常细致，对于词汇、句型和语法的修改意见很清晰，有利于学生基础水平的提高，能够有效指导学生写作；有利于学生自主学习，尤其是有学习主动性的学生，通过一篇作文的反复修改，就能极好地夯实英语基础知识；现代高科技的使用，能够大范围地检验学生的作文水平，最大限度地帮助所有学生的写作。因此，在写作训练中，学习者应更加重视网络即时反馈，充分利用数字化平台促进写作水平的提高。

二、同伴反馈

学习者在进行写作训练时，也可采用同伴反馈的方式来促进写作能力的提升。对于同伴反馈，国内外专家都做出了相关研究。Tsui 与 Ng 将同伴反馈定义为"一种学习者对同伴作文进行阅读、评价、并给出反馈意见的合作学习活动。在此过程中，学习者通过支架作用，提高彼此的写作水平"。国内学者也通过实证研究证明，学生参与反馈，不仅可以使他们更加主动地参与到写作评价过程中，而且能够在评价同伴的作文中取长补短，从而提高自己的语言表达水平。

同伴互评在学习实践中验证为写作学习的有效途径。笔者也选取所在单位公选课《英语考研写作》的修课学生为研究对象。该公选课设置两个班，选课学生数量分别为 53 人与 39 人，实验中分别设置为控制班（53）与实验班（39）。实验前对两个班学生的英语水平测试成绩进行独立样本 t 检验，结果显示控制班与实验班学生写作水平无明显差异。该实验历经一个学期。实验过程中，两个班由同一名教师授课，授课内容一致。实验过程中，学生共接受三项写作任务，每项任务均经过"初稿—反馈—修改稿—反馈—最终稿"的环节。作文反馈均在课下进行，但是两个班学生接受不同的反馈方式。控制班学生完成作文的初稿之后，由教师进行批阅，教师给予学生作文相应分数并给出评语，教师将作文返还学生，并在课堂上短时集中讲解作文中出现的主要问题，然后学生修改文章写出修改稿，再交至老师进行评阅，经过教师反馈后，学生进行修改写出最终稿。实验班采用同伴评价与教师评价相结合的方式。在经过正常授课过程后，学生写出第一稿，课下学生之间形成合作同伴，相互阅读彼此的作文，并对其中出现的优点与问题进行讨论与评价，对文章的篇章结构与遣词造句等方面进行全方位的讨论与交流，然后学生写出修改稿，再由老师进行反馈，并依据教师反馈写出最终稿。

笔者分别对控制班与实验班的学生进行了写作水平测验的前测与后测，收集学生第一次写作任务的初稿和最终稿，并在实验结束时选取学生进行了半开放式访谈。本研究对实验数据进行分析，将控制班与实验班学生的写作水平测验成绩进行对比，对学生写作文本进行言语失误解码对比分析，并对访谈内容的质性数据进行描述分析。

最终，写作水平测试成绩对比显示，控制班学生在通过一个学期的英语写作学习后成绩比实验前有显著提高（$p<0.05$）（见表 6-2）。实验班学生在通过一学期的同伴反馈后，成绩比实验前成绩有显著提高（$p<0.05$）（见表 6-3）。实验班与控制班运用了不同的反馈方式，因此，通过对比两组学生写作水平提高的程度能够反映同伴反馈与教师反馈对学生写作水平的影响强弱。通过对比分析，实验班学生成绩比控制班学生成绩提高幅度大（见表 6-4），即同伴反馈使学生写作水平有更大提高。

表6-2 控制班学生写作水平测验前测、后测成绩对比

	N	Mean	Std. Deviation	t	Sig. (2-tailed)
pre-test	53	30.208	6.500	-6.681	.000
post-test	53	36.226	6.145		

表6-3 实验班学生写作水平测验前测、后测成绩对比

	N	Mean	Std. Deviation	t	Sig. (2-tailed)
pre-test	39	27.256	9.159	-9.743	.000
post-test	39	42.615	6.624		

表6-4 实验组与控制组前测、后测成绩提高程度对比

	Group	N	Mean	Std. Deviation	t	Sig. (2-tailed)
Post-test	EG	39	15.359	9.845	5.459	.000
Pre-test	CG	53	6.019	6.559		

采用桂诗春与杨惠中的 CLEC 中言语失误分类表对两组学生的语言错误进行解码分析，将作文中的言语失误归类为词形、动词短语、名词短语等11类失误，每类下又细分为拼写、大小写、时态、格等61项言语失误。通过选取实验班和控制班学生第一篇作文的初稿与最终稿，研究人员对文章中的言语失误编码量化，进行了言语失误数量对比。控制班初稿语言失误数量为1 075，最终稿失误数量为797，失误改正率为25.86%。而实验班初稿语言失误数量为1 118，最终稿失误数量为671，失误改正率为39.98%，错误改正率高于控制班。同伴反馈更能够帮助学生分析、改正作文中的言语失误。访谈结果显示大多数人认可同伴互评的积极作用，认为这种评价方式为同学之间提供了更多交流、合作与互相学习的机会，有针对性地进行评价使学生更加清晰的了解自己作文中的问题，比教师的总体评价更有收获。

因此，在今后英语写作学习中，教师应有意识地将传统的单一教师评价与学生同伴反馈有机结合，充分发挥同伴反馈的积极作用，减轻教师负担，学习者也应更加重视与同伴之间的交流与反馈，从而更加有效地提高学习者的英语写作水平。

除上面提到的网络评价与同伴评价，学习者的写作训练过程中，教师评价一直发挥着重要的主导作用，学习者应在教师反馈中找到提高的关键点助力写作水平的提升。学习者也应进一步将智能写作平台与教师的写作教学相融合、优化其作用，提升写作水平。

附　　录

附录一　练习参考答案

Key to the Exercises

Chapter One
I. Multiple choice
1~5 C D C B C　　6~10 C C B C D
11~15 A D D D D　16~20 B D C C B
II. Reading Comprehension
Passage One　1~10　G K J L H D E O F I
Passage Two　11~20　O F L E A N C I J B

Chapter Two
I. Translation
A. Translate the following sentences into English

1. A collection of data is called a data set, and a single observation a data point.

2. A computer is a device which takes in a series of electrical impulses representing information.

3. A computer work many times more rapidly than nerve cells in the human brain.

4. A cork floating on water is not swept along with the water. Rather, it moves up and down with the wave motion.

5. A force involves direction as well as magnitude.

6. A polymer is a substance of high molecular weight, well above the size of

the compounds considered so far.

7. A port is a harbor with the necessary terminal facilities to speed up the moving of cargo and passengers.

8. A power reactor has no need of air, for the heat generated in the uranium pile is the result of unclear fission, not of combustion.

9. A second panel that will visually display any alarm condition in the building can be provided in the Mechanical System Control Office.

10. A special fund has been set up to help these nations use new chemicals and technology.

B. Translate the sentences into Chinese

1. 轴承按恒预载荷设计，在机器工作过程中，轴承载荷不会变化。
2. 为获得最佳性能，保证长期无故障使用，请仔细阅读说明书。
3. 网络模块硬件安装指南。
4. 操作和维修弧焊设备有潜在的危险。
5. 如机器在需要时间内不停止运作，热过载装置将会启动。
6. 一定要把设备安装在垂直不易振动的墙上。
7. CY15 型抽油机的结构紧凑。
8. 该机器操作时安全可靠，便于维修，能在恶劣条件下工作。
9. 电机皮带轮上备有锥套，便于安装和拆卸。
10. 请注意电机与主轴同心度，以免产生振动或引起轴承发热等情况。

II. Reading Comprehension

1~5　B H I A B　6~10　D B I C K　11~15　G A G J E

Chapter Three

I. Topic Sentences

(1) It was the best of times, it was the worst of times.

(2) "But people are not born as a failure," he said. "A man can be destroyed but not defeated."

(3) We regardless of the shackles of mind, indulge in the world buckish, focus on the beneficial principle, we have lost themselves.

(4) It is my spirit that addresses your spirit; just as if both had passed through the grave, and we stood at God's feet, equal — as we are!

(5) Shakespeare is above all writers, at least above all modern writers, the poet of nature.

II. Paragraph Writing

(1) Paragraph for Picture Description

From the picture, we know that more and more young people are showing their admiration in an excessive way. On the one hand, the left picture tells us that the young man writes the word "BECKHAM" on his face. On the other hand, the right picture informs us that the other young man is spending RMB300 on his hair in a Beckham-style. It can easily be seen that blind idolatry is not uncommon today.

(2) Sample Writing

I believe that it is possible to live a green, sustainable life. To accomplish this goal, we need to be familiar with the small adjustments we can make in our every day lives. The first thing that comes to my mind is that, instead of using cars, we should set about traveling by public transport whenever available. Secondly, we should take care not to take electric power for granted. When we leave a room, all the lights should be turned off. Infact, anything electrical that is not in use should be unplugged. Thirdly, we can recycle. Many things that we use are recyclable. If we get a container to collect there cyclable things, we can contribute to the conservation of natural resources and reduce the and reduce the amount of pollution and green house gas generated. In addition, a lot of things can be reused, such as fabric shopping bags and there verse side of printed paper.

(3) A Letter of Condolence

My Dearest Pauline,

I was over whelmed with sadness to hear about the death of Frank in battle. I long for words to say how much I sympathize with you, but no near adequate in moments like these. I will say, though, that my heart goes out to you. I will always remember the deep enjoyment I had in knowing Frank, such a kind, gentle soul.

He was an extraordinarily impressive man and a very brave soldier. He filled so many of us with admiration by his willingness to give his life for world peace and freedom. His life will endure as a model for us all. I am so proud of him.

You can depend on my love and support during this sad time.

With my deepest love and sympathy,

Jenny

(4) Sample Writing

Friendship is often compared to a flower. In general, flowers need sunlight and water to grow. If you don't expose flowers regularly to enough sunlight and water, they will wither and even die. The same applies to friendship. If you take a friendship for granted, not spending time and energy nurturing/taking care of it, you may one day find your friendship has ceased to exist. Conflict can be compared to a blow to a flower. Friendships, especially young friendships, are unable to endure conflicts just as flowers can not survive repeated blows. If you have made promises to spend your time with your friend, keep your word. Other wise it will hurt your friend's feelings. Old friends may be able to for give your faults, but you can not expect new friends to do the same. You must keep in mind that most friendships have a breaking point and take care not to allow any conflict to go beyond that point.

(5) Sample Writing

Yilu Zhao

No. 2 High School of East China Normal University

155 Jinshajiang Road

Shanghai 200062

China

December 1, 1993

Office of Undergraduate Admissions

Yale University

38 Hillhouse Avenue

New Haven, CT 06511

USA

Dear Sir/Madam,

I am writing to express my interest in studying history at Yale University, especially your Directed Studies program.

History has always fascinated me, and I firmly believe that the best way to study Western history is to go to a top university in the West, which would greatly help put things into perspective. I understand that your Directed Studies program will guide students through the Western canons of philosophy and literature as well as history, which is exactly the education I yearn for.

History is usually written from the viewpoint of a country. I expect that, at classes in Yale, my historical concepts will differ from, and even clash with, my fellow American students. This will be an enriching experience for all of us.

My ultimate goal is to become a journalist reporting on Western news to the Chinese audience and Chinese news to the West in ways that can promote mutual understanding. A solid grasp of both Chinese and Western history will be a very necessary first step.

Attached please find the duly filled-in application form, my resume, two essays and three letters of recommendation.

I would be much obliged if I could be considered for any kind of financial assistance or scholarship, which would help me greatly in the completion of the degree.

Again, I sincerely thank you for your time and kind consideration.

Sincerely,
Yilu Zhao

(6) Sample Writing

Howard Hughes was an American entrepreneur and an aviation pioneer. During WWⅡ, he entered into a contract with the US government to make planes that would be able to transport troops and materials across the Atlantic Ocean. The prototype he finally produced was nick named the Spruce Goose. It was made entirely of wood, and it was the largest airplane every built. On November 2, 1947, the Spruce Goose made its first and only flight, and after that it was put into storage and then on display for the public. Many think that the Spruce Goose was a failure and a waste of time and money. But if we think of the fact that many of its design features have been in corporated into the modern cargo plane, we will not be so quick to blame Howard Hughes. He was simply ahead of his time.

(7) Sample Writing

There are many benefits of/to bringing the maker movement into the classroom. First and foremost it calls for students to turn from being passive users into active discoverers by stimulating their imagination and creativity. It also allows students to work on "real life" problems in a math or science classroom. This helps students realize the practical aspects of education and can transform their motivation. Moreover, students can learn how to interact with each other effectively, generating a sense of engagement and mutual acceptance. Added to all this, the completion of each project boosts the confidence of students in their capacity to build something useful. In short, the maker movement injects creativity, encouragement, the spirit of teamwork and a sense of achievement into the classroom, opening up a vast and exciting new frontier in the world of education.

Chapter Four

Sample Writing

Task One

Used Laptop for Sale

I have a Lenovo laptop for sale, which I bought last September.

I strongly recommend to you this used laptop based on the following reasons: First, it is a super thin laptop, which makes it portable and practical. Second, due to my careful maintenance, the laptop is still in good condition, running very fast. Third, with its high quality CPU, this laptop can be used for you to write and edit documents, listen to music and watch videos. And it can also satisfy the need to play computer games. Last but not least, in my opinion, 2000 yuan for this laptop is really an attractive price. For those who would like to have a practice PC without paying too much, this used computer is an ideal choice. After all, it can not only satisfy your various needs in your study and daily life, but also save you a lot of money.

Whoever is interested and intends to know more relevant details can contact me by calling 86543217 or sending emails to liming@163.com

Li Ming

Task Two

After graduation, almost all college students will unavoidably be faced with the problem of career choice, which is really a dilemma and views on this issue are not identical. Some hold that top priority should be given to starting a business of your own, while others think that finding a job is the best choice that influences their future.

From my personal perspective, I definitely prefer the latter. First and foremost, a good start for one's own business requires plenty of money along with adequate work experience, which is often what college students are short of. Taking a job will enable us to learn from the seniors and accumulate work experience. Theoretical knowledge will provide graduates with the ability to consider things comprehensively, however, only by integrating with practice can it be useful for their future development. Moreover, we can be involved in a more complex interpersonal relationship and cultivate necessary skills in communication and cooperation with others. Lastly, young entrepreneurs, as college graduates, are under even greater pressure than finding a job elsewhere.

Therefore, it is an undeniable fact that we should accumulate as much experience as possible by finding a job somewhere and working for others and wait for the appropriate time to start our own business.

Task Three

Dear Cook,

I am quite delighted to hear that you have arrived in Beijing and will begin your teaching career in our university. And today, I am writing for the purpose of recommending certain tourist attractions.

The long history and a host of historical buildings characterize Beijing, the capital city of China. Thus, it is advisable for you to visit places including the Summer Palace, the Great Wall and the Forbidden City. These attractions are particularly worth visiting, because these places will bring you opportunities to acquire the historical knowledge of China, arouses your enthusiasm for Chinese culture and help you to appreciate the distinctive Chinese architectures.

I am convinced that you will enjoy comfortable, fruitful and wonderful trips in these attractions.

Your truly,
Li Ming

Task Four

These two pictures are particularly worth concern for the reason that the painter focuses his eyesight on what the truly reading is. In the first cartoon, there is a youngster, sitting leisurely and comfortably in a chair and flaunting his large number of books, with no book in hands. However, in the right picture, although the guy has just a few books, he has made his mind to try his utmost to read 20 books in this year. Several Chinese characters, finally, can be noticed, which say "having books" and "reading books".

In the contemporary society, a host of people prefer to purchase, store and even flaunt their books, but they may never read any books. This trend is rather ridiculous. As a matter of fact, every one should bear in mind that books should be read not be boasted. As a positive habit, reading books brings us knowledge, arouses our enthusiasm for future life and helps us to enhance our quality. It is books that enable us to build up not only knowledge, but also a confidence, optimism and courage to face any adversities in life, work and study. Unfortunately, many people have books but never read, which has constituted an obstacle that hinders their growth and progress.

I, as a college student, am convinced that the society as a whole should forge a wholesome atmosphere to advocate, educate and encourage all people to not only purchase books, but also to be absorbed in reading books.

Chapter Five
Passage Writing
1. Sample writing

Dear Mr. Brown,

I am writing on behalf of the English Department to invite you to give a lecture in our college.

We know that you are an expert on Australian literature. As English majors, our students would like to know something about Australian literature. We would be very grateful if you could give a talk on "Contemporary Australian literature" to students of the English Department on Saturday, June 4. If this subject does not suit you, any other similar topic would be welcome as well.

We have already had several very interesting talks from some distinguished visitors from various countries and we look forward early to the opportunity to benefit from your experience and wisdom.

Yours truly,
Linda

2. Sample writing

Dear Lucy,

I am writing to express our heartfelt thanks for taking good care of my cat Cathy while we were on holiday.

She was such a happy cat when we got home; we knew she must have had lots of loving attention. When we used to pick up from the kennel she was always unhappy. You not only saved us some money, but you also spared us the worry of how she was doing while we were away.

Your kind help is very much appreciated.

Yours truly,
Tom

3. Sample writing

Dear brother,

Kindly excuse me for my not being able to attend your graduation ceremony next Wednesday as I have promised.

You know, there will be a meeting of great importance to my company next week in Nanjing. But the person who was originally appointed to it is now seriously ill in hospital. And I have been asked to take his place to attend the meeting and make a speech on behalf of my company. On the one hand, it is a task assigned by my boss out of his trust in me. On the other hand, I do regard it as an opportunity to both display and enhance my abilities. So I am afraid I cannot be present at your graduation ceremony.

Though I have decided to send you a gift to celebrate your graduation, I really regret that I cannot give you my sincere congratulations on the spot, for I know any gift can never parallel a warm word spoken personally by a family member. I do feel terribly sorry. Please forgive me.

Yours sincerely,
Li Ming

4. Sample writing

Dear Lucy,

Heartfelt congratulations on your graduation from the Graduate School.

I have good reasons to feel proud of you. I know the degree of master meant many years of assiduous study and hard work. I have heard of your excellent record in research and extracurricular activities. In this you took the right road to emerge as a fully developed young lady to society.

I take pride in your achievements and avail myself of this opportunity to extend to you my best wishes for your success and happiness.

Yours sincerely,
Li Ming

5. Sample writing

Dear Mr. Stone,

  I take great pleasure in introducing Lucy Brown, one of my best friends to you. She is going to pursue her education as a postgraduate in your university after her graduation here. She and I had studied together for four years. She is hard-working girl. Now that we have finished our study here we had to part with each other.

  Will you please give her some guidance in regard to the entrance examination? Any information you can provide, as well as your introduction for him to meet the future tutor shall be appreciated very much.

Yours truly,
Li Ming

6. Sample writing

Dear Tom,

  I am afraid that I won't be in our dormitory tonight because my father has come here to see me and I plan to sleep in the room he has booked in a nearby hotel. I had wanted to tell you that in person but you are not back yet. So I have to leave this note for you.

  My father has brought me some local specialties from my hometown. I've left some on your desk. Help yourself and I hope you'll enjoy them.

  Take care of yourself.

Yours,
Li Ming

附录二 科技类专业词汇

后验估计	a posteriori estimate
先验估计	a priori estimate
验收测试	acceptance testing
可及性	accessibility
累积误差	accumulated error
驱动器	actuator
适应层	adaptation layer
容许误差	admissible error
集结矩阵	aggregation matrix
放大环节	amplifying element
信号器	annunciator
近似推理	approximate reasoning
配置问题	assignment problem
联想机	association
渐进稳定性	asymptotic stability
姿态捕获	attitude acquisition
姿态扰动	attitude disturbance
可扩充性	augment ability
自治系统	autonomous system
基座坐标系	base coordinate system
方位对准	bearing alignment
盲目搜索	blind search
边界值分析	boundary value analysis
蝶阀	butterfly valve
清晰性	clarity
串联补偿	cascade compensation
突变论	catastrophe theory
集中性	centrality
链式集结	chained aggregation
混沌	chaos
特征轨迹	characteristic locus
化学推进	chemical propulsion
分类器	classifier
闭环极点	closed loop pole
聚类分析	cluster analysis
粗-精控制	coarse-fine control
蛛网模型	cobweb model
系数矩阵	coefficient matrix
认知科学	cognitive science
认知机	cognition
组合决策	combination decision
指令位姿	command pose
相伴矩阵	companion matrix
房室模型	compartmental model
兼容性	compatibility
补偿网络	compensating network
补偿，矫正	compensation
柔顺，顺应	compliance
组合控制	composite control
组态	configuration

附录二 科技类专业词汇

连接性　connectivity
守恒系统　conservative system
一致性　consistency
约束条件　constraint condition
消费函数　consumption function
连续工作制　continuous duty
控制精度　control accuracy
控制柜　control cabinet
控制力矩陀螺　control moment gyro
控制盘　control panel
控制时程　control time horizon
控制仪表　controlling instrument
合作对策　cooperative game
协调策略　coordination strategy
协调器　coordinator
转折频率　corner frequency
临界阻尼　critical damping
临界稳定性　critical stability
截止频率　cut-off frequency
控制论　cybernetics
循环遥控　cyclic remote control
阻尼振荡　damped oscillation
阻尼器　damper
阻尼比　damping ratio
数据采集　data acquisition
数据加密　data encryption
数据处理器　data processor
决策空间　decision space
解耦参数　decoupling parameter
延时遥测　delayed telemetry
导出树　derivation tree
微分反馈　derivative feedback
描述函数　describing function
希望值　desired value

目的站　destination
检出器　detector
偏差　deviation
偏差报警器　deviation alarm
诊断模型　diagnostic model
微分对策　differential game
微分环节　differentiation element
数字滤波器　digital filer
数字化　digitization
尺度传感器　dimension transducer
直接协调　direct coordination
判别函数　discriminant function
扰动补偿　disturbance compensation
多样性　diversity
可分性　divisibility
领域知识　domain knowledge
主导极点　dominant pole
对偶原理　dual principle
双自旋稳定　dual spin stabilization
能耗制动　dynamic braking
动态特性　dynamic characteristics
动态偏差　dynamic deviation
计量经济模型　econometric model
经济控制论　economic cybernetics
经济效益　economic effectiveness
经济评价　economic evaluation
经济指数　economic index
经济指标　economic indicator
有效性　effectiveness
效益理论　effectiveness theory
需求弹性　elasticity of demand
电子料斗秤　electronic hopper scale
仰角　elevation
异常停止　emergency stop

经验分布　empirical distribution
内生变量　endogenous variable
均衡增长　equilibrium growth
平衡点　equilibrium point
等价类划分　equivalence partitioning
工效学　ergonomics
误差　error
纠错剖析　error-correction parsing
估计量　estimate
估计理论　estimation theory
评价技术　evaluation technique
事件链　event chain
外生变量　exogenous variable
外扰　external disturbance
故障诊断　failure diagnosis
可行性研究　feasibility study
可行协调　feasible coordination
可行域　feasible region
特征检测　feature detection
特征抽取　feature extraction
反馈补偿　feedback compensation
有限自动机　finite automaton
定值控制　fixed set point control
流量传感器　flow sensor
流量变送器　flow transmitter
涨落　fluctuation
强迫振荡　forced oscillation
变频器　frequency converter
频域响应　frequency response
全阶观测器　full order observer
功能分解　functional decomposition
闸阀　gate valve
生成函数　generation function
地磁力矩　geomagnetic torque

球形阀　globe valve
陀螺漂移率　gyro drift rate
和谐偏差　harmonious deviation
和谐策略　harmonious strategy
隐蔽振荡　hidden oscillation
层次结构图　hierarchical chart
递阶控制　hierarchical control
递阶规划　hierarchical planning
内稳态　homeostasis
横向分解　horizontal decomposition
图像识别　image recognition
冲量　impulse
脉冲函数　impulse function
点动　inching
品质因数　index of merit
工业自动化　industrial automation
推理机　inference engine
信息采集　information acquisition
固有调节　inherent regulation
初始偏差　initial deviation
发起站　initiator
入轨姿势　injection attitude
不稳定性　instability
积算仪器　integration instrument
智能终端　intelligent terminal
互联系统　interacted system
互联　interconnection
断续工作制　intermittent duty
内扰　internal disturbance
同构模型　isomorphic model
迭代协调　iterative coordination
喷气推进　jet propulsion
分批控制　job-lot control
知识获取　knowledge acquisition

知识同化	knowledge assimilation
梯形图	ladder diagram
极限环	limit cycle
直行程阀	linear motion valve
线性规划	linear programming
称重传感器	load cell
局部最优	local optimum
长期记忆	long term memory
磁卸载	magnetic dumping
幅值比例尺	magnitude scale factor
人机协调	man-machine coordination
手动操作器	manual station
边际效益	marginal effectiveness
匹配准则	matching criterion
最大超调量	maximum overshoot
极大值原理	maximum principle
机理模型	mechanism model
最小实现	minimal realization
模态集结	modal aggregation
模态变换	modal transformation
模型置信度	model confidence
模型逼真度	model fidelity
模型验证	model verification
可动空间	motion space
最近邻	nearest-neighbor
必然性测度	necessity measure
负反馈	negative feedback
非线性环节	nonlinear element
通断控制	on-off control
开环极点	open loop pole
最优轨迹	optimal trajectory
轨道摄动	orbit perturbation
轨道交会	orbital rendezvous
序参数	order parameter
振荡周期	oscillating period
交叠分解	overlapping decomposition
模式基元	pattern primitive
峰值时间	peak time
感知器	perceptron
周期工作制	periodic duty
摄动理论	perturbation theory
相位超前	phase lead
反接制动	plug braking
旋塞阀	plug valve
点位控制	point-to-point control
极点配置	pole assignment
零极点相消	pole-zero cancellation
多项式输入	polynomial input
压力变送器	pressure transmitter
主频区	primary frequency zone
优先级	priority
生产预算	production budget
产生式规则	production rule
利润预测	profit forecast
射频敏感器	radio frequency sensor
随机扰动	random disturbance
随机过程	random process
速率积分陀螺	rate integrating gyro
比值操作器	ratio station
实时遥测	real time telemetry
整流器	rectifier
降阶观测器	reduced order observer
冗余信息	redundant information
再入控制	reentry control
调节装载	regulating device
调节	regulation
关系代数	relational algebra
继电器特性	relay characteristic

中文	English	中文	English
交会和对接	rendezvous and docking	切换点	switching point
归结原理	resolution principle	系统工程	system engineering
响应曲线	response curve	转速表	tachometer
回差矩阵	return difference matrix	作业周期	task cycle
回比矩阵	return ratio matrix	示教编程	teaching programming
风险分析	risk decision	遥测	telemetry
机器人学	robotics	目的系统	teleological system
根轨迹	root locus	温度传感器	temperature transducer
旋转变压器	rotating transformer	模板库	template base
饱和特性	saturation characteristics	治疗模型	therapy model
自组织系统	self-organizing system	温度计	thermometer
自校正控制	self-tuning control	厚度计	thickness meter
敏感元件	sensing element	分时控制	time-sharing control
灵敏度分析	sensitivity analysis	时变参数	time-varying parameter
感觉控制	sensory control	自上而下测试	top-down testing
伺服控制	servo control	拓扑结构	topological structure
相似性	similarity	跟踪误差	tracking error
仿真实验	simulation experiment	权衡分析	trade-off analysis
仿真速度	simulation velocity	瞬态偏差	transient deviation
单轴转台	single axle table	变送器	transmitter
单级过程	single level process	趋势分析	trend analysis
奇异摄动	singular perturbation	双时标系统	two-time scale system
受役系统	slaved system	单位圆	unit circle
电磁阀	solenoid valve	单元测试	unit testing
调速系统	speed control system	上级问题	upper level problem
稳定极限	stability limit	效用函数	utility function
状态方程模型	state equation model	价值工程	value engineering
定点精度	station accuracy	速度传感器	velocity transducer
稳态偏差	steady state deviation	纵向分解	vertical decomposition
逐步精化	stepwise refinement	权因子	weighting factor
强耦合系统	strongly coupled system	加权法	weighting method
主观频率	subjective probability	零输入响应	zero-input response
自持振荡	sustained oscillation	零状态响应	zero-state response

附录三 常用前缀、后缀与词根

一、常见前缀

1. 反义前缀

（1）表示否定意义的前缀

dis‑ = not, deprive of 表示"不""剥夺""取消"

dis‑ + agree（一致，同意）→disagree 不一致，意见不合

dis‑ + arm（武装）→disarm 解除武装

dis‑ + approve（同意，批准）→disapprove 不赞成，不准

il‑, im‑, in‑, ir‑ = not 表示"非""不"

il‑ + literate（有读写能力的）→illiterate 文盲的

im‑ + possible（可能的）→impossible 不可能的

in‑ + valuable（有价值的）→invaluable 无价的，非常珍贵的

ir‑ + responsible（对……负责任的）→irresponsible 不负责任的

ir‑ + religious（宗教的，虔诚的）→irreligious 无信仰的，不虔诚的

ir‑ + regular（规则的）→irregular 不规则的

（2）表示相反、对立意义的前缀

anti‑ = against, opposite to, back 表示"反""对""往回"

anti‑ + warlike（好战的）→antiwarlike 非好战的

（3）表示错误意义的前缀

mis‑ = wrongly, badly 表示"错误"

mis‑ + advise（劝告）→misadvise 给予错误的劝告

mis‑ + place（安放）→misplace 误置，误放

mis‑ + understand（理解）→misunderstand 误解

2. 表示位置方向的前缀

（1）a‑ = on, toward 表示"在……之上""向着"

a‑ + side（旁边）→aside 在旁边

（2）de－＝down 表示"向下"
de－＋scend（上涌）→descend 下降
de－＋grade（级别）→degrade 降级
（3）ex－＝out 表示"向外"
ex－＋press（压）→express 表达
ex－＋port（港口）→export 向外运送，出口
（4）fore－＝before 表示"先""前"
fore－＋arm（手臂）→forearm 前臂
fore－＋ground（背景）→foreground 前景
（5）inter－＝between，among 表示"之间"
inter－＋national（国家的）→international 国际的
inter－＋action（行动）→interaction 互动
inter－＋net（网）→internet 互联网
（6）mid－＝middle 表示"中间的"
mid－＋night（夜）→midnight 半夜
mid－＋summer（夏天）→midsummer 仲夏
mid－＋term（学期）→midterm 期中
（7）post－＝after 表示"在……之后"
post－＋war（战争）→postwar 战后的
post－＋script（手稿）→postscript 附笔
（8）sub－＝under 表示"下""副"
sub－＋marine（海洋的）→submarine 海底的，潜水艇
sub－＋way（道路）→subway 地铁
sub－＋title（标题）→subtitle 副标题

3. 表示数量的前缀
（1）bi－＝double，two 表示"两""双"
bi－＋lingual（舌音的）→bilingual 双语的
bi－＋monthly（每月一次的）→bimonthly 双月的
（2）tri－＝three 表示"三"
tri－＋angle（角，角度）→triangle 三角形
（3）hemi－，semi－＝half 表示"半"
hemi－＋sphere（球体）→hemisphere 半球
semi－＋circle（圆圈）→semicircle 半圆形
（4）micro－＝small 表示"微小的"

micro－＋wave（波）→microwave 微波

micro－＋economics（经济学）→microeconomics 微观经济学

micro－＋analysis（分析）→microanalysis 微量分析

（5）macro－＝large 表示"大的"

macro－＋effect（效应）→macroeffect 宏观效应

macro－＋economics（经济学）→macroeconomics 宏观经济学

macro－＋molecule（分子）→macromolecule 高分子

（6）multi－＝many，much 表示"多的"

multi－＋color（颜色）→multicolor 多种颜色的

multi－＋channel（渠道）→multichannel 多通话线路的

multi－＋purpose（目的）→multipurpose 多目标的，用途广的

二、常见后缀

1. 名词性后缀

（1）－age 为抽象名词后缀，表示行为，状态和全体

percentage 百分数，百分率；voltage 电压，伏特数；lavage 灌洗，洗出法；curettage 刮除法；shortage 不足，缺少

（2）－cy 表示抽象名词

accuracy 准确，精确度；infancy 婴儿期

（3）－ence、－ance 表示性质和动作

difference 不同；interference 干扰，干预；influence 影响，感化；occurrence 发出，出现；violence 激烈，暴力；existence 存在；significance 意义，意味

（4）－ency、－ancy 抽象名词后缀

deficiency 不足，不全；tendency 趋势，趋向；frequency 频率；pregnancy 妊娠；emergency 紧急，急救；fluency 流利，流畅；sufficiency 足够，充足；constancy 坚定，经久不变

（5）－er 表示…人、…者

diameter 直径；receiver 接收者，接受者；beginner 初学者，创始人；reader 读者；cooker 厨具

（6）－ics 表示…科学

Physics 物理学；pediatrics 儿科学；obstetrics 产科学，orthopedics 矫形科学

（7）－ian 表示…人

physician 医师，内科医师；technician 技术员

(8) -ing 由动词变化而来的动名词

nursing 护；typing 分型，分类；mapping 绘制…图；bleeding 出血；vomiting 呕吐；positioning 把…放在适当的位置；matching 和…相配

(9) -ion 由动词构成的名词

occasion 偶然原因；division 分割，分开；vision 视力，视觉；distortion 扭曲，变形

(10) -ism 表示制度、主义及现象等的抽象名词

mechanism 机理，机制；idealism 理想主义

(11) -ist 表示人称名词

specialist 专家；internist 内科医生；biologist 生物学家；economist 经济学家；chemist 化学家

(12) -ization 由动词构成的抽象名词

organization 组织，机构，机化；internationalization 国际化；realization 实现；modernization 现代化；normalization 正常化

(13) -ment 表示动作，行为或具体事物

measurement 测量，量度；experiment 实验；instrument 仪器，器械；fragment 片段，断片；replacement 替代，置换；development 发展；movement 动作，活动；equipment 装置，设备；improvement 改善

(14) -ness 加在形容词后构成抽象名词

thickness 厚度；effectiveness 有效；usefulness 有用的；coldness 寒冷；darkness 黑暗

(15) -ship 表示状态

relationship 关系，联系；interrelationship 相互关系，相互联系。

(16) -th 加在形容词后构成名词

length 长度；width 宽度；depth 深度；truth 真理

(17) -ty 表示性质

responsibility 责任，责任心；capacity 容量，能力；safety 安全性；permeability 渗透性；unity 整体，统一性；similarity 类似，相似

2. 形容词性后缀

(1) -able 与 -ible 表示可能的，可以的

acceptable 易接受的；movable 可移动的；alterable 可改变的，可改动的；available 可用的，可得到的；uncomfortable 不舒服的；visible 可见的；irreversible 不可逆的；impossible 不可能的；inaudible 听不见的

(2) -al、-ant、-ent 表示有…的属性

natural 自然的；special 特别的，特殊的；central 中央的；terminal 末端的；typical 典型的；digital 数字的；capital 首要的，重要的；vocal 有声的，声带的

Significant 有意义的，重要的；resistant 抵抗的，反抗的；important 重要的；constant 坚定的，持久的，permanent 永久的

consistent 坚定的；different 不同的；sufficient 足够的；convenient 便利的，方便的；evident 明显的；fluent 流利的，流畅的；efficient 有效的；frequent 常常的，频繁的

（3）-ary 表示与…有关的

ordinary 平常的，普通的；anniversary 周年的；voluntary 自愿的，随意的

（4）-ed 用于名词或动词加 ed 转化为形容词

coded 加密的；limited 有限的；lubricated 滑润的；surrounded 围住的，被围绕的

（5）-ful 由名词构成形容词，表示充满…的

useful 有用的；successful 成功的；plentiful 丰富的；helpful 有帮助的；beautiful 漂亮的；powerful 充满力量的

3. 动词性后缀

（1）-ate 结尾的词汇通常为动词

deviate 背离、偏离；decelerate 减速；accelerate 加速；operate 操作；vibrate 振动、颤动；migrate 移动，移民；participate 参与；anticipate 预期、期望；abbreviate 缩写；celebrate 庆祝

（2）-en 形容词构成动词，表示变、加、使…

weaken 变弱、变衰弱；soften 使…软化；thicken 使…变厚；strengthen 加强；shorten 使…变短；deepen 加深、深化；harden 使…变硬；lengthen 使…延长；loosen 放松、解开；lighten 减轻；lessen 减少；sharpen 变尖锐；broaden 拓宽；widen 变宽

（3）-ize 加在形容词或名词上，表示…化

modernize 现代化；minimize 缩小；neutralize 中和；standardize 标准化；depolarize 去极化；

4. 副词性后缀

（1）-ly 词缀最常用，加在形容词后构成副词，表示…地

simultaneously 同时地；concurrently 同时地；widely 广泛地；exclusively 专用地、唯一地；scarcely 仅仅、刚刚；immediately 立即

(2) -ward(s) 加在前置词上，构成副词，表示方向。

三、常见的词根

(1) aer, ar, 含义是"空气，大气"aeroplane, aerial

(2) ag, act, ig, 含义是"做，动作"active, agent, reaction

(3) alt, 含义是"高"，altitude

(4) alter, altern, altr, 含义是"其他，变更"alternate

(5) bio, bi, bion, 含义是"生物，生命"biology, bionics

(6) brev, bri, brief, 含义是"短"brief, abbreviation, abridge

(7) cap, capt, cept, cip, 含义是"取，获"capture, except, concept, capacity

(8) ced, ceed, cess, 含义是"行，让步"proceed, succeed, excess

(9) centr, 含义是"中心"concentrate, eccentric

(10) clain, clam, 含义是"呼喊"claim, proclaim, exclaim

(11) clos, clud, 含义是"闭合"conclude, enclose, include

(12) col, cult, 含义是"耕耘"colony, cultivate, agriculture

(13) cor, cord, 含义是"心"cordial, record, accord

(14) curr, cur, cour, 含义是"跑，动作"current, occur, concurrence

(15) dic, dict, 含义是"说，示"dictate, edit, indicate, predict

(16) doc, doct, 含义是"教"doctor, document

(17) duc, duct 含义是"引导，传导"introduce, produce, conduct, deduct

(18) fact, fac, fect, dic, dit, 含义是"做，创造"factory, effect, profit, faculty, perfect

(19) fend, fens, 含义是"打，击"defence, offence

(20) fer, 含义是"搬运，移转"transfer, defer

(21) fin, finit, 含义是"终，极"final, finish, confine

(22) firm, 含义是"坚固"firm, confirm, affirm

(23) fix, 含义是"固定"prefix, affix

(24) flect, flex, 含义是"弯曲"flexible, reflex

(25) flor, flour, flower, 含义是"花"flower, flourish

(26) form, 含义是"形"uniform, formula, transform, reform, deform

(27) forc, fort, 含义是"力，强度"force, enforce, effort

(28) gen, genit, 含义是"生产，发生"generate, generation

(29) gram, graph, 含义是"书写, 记录" telegram, diagram, photograph

(30) grad, gress, gred, gree, 含义是"步, 阶段" gradually, degree, progress

(31) hab, habit, hibit, 含义是"保持, 住" inhabit, exhibit, prohibit

(32) her, hes, 含义是"粘附" adhere, cohesion

(33) ject, jet, 含义是"抛射" project, inject

(34) jour, 含义是"日, 一天" journal, journey, adjourn

(35) jug, junct, 含义是"结合, 连合" conjunction, junction

(36) labour, labor, 含义是"劳动, 工作" labourer, elaborate, collaborate

(37) lect, leg, lig, 含义是"挑选, 采集" collect, select, lecture

(38) lif, liv, 含义是"生活, 生存" life, alive, live

(39) loc, 含义是"场所, 位置" location, dislocate

(40) long, leng, ling, 含义是"长的" length, prolong, linger

(41) loqu, locut, 含义是"说话" colloquial, eloquent

(42) mand, mend, 含义是"命令" command, demand, recommend

(43) man, manu, 含义是"手, 手法" manage, manual

(44) memor, menber, 含义是"记忆" memory, remember, memorial

(45) mind, ment, 含义是"心" mind, remind, mental

(46) merc, merch, 含义是"贸易" commerce, merchant

(47) meas, mens, meter, metr, 含义是"测量, 度量" measure, meter, diameter

(48) min, 含义是"小" diminish, minority

(49) miss, mit, 含义是"派遣, 送" mission, dismiss, transmit, missile

(50) mob, mot, mov, 含义是"动" movement, motion, mobile, remove

(51) nect, nex, 含义是"捆扎" connect, disconnect, annex

(52) not, 含义是"记号, 注意" note, denote, annotation

(53) onom, onym, 含义是"名字" synonym, antonym, anonymous

(54) pair, par, 含义是"a) 相同, 对等 b) 准备" compare, prepare

(55) pel, puls, 含义是"追逐" expel, impel

(56) pend, pens, pond, 含义是"悬挂" depend, independent, ex-

pense

(57) phon，含义是"声音"symphony，telephone，microphone

(58) plac，含义是"位置，场所"place，replace

(59) peopl，popul，publ，含义是"人民，民众"public，republic，popular，people

(60) port，含义是"搬运"export，import，deport

(61) press，含义是"压，压制"pressure，express，oppress，impression

(62) prob，proof，prov，含义是"实验，验证"prove，approve，

(63) quer，quest，quir，quis，含义是"寻找，探问"inquiry，question，inquisition

(64) rang，rank，含义是"排列"arrange，rank，

(65) rect，right，rig，含义是"正，直"correct，direct，erect

(66) riv，含义是"河流，流远"river，arrive，derive

(67) rupt，含义是"破坏，毁坏"eruption，bankrupt，corruption

(68) sci，含义是"认识，知识"science，conscious

(69) scrib，script，含义是"书写，记录"describe，script

(70) sens，sent，含义是"感觉，情感"sensation，sentiment

(71) sign，含义是"标记，符号"signal，signature，design

(72) sembl，simil，含义是"相似，类似"similar，resemble，assimilate

(73) soci，含义是"结合，社交"social，association

(74) spec，spect，spitc，spis，含义是"看，视"inspect，spectator，conspicuous，respect

(75) struct，含义是"建筑，构造"structure，construct，instruct，destruction

(76) tect，teg，含义是"遮蔽，掩盖"detect，protect

(77) temp，tens，含义是"时间，时机"tense，contemporary，temporal

(78) tend，tes，tent，含义是"倾向，伸张"tendency，extend，intend

(79) test，含义是"证明，证实"testify，protest，contest

(80) text，含义是"编织，构成"textile，texture，context

(81) tract，trail，含义是"拖拉，吸引"attract，tractor，

abstract, contract

(82) tribut, 含义是"给予" contribution, distribute

(83) us, ut, 含义是"用，使用" usable, utilize, abuse

(84) vac, van, 含义是"空，虚" vacancy, vanity, evacuate

(85) vad, vas, wad, 含义是"走，去" invade, wade, evade

(86) vers, vert, 含义是"旋转，反转" convert, inversion, reverse, divert

(87) vid, vis, vey, view, 含义是"观看，看见" television, visible, evident, interview, survey

(88) viv, vit, 含义是"生，活" vivid, vital, survival

(89) war, ward, 含义是"注意，保护" aware, wary, ward

(90) way, 含义是"路" way, away, subway, always

附录四　常用英语谚语与名人名言

1. 常用英语谚语

A friend in need is a friend indeed.
患难见真交。
A good book is a good friend.
良书如挚友。
A good medicine tastes bitter.
良药苦口。
A journey of a thousand miles begins with a single step.
千里之行始于足下。
A life without a friend is a life without a sun.
人生若无友，就如同生命中没有太阳。
A straight foot is not afraid of a crooked shoe.
身正不怕影子斜。
A trouble shared is a trouble halved.
两人分担，困难减半。
All roads lead to Rome.
条条大路通罗马。
All things are difficult before they are easy.
万事开头难。
An apple a day keeps the doctor away.
一日一苹果，医生远离我。
An hour in the morning is worth two in the evening.
一天之计在于晨。
A young idler, an old beggar.
少壮不努力，老大徒伤悲。

Bad news has wings.
好事不出门，坏事传千里。
Cats hind their paws.
大智若愚。
Doing is better than saying.
与其挂在嘴上，不如落实在行动上。
Early to bed and early to rise makes a man healthy, wealthy and wise.
早睡早起身体好。
Easier said than done.
说起来容易做起来难。
East, west, home is best.
金窝、银窝，不如自己的草窝。
Every man has his price.
天生我才必有用。
Facts speak louder than words.
事实胜于雄辩。
Failure is the mother of success.
失败乃成功之母。
First think, then act.
三思而后行。
God helps those who help themselves.
自助者，天助之。
Gold will not buy anything.
黄金并非万能。
Great hopes make great man.
远大的抱负，造就伟大的人物。
Great minds think alike.
英雄所见略同。
Hardworking is the mother of success.
勤奋是成功之母。
He who makes no mistakes makes nothing.
想不犯错误，就一事无成。
Hope for the best, but prepare for the worst.
抱最好的愿望，做最坏的打算。

Imagination is more important than knowledge.
想象力比知识更重要。
It is better to be a head of dog than a tail of a lion.
宁为鸡头，不为凤尾。
It is never too late to learn.
活到老，学到老。
Keep something for a rainy day.
未雨绸缪。
Kill two birds with one stone.
一石双鸟。一举两得。
Knowledge is power.
知识就是力量。
Learn to walk before you run.
循序渐进。
Living without an aim is like sailing without a compass.
没有目标的生活如同没有罗盘的航行。
Love me, love my dog.
爱屋及乌。
Money is a good servant but a bad man.
只做金钱的主人，莫做金钱的奴隶。
Money is not everything.
金钱不是万能的。
Never do things by halves.
做事不能半途而废。
Never put off till tomorrow what you can do today.
今日事，今日毕。
No competition, no progress.
没有竞争，就没有进步。
No man is wise at all times.
智者千虑，必有一失。
No man is born wise but learned.
人非生而知之。
No pains, no gains.
不劳则无获。

No sweet without sweat.

苦尽甘来。

Nothing is difficult to the man who will try.

世上无难事，只要肯登攀。

Nothing is impossible to a willing mind.

世上无难事，只怕有心人。

Nothing seek, nothing find.

无所求则无所获。

Opportunity knocks only once.

机不可失，时不再来。

Opportunities seldom knock twice.

机不可失，时不再来。

Practice makes perfect.

熟能生巧。

Pride goes before a failure.

骄兵必败。

Reading makes a full man.

读书长见识。

Rome was not built in a day.

冰冻三尺，非一日之寒。

Seeing is believing.

百闻不如一见。

Stick to it, and you'll succeed.

只要人有恒，万事都能成。

There is but a secret to success—Never give up!

成功只有一个秘诀—永不放弃！

There is no smoke without fire.

无风不起浪。

Time and tide wait for no man.

岁月不待人。

Time flies.

时光已逝．

To live is to learn; to learn is to better live.

活着为了学习，学习为了更好地活着。

Two heads are better than one.
三个臭皮匠顶个诸葛亮。
Where there is a will, there is a way.
有志者,事竟成。
Well begun is half done.
好的开端是成功的一半。
When god closes a door, he opens a window.
上帝关上一扇门,会为我们打开一扇窗。
Where there is life, there is hope.
生命不息,希望常在。
Wisdom in the mind is better than money in the hand.
脑中有知识,胜于手中有金钱。
You have to believe in yourself. That's the secret of success.
必须相信自己,这是成功的秘诀。

2. 名人名言

Love look not with the eyes, but with the mind. ——William Shakespeare
爱不是用眼睛看,而是用心去感受。——莎士比亚
Let life be beautiful like summer flowers and death like autumn leaves. ——Tagore
生如夏花之绚烂,死如秋叶之静美。——泰戈尔
Goals determine what you're going to be. ——Julius Erving
人生的奋斗目标决定你将成为什么样的人。——欧文
The fox changes his skin but not his habits. ——Suetonius
江山易改,本性难移。——苏埃托尼乌斯
Life has a value only when it has something valuable as its object. ——Hegel
目标有价值,人生才会有价值。——黑格尔
The silent night has the beauty of the mother and the clamorous day of the child.
静悄悄的黑夜具有母亲的美丽,而喧闹的白天具有孩童的美丽。——泰戈尔
Dark and difficult times lie ahead, soon we must all face the choice between what is right and what is easy. ——J. K. Rowling
黑暗和困难笼罩着前行的道路,很快我们就要在正确的和轻松的(道路)之间进行选择。——J·K·罗琳

The proper function of man is to live, but not to exist. ——Jack London
人应该生活,而非单纯生存。——杰克·伦敦
People with tact have less to retract. ——Arnold Glasgow
智者悔少。——阿诺德·格拉斯哥
To do injustice is more disgraceful than to suffer it. ——Plato
制造不公平比承受不公平更可耻。——柏拉图
The worst bankrupt is the person who lost his enthusiasm. ——Arnold
丧失热情是一个人最惨的破产。——阿诺德
The miracle is this—the more we share, the more we have. ——Leonard Nimoy
神奇的是,我们分享的越多便拥有的越多。——伦纳德·尼莫伊
The only thing we have to fear is fear itself. ——Franklin D. Roosevelt
唯一我们不得不恐惧的事情是恐惧本身。——富兰克林·罗斯福
If money be not you servant, it will be your master. The covetous man can not so properly be said to possess wealth, as that may be said to possess him. ——Francis Bacon
如果钱财不是你的仆役,那就是你的主人。贪财的人与其说是他拥有钱财,不如说是钱财占有他。——弗兰西斯·培根
He who loses wealth loses much; he who loses a friend a friend loses more; but he who loses loses courage loses all. ——Cervantes
损失财产的人损失很大,失去朋友的人损失更多,而失去勇气的人则失去了一切。——塞万提斯
He conquers twice, who upon victory overcomes himself. ——Francis Bacon
在胜利后能够控制自己的人获得了第二次胜利。——弗兰西斯·培根
Reading makes a full man, conference a ready man, and writing an exact man. ——Francis Bacon
读书使人充实,讨论使人机敏,写作使人严谨。——弗兰西斯·培根
We cannot all be masters, nor all masters cannot be truly followed. ——Shakespeare
不是每个人都能做主人,也不是每个主人都能值得仆人忠心的服侍。——莎士比亚
No man is rich enough to buy back his own past. ——Wilde
没有人可以富有到能够赎回自己的过去。——王尔德

参 考 文 献

[1] Krashen S. The Input Hypothesis: Issues and Implication [M]. New York: Longman, 1985.

[2] Landauer T K, D Laham, P Fohz. Automatic essay assessment [J]. Assessment in Education, 2003 (10).

[3] Mendonca C Q, Johnson K E. Peer review negotiations: revision activities in ESL writing instruction [J]. TESOL Quarterly, 1994.

[4] O'Malley J M, Chamot A U. Learning Strategies in Second Language Acquisition [M]. Camb ridge University Press, 1990.

[5] Swain M. Communicative competence: some roles of comprehensible input and comprehensible output in its development [M] // S. Gass C Madden. Input in Second Language Acquisition. Rowley, MA: Newbury House, 1985.

[6] Tsui B M, Ng M. Do secondary L2 writers benefit from peer comments? [J]. Journal of Second Writing, 2000 (9).

[7] 蔡基刚. 英汉写作对比研究 [M]. 上海: 复旦大学出版社, 2001.

[8] 蔡基刚. 英汉写作修辞对比 [M]. 上海: 复旦大学出版社, 2003.

[9] 陈向明. 实践性知识: 教师专业发展的知识基础 [J]. 北京大学教育评论, 2003 (1).

[10] 教育部考试中心. 2014年全国硕士研究生入学统一考试: 英语(1)考试大纲（非英语专业）[M]. 北京: 高等教育出版社, 2013.

[11] 李红英. I Have a Dream 及物性特征选择与主题凸显等效分析 [J]. 浙江海洋学院学报（人文科学版），2008 (3).

[12] 李荫华. 全新版大学进阶英语综合教程 [M]. 上海: 上海外语教育出版社, 2017.

[13] 刘建达. 现代技术与语言测试--应用、影响及发展方向 [J]. 外语电话教学, 2013 (7).

［14］刘璐.《假如给我三天光明》的生命意识研究［J］.佳木斯大学社会科学学报，2017（2）.

［15］路文军.元认知策略与英语写作的关系［J］.外语与外语教学，2006（9）.

［16］马秉义.英汉主语差异初探［J］.外国语，1995（5）.

［17］批改网.百万同题英语写作大数据报告［R］.北京：北京语言智能协同院，2015.

［18］全国大学英语四六级考试委员会.全国大学英语四六级考试大纲（2016年修订版）［M］.上海：上海交通大学出版社，2016.

［19］苏慧，王占斌.塞缪尔·厄尔曼散文Youth的点评与欣赏［J］.语文学刊，2009（6）.

［20］陶振英，等.浅析汉语谓语和英语谓语的差异［J］.商丘师专学报，1999（10）.

［21］王长喜.长喜考研英语12句作文法［M］.北京：学苑出版社，2006.

［22］王初明.影响外语学习的两大因素与外语教学［J］.外语界，2001（6）.

［23］王初明.正确认识外语学习过程是提高外语教学质量的关键［J］.外语与外语教学，2001（10）.

［24］王海啸.体验式外语学习的教学原则——从理论到实践［J］.中国外语，2010（7）.

［25］王敏.大学英语主题写作主谓搭配认知研究［J］.湖北经济学院学报（人文社会科学版），2014（5）.

［26］王娜.基于数字化写作平台的写作动机与能力实证研究［J］.外语电话教学，2012（5）.

［27］陈娟文，王娜.基于数字化学习资源的英语写作能力培养［J］.现代教育技术，2016（5）.

［28］王守仁.进一步推进和实施大学英语教学改革－－关于《大学英语课程教学要求（试行）》的修订［J］.中国外语，2008（1）.

［29］王守仁.坚持科学的大学英语教学改革观［J］.外语界，2013（6）.

［30］王守仁.充分认识通用英语的育人价值－－兼谈《大学英语教学指南》的研制［M］.青岛：外语教学与研究出版社，2015.

［31］王守仁.《大学英语教学指南》要点解读［J］.外语界，2016（3）.

［32］王佐良，丁往道.英语文体学引论［M］.北京：外语教学与研究出

版社,1987.

[33] 吴一安,唐锦兰.融入自动评价系统的英语写作实验教学对高校教师的影响研究[J].外语电话教学,2012(7).

[34] 吴一安.优秀外语教师专业素质探究[J].外语教学与研究,2005(3).

[35] 肖立齐.肖立齐考研英语复习教程[M].北京:外文出版社,2003.

[36] 新东方考研英语命题研究组.新东方考研英语高分写作[M].北京:群言出版社,2007.

[37] 于爱莲.从 I Have a Dream 中看演讲文体的修辞风格[J].咸阳师范学院学报,2005(12).

[38] 张锦辉.基于"最近发展区"理论的英文写作同伴反馈的实证研究[J].吉林广播电视大学学报,2013(7).

[39] 张莲.英语专业课程改革与教师发展良性互动机制的构建[J].外语与外语教学,2013(3).

[40] 张玉娟,陈春田,等.新世纪使用英语写作[M].北京:外语教学与研究出版社,2013.

[41] 赵元任,吕叔湘.汉语口语语法[M].北京:商务印书馆出版,1979.

[42] 中国外语测评中心.国际人才英语考试官方指南[M].北京:外语教学与研究出版社,2017.

[43] 竹玛,许文涛.大学英语四级考试全真试题及超详解[M].北京:北京燕山出版社,2014.

[44] 朱旭东.论教师专业发展的理论模型建构[J].教育研究,2014(6).

[45] http://www.koolearn.com

[46] https://wenku.baidu.com

[47] https://www.pigai.org

[48] http://etic.claonline.cn

[49] http://www.chinadaily.com.cn

[50] https://www.wendu.com